Productive Transformation in Africa

"Policy officials, advisors, and practitioners will especially value this book, which distils a quite unparalleled mix of lengthy high-level experience of developmental decision-making in Africa, immersion in the historical evidence and research literature on structural change globally, and profound individual wisdom. Arkebe's insistence on the need—and opportunities—for selective intervention targeting not broad sectors but specific economic activities most likely to generate broader and longer lasting gains should be a wake-up call to all."

—Christopher Cramer, *Professor of the Political Economy of Development, SOAS University of London*

"Arkebe Oqubay's latest volume is a *tour de force* that is a must read for those charged with leading Africa's developmental strategy as well as for analysts and scholars. The book draws on the analytical insights of the heterodox classics, as well as carefully chosen case studies of the experiences of specific countries and of broader sectoral trends to make a convincing case for a broadening of the current uneven and pragmatic recovery of industrial policy in parts of the African continent into a broader effort to advance structural transformation informed by a mindset of "possibilism" in contrast to Afro-pessimism. Each of the book's many specific findings and recommendations merit serious reflection by policy makers at national, regional economic community and AU/AfCFTA levels alike. The volume amasses a wealth of information and analysis which will stand as a landmark study for many years to come."

—Rob Davies, *Honorary Professor, Nelson Mandela School of Public Governance, University of Cape Town and a former Minister of Trade and Industry of the Republic of South Africa*

"This book is a major contribution to the political economy of development and African industrialisation. Drawing on decades of scholarship, policymaking experience, and new empirical evidence, Arkebe Oqubay offers a rigorous and hopeful analysis of how African economies can achieve structural transformation through strategic, selective, and activist industrial policies. Moving beyond aggregate growth metrics, the book centres productive capacity, technological learning, and sector-specific strategies, while challenging Afro-pessimism through comparative insights from Africa and successful late industrialisers. Anchored in Hirschman's "possibilism," the book provides a coherent framework that links history, practice, and future pathways—making it essential reading for policymakers, practitioners, and scholars committed to sustainable and inclusive development in Africa."

—Carlos Lopes, *Honorary Professor, Nelson Mandela School of Public Governance, University of Cape Town, and Former Executive Secretary, UNECA*

"Successful industrial policy is not self-evident. This book offers a strong defence of the case in favour using Mauritius and Morocco as case studies, highlighting some of the necessary conditions for replication."

—Stefan Dercon, *Professor of Economic Policy and Director of CSAE, University of Oxford, and Former Chief Economist of UK DFID*

"Essential and timely, this book confronts the industrial policy challenges facing Africa amid demographic shifts and uneven industrialisation. It argues that sectoral targeting, productive investment, industrial ecosystem development, and domestic resource mobilisation are critical. Drawing on cases from several African countries, it offers practical lessons in designing and practising productive transformation—rejecting "one size fits all" prescriptions while affirming the state's developmental role. Highly recommended for African policymakers and practitioners."

—Donald Kaberuka, *Former President of the African Development Bank and Finance Minister of Rwanda*

Arkebe Oqubay

Productive Transformation in Africa

Industrial Policies for Sustainable Economic Development

palgrave
macmillan

Arkebe Oqubay
SOAS University of London
London, UK

ISBN 978-3-032-23940-2 ISBN 978-3-032-23941-9 (eBook)
https://doi.org/10.1007/978-3-032-23941-9

This Palgrave Macmillan imprint is published by the registered company Springer Nature Switzerland AG.
The registered company address is: Gewerbestrasse 11, 6330 Cham, Switzerland

Arguments. Practices. Path Forward.
What we know about development strategies and policymaking

Preface

It has been over a decade since the publication of the pioneering work on industrial policy and structural transformation, *Made in Africa* (Oxford University Press, 2015), which boldly called for Africa's productive transformation and industrialisation. ***Productive Transformation Africa*** aims to build on this groundbreaking work and bridge existing gaps in the literature by providing extensive empirical evidence, supported by reliable datasets, and by focusing on the design and implementation of industrial policy and the challenges of industrialisation in Africa.

This monograph explores over six decades of African industrialisation, offering detailed insights into the challenges, diagnostics, and opportunities of African industrial development, as well as the prospects for broader and sustainable structural transformation. The book is published at a moment when green transformation has become integral to productive transformation, and when the economic futures of African nations are central to the African development agenda.

This book has benefitted from several forums and discussions. First and foremost, it draws on research supported by a British Academy grant (GP/400322), the Greening of African Economic Development. Additionally, part of this book's content was prepared for my annual lecture at the CSAE Conference 2024, held at the University of Oxford, on the topic of "Producing Transformation in Africa: What We Know about Development Strategies and Policymaking." Several perspectives in this book were discussed during my Amsden Memorial Lecture at an event hosted by Pretoria-based Trade and Industrial Policy Strategies (TIPS) and the DSI/NRF South African Research Chair in Industrial Development

(SAARCHi-ID) at the University of Johannesburg. Many ideas have emerged from research outputs supported by SAARCHi-ID at the University of Johannesburg. The book features two analytical aspects: supporting reviews with extensive empirical evidence and comparative research, backed by relevant case studies from various sectors and countries, to illustrate variations and real-world experiences.

The author hopes that the book will inspire new research initiatives and debates that will ultimately contribute to the development of effective strategies and informed policymaking.

British Academy Global Professor
SOAS University of London

Arkebe Oqubay

Acknowledgements

I want to express my sincere gratitude to Professor Christopher Cramer for his constructive conversation and valuable comments, which helped improve the draft manuscript. I am grateful to Dr Tesfachew Taferre and Dr Ayalew Mamo for their critical insights and comments. I also wish to thank Vice-Chancellor Professor Adam Habib, Professor John Sender, Professor Carlos Oya, and Professor Laura Hammond of SOAS, University of London, for their longstanding academic collaboration and friendship. Additionally, I thank Professor Justin Yifu Lin of Peking University, Professor Ha-Joon Chang and Professor Richard Kozul-Wright of SOAS University of London, and Professor Peter Nolan of the University of Cambridge. My appreciation extends to Professor Stefan Dercon, Professor Adnan Khan, and colleagues at CSAE.

Our collaborative work with John Mathews, as featured in The Oxford Handbook of the Greening of African Economic Development (Oxford University Press, 2025), and in the British Academy research project "The Greening of African Economic Development" has significantly deepened my understanding of green transformation. Their input has enhanced the quality and scope of this book. The charts are based on data compiled by the research project "The Greening of African Economic Development," funded by the British Academy and based at SOAS, University of London.

I am grateful to the Centre for International Knowledge Development (CIKD) and the Global South Research Centre (GSRC) for exchanges of ideas and support. I would also like to thank Professor Su Changhe and Professor Yu Zheng of Fudan University, as well as Professor Liu Hong of

Nanyang Technological University (Singapore), for their valuable contributions.

I thank Wyndham Hacket Pain, commissioning editor at Palgrave Macmillan, for his support during the review and publication process. I also thank the anonymous reviewers for their insightful feedback.

I am grateful to Dr Uduak Akpan at SOAS University of London for his assistance in compiling the data. I also thank Dr Nigisty Gebrechristos for her comments on the draft chapter. Additionally, I thank Samuel and Binyam Arkebe for sharing numerous discussions and insights on both themes—African industrialisation and the China–Africa dimension. Many thanks to all who have contributed directly or indirectly, participated in the exchanges, and influenced the content of the book, although I have not been able to mention all their names.

Contents

About the Author

Arkebe Oqubay, PhD is a distinguished scholar-practitioner. He holds the British Academy Global Professor position at SOAS University of London. He leads a landmark research project, *The Greening of Africa's Economic Development*, funded by the British Academy. He is a former Senior Minister and Special Advisor to three successive Prime Ministers of Ethiopia and has been at the centre of policymaking in Ethiopia for over 30 years. Arkebe has been recognised internationally for his bold reforms, innovative and strategic leadership role in Ethiopia's economic transformation, and for championing the country's pioneering industrial development model, which has been replicated across many African countries. He is the former Mayor of Addis Ababa, acclaimed as the Best African Mayor in 2005 and a finalist for the World Mayor award, and he has led the boards of key public enterprises, including Ethiopian Airlines.

Dr Arkebe is a leading advocate for Africa's industrialisation, economic transformation, and sustainability. He continues to provide crucial policy advice to African governments and consults for international organisations. His publication with Oxford University Press includes the acclaimed *Made in Africa* (2015), *How Nations Learn: Technological Learning, Industrial Policy, and Catch-up* (2019), *China-Africa and an Economic Transformatio*n (2019), *The Oxford Handbook of the Ethiopian Economy* (2019), *The Oxford Handbook of the South African Economy* (2021), *The Oxford Handbook on Industrial Policy* (2020), *The Oxford Handbook of Industrial Hubs and Economic Development (2020), The Oxford Handbook on the Greening of Economic Development (2025), The Oxford Handbook of the Moroccan Economy (2026), and Greening African Economic Development* *(forthcoming)*. His recent publications with Palgrave Macmillan include *Industrial Hubs and Economic Catch-Up: Productive Transformation and Governance* (2025), *Industrial Policy and Economic Development: Theory, Strategy, and Practice* (2025), and *Greening African Economic Development* (forthcoming research monograph). .

He is the recipient of various international awards, including the Order of the Rising Sun, Gold and Silver Star, bestowed upon him by the Emperor of Japan in recognition of his dedicated contributions to Africa's industrialisation. He was also Africa's sole candidate for the post of Director-General of the United Nations Industrial Development Organisation (UNIDO), unanimously endorsed by the African Union.

List of Abbreviations and Acronyms

ABC	Agricultural Bank of China
AfCFTA	African Continental Free Trade Area
AfDB	African Development Bank
AI	Artificial intelligence
AIIB	Asian Infrastructure Investment Bank
AMU	Arab Maghreb Union
ASEAN	Association of Southeast Asian Nations
BII	British International Investment
BNDES	Brazilian Development Bank
CBAM	Carbon Border Adjustment Mechanisms
CDB	China Development Bank
Africa CDC	Africa Centres for Disease Control and Prevention
CEN-SAD	Community of Sahel–Saharan States
CIKD	Centre for International Knowledge on Development
COMESA	Common Market for Eastern and Southern Africa
DBM	Development Bank of Mauritius
DFIs	Development finance institutions
DRC	Democratic Republic of Congo
EAC	East African Community
ECCAS	Economic Community of Central African States
ECOWAS	Economic Community of West African States
EIB	European Investment Bank
ELI	Export-led industrialisation
EVs	Electric vehicles
FDI	Foreign direct investment
FOCAC	Forum on China-Africa Cooperation
FTA	Free Trade Area

GII	Global Innovation Index
HIPC	Heavily indebted poor countries
ICBC	Industrial and Commercial Bank of China
IDC	South African Industrial Development Corporation
IFC	International Finance Corporation
IFIs	International financial institutions
IGAD	Inter-governmental Authority on Development
ISI	Import-substitution industrialisation
MENA	Middle East and North Africa
MHT	Medium-high and high technology
MNCs	Multinational Corporations
MVA	Manufacturing value added
NDB	New Development Bank
NEPAD	The New Partnership for Africa's Development
NEPAD	New Partnership for Africa's Development
OCP	Office Cherifien des Phosphates
OECD	Organisation for Economic Co-operation and Development
PCI	Productive capacity index
PPP	purchasing power parity
PRPs	Performance-related payments
REC	Regional economic community
SADC	Southern African Development Community
SAP	Structural adjustment programs
SASOL	South African Synthetic Oil Limited
SDGs	Sustainable Development Goals
SSA	Sub-Saharan Africa
TAZARA	Tanzania-Zambia Railway
TOR	Terms of reference
TVET	Technical and vocational education and training
WIPO	World Intellectual Property Organisation

List of Figures

List of Tables

PART I

Arguments and Perspectives

CHAPTER 1

Introduction to African Industrialisation and Productive Transformation

1 Background and Context

Africa's economic future hinges critically on productive transformation—the structural shift from low-productivity agriculture towards higher-productivity manufacturing and services. Yet the continent's industrialisation prospects remain intensely debated among development scholars and policymakers. The achievements of Mauritius's textile and apparel industry (1970s–1990s) and Morocco's automotive sector (2000s–2010s) provide compelling evidence that manufacturing-led productive transformation is achievable in African contexts. This evidence gains added significance when considered alongside aggregate trends: manufacturing value added (MVA) has grown consistently since the mid-1990s, directly challenging the premature deindustrialisation narrative and demonstrating that Africa's industrial trajectory, while distinct from historical patterns elsewhere, remains fundamentally viable and increasingly dynamic.

Africa thus stands at a critical juncture in its economic development. After decades of diverse and uneven progress, the continent has embarked on a journey of industrialisation and structural transformation that defies simplistic narratives. This book examines the complex, varied, and often contradictory patterns of Africa's productive transformation through rigorous analysis of structural change, industrial policy interventions, and the political economy of catch-up development.

A. Oqubay, *Productive Transformation in Africa*,
https://doi.org/10.1007/978-3-032-23941-9_1

The prevailing discourse on African development has long oscillated between Afro-pessimism and Afro-optimism. Neither perspective captures the nuanced reality of Africa's economic transformation. Since the millennium, several African countries have demonstrated unprecedented political determination to promote economic diversification and industrialisation. Ethiopia's industrial parks strategy, Rwanda's emphasis on knowledge-based services, Morocco's automotive manufacturing hub, and Kenya's position as East Africa's industrial and financial centre exemplify deliberate, state-led efforts to reshape productive structures. These initiatives mark a fundamental departure from the Washington Consensus orthodoxy that dominated African policymaking in the 1980s and 1990s, signalling a return to active industrial policy adapted to contemporary global conditions.

Yet this renewed commitment unfolds against profound structural constraints. Africa's manufacturing sector remains stubbornly small, accounting for less than 10% of GDP in most countries, with limited growth over recent decades. Labour productivity gaps between Africa and other developing regions have widened. Most troublingly, employment continues shifting from agriculture, not into manufacturing but into low-productivity services, challenging conventional models of structural transformation.

Understanding Africa's industrial trajectory requires moving beyond aggregate statistics and simple comparisons with Asia's developmental experience. Africa's pursuit of industrialisation exhibits three defining features: *variation* across countries in strategies, outcomes, and policy effectiveness; *unevenness* in the pace and depth of transformation between and within countries; and *diversity* in the specific pathways, sectoral patterns, and institutional arrangements through which productive transformation occurs or fails to occur.

The analytical framework employed here draws on development economics, structuralist thought, and evolutionary economics. We examine how countries build productive capabilities, diversify their economic structures, and close technology gaps with frontrunners. Industrial policy—purposeful government intervention to shape the composition and trajectory of economic activity—occupies a central place in our analysis. We investigate not only what policies African governments have pursued but also how implementation challenges, political economy constraints, and institutional capacities have shaped outcomes.

Africa's position in the global economy presents both opportunities and constraints. The external environment has evolved substantially since

Asia's classical late industrialisation period. Global value chains have reconfigured production geography, creating new entry points but also new dependencies. China's emergence as both major investor in Africa and competitor in third markets has fundamentally altered the landscape. Climate imperatives and the push towards decarbonisation present obstacles to conventional industrial pathways while opening opportunities for green industrialisation.

Amid these challenges, Africa possesses distinctive underutilised advantages. The continent's demographic trajectory—with the world's youngest and fastest-growing population—represents enormous potential for domestic markets and productive labour forces. Rapid urbanisation creates agglomeration economies and shifts consumption patterns. Regional integration efforts, though incomplete, expand market size. Technological change offers leapfrogging possibilities, from mobile money to renewable energy. Fundamentally, Africa's position as a late-late developer provides opportunities to learn from earlier industrialisers' successes and failures.

This book examines these dynamics through detailed analysis of sectoral transformations, comparative policy studies, and theoretical engagement with debates on structural change and economic development. We pay particular attention to the political economy of industrialisation—the coalitions, institutions, and power relations that enable or constrain transformation. Understanding why some countries have made greater progress requires examining not just technical policy choices but the deeper political settlements and state capabilities underpinning developmental projects.

The argument proceeds through systematic analysis of Africa's structural transformation patterns, industrial policy experiences, and future prospects. We document what has changed in Africa's productive structures over recent decades, identify mechanisms through which change has occurred or been blocked, and assess policy instruments and institutional arrangements that have proven effective. Throughout, we maintain analytical rigour while remaining attentive to Africa's heterogeneity—recognising that generalisations about "Africa" often obscure more than they reveal.

The stakes could not be higher. Africa's population is projected to reach 2.5 billion by 2050, with 40% of the world's population in Africa by century's end, nearly two-thirds living in cities. The overwhelming majority of new labour force entrants will require productive employment.

Accelerated structural transformation can convert demographic momentum into opportunity.

This book offers a sober, but optimistic, assessment. Africa's industrial transformation remains incomplete and fragile, but it is underway. The challenge facing policymakers, scholars, and development practitioners is understanding the mechanisms of structural change deeply enough to design and implement effective acceleration strategies. This requires moving beyond ideological debates about state versus market to focus on practical challenges: productive transformation, capability building, boosting productive investments and exports, developing technological capabilities, and navigating the political economy of development across diverse African contexts.

2 Analytical Framework

The book conceptualises industrial policies as strategies for accelerating productive transformation, and as broader in scope as a means of structural change and economic catch-up, than is often presented in the mainstream literature. It involves multiple areas, including productive capacities, a focus on the production side, demand-stimulating measures, and macroeconomic policies that support structural change, development goals, and the development of innovative and technological capabilities. Importantly, this book has a bias towards possibilism—the belief that even within structural constraints, strategic action, learning, capability development, and institution-building can lead to progress in development. It is founded on a development perspective that African states have choices, that policy space exists and can be expanded, and that cooperation—when deliberately and strategically directed at catalysing African industrialisation—can promote the continent's economic transformation.

Africa's industrialisation and economic transformation have garnered significant attention in debates among researchers and policymakers. This discussion arises from the slow pace of structural change on the continent and the realisation that late industrialisation offers a promising route, as demonstrated by the experiences of East Asia and, more recently, China's remarkable economic growth. In light of the increasing frequency and severity of global crises and uncertainties, such as the COVID-19 pandemic, the vulnerability of many developing economies has been highlighted. The resurgence of industrial policy in advanced economies has also brought the issue of industrialisation to the forefront.

The book uses terms such as "structural change," "structural transformation," "productive transformation," and "economic transformation" interchangeably. However, we distinguish between "structural change" and "structural transformation." As countries grow and develop, their economic structures evolve, with the relative importance of different sectors to national GDP changing. For example, the economic structures of many African countries have shifted over the last six decades—agriculture is no longer dominant, and industry (construction, mining, and manufacturing) is beginning to reach 25–30%, with services now being the most prominent in national output. This represents "structural change" or the shift in the economy's structure, but such structural changes do not necessarily indicate movement up the value, technology, and productivity ladder. Conversely, "structural transformation" is widely understood to be qualitatively different from structural change, as it signifies a shift from low-value, low-technology, and low-productivity sectors or activities towards high-value, high-productivity, and high-technology industries or activities.

Viewed from this perspective, African countries still lag behind in structural transformation, despite notable shifts in their economies from agriculture to industry and services. In many African nations, the dominant sector (services) consists of labour-intensive, low-value, low-productivity, non-tradable services that closely resemble agriculture, where production is mainly low-productivity, low-value subsistence farming, and rural economic activities. Wage levels for labourers in the informal urban services sector are only slightly higher than incomes from rural economic activities. Genuine transformation requires productivity (i.e., labour productivity) and industrial policies, as the former enable countries to climb the value, technology, and productivity ladder, while the latter direct capital and labour towards higher-value, higher-productivity activities. Progress up the ladder can occur either across sectors or within a specific industry among different products.[1]

This book explores Africa's industrialisation during a crucial historical period, amid the rise of the Global South and concerns surrounding multilateralism and global governance systems (CIKD 2024). It aims to examine and provide perspectives on African industrialisation by addressing critical issues. First, it investigates the historical development and

[1] For further insights, refer to *Made in Africa* (2015, Chap. 2) and *The Oxford Handbook of Industrial Policy* (2020, Chaps. 2 and 3).

current situation of African industrialisation within the context of shifting global trends. Moreover, it considers the challenges of industrialisation in Africa through analysis of sectors and policies, and explores potential pathways forward. The book primarily concentrates on practical policy directions and seeks to contribute to the ongoing debate on African industrialisation by emphasising policy-relevant issues. Furthermore, the Global South has become a driving force in the world economy and a source of industrial vigour; however, its potential remains largely untapped, particularly at a time when developing and emerging economies face significant vulnerabilities (Akyüz 2017).

There are two main perspectives on industrial policies—the market-based approach, which includes the neoliberal view seeing industrial policies as tools for opening markets, privatisation, and economic liberalisation, and the neoclassical perspective, which limits the role of industrial policies to correcting market failures. An alternative viewpoint—embracing heterodox and structuralist development economics—considers industrial policy from an activist, productive-transformation perspective, emphasising the developmental and strategic importance of the state and the productive role of firms, which drive innovation and industrialisation.

However, the discourse on industrial policy and scholarly debates have evolved over the decades, reflecting global economic shifts, changes in the international power structure, and the ideological fervour of the period.[2] Our perspective in this book is based on a broader understanding of industrial policy as an effective tool for industrialisation and structural transformation in the twenty-first century, or essentially as a policy framework for productive transformation. Oqubay highlights (2020: 18):

> From a long-term, strategic perspective, industrial policy underpins structural transformation and catch-up, sustained economic growth, productivity gains, technological advances, and broader socio-economic transformation. The approach taken is based on a broader conceptualisation of industrial policy, incorporating production, international trade, technology, and innovation, rather than a narrower definition confined to government interventions or policy instruments. This means that the purpose and patterns of industrial policy, as well as the perspectives underlying them, are of paramount importance.

[2] List ([1841] 1856), Hirschman (1958), Amsden (1989, 2001), Kaldor (1967), Chang (1994, 2002), Lee (2019), Oqubay (2015, 2025).

Several discussions and empirical evidence are reviewed in *The Oxford Handbook of Industrial Policy* (Oxford University Press, 2020). Oqubay et al. (2020: 18) adds:

> First, it presents industrial policy as a vehicle of structural transformation and wealth creation, in which manufacturing (and other dynamic, high-productivity, and knowledge-intensive activities) exhibits increasing returns (both static and dynamic) and drives structural change. It highlights the strategic role of exports, particularly as a source of international learning and a means of alleviating balance-of-payment constraints. Second, it underlines the dynamics of industrial policy as a conduit for technological learning and the development of innovation capability. Finally, it shows that unevenness and adaptability have been key aspects of the practice of industrial policies over the last two centuries, suggesting their continuing relevance for structural change, structural transformation, and catch-up, even in the radically transformed global economic landscape of the twenty-first century, where policy space is more restricted than in the past.

Multiple considerations and perspectives underpin this book's perspective and approach. First, structuralist development economics, which emphasises structural transformation and economic catch-up, provides essential conceptual frameworks for analysing Africa's industrialisation, highlighting that industrialisation and manufacturing are engines of structural change (Kaldor 1967, 1980; Thirlwall 2013). Furthermore, developing countries rarely follow a linear development path. Instead, they may pursue different trajectories and catch up by exploiting their latecomer advantages through particular institutional innovations (Gerschenkron 1962; Amsden 1989; Lee 2019).

Second, the diversity and heterogeneity of African economies, along with each nation's unique characteristics—such as political economy, economic structure, endowments, and history—are essential factors. There is no universal solution for Africa's industrialisation; each country has to find its own development path that fits its specific circumstances. The book's approach supports realistic optimism, or Hirschman's "possibilism," rather than the widespread deep pessimism prevalent in contemporary discourse (Cramer et al. 2020). It also draws on international political economy to examine the aspects of international development cooperation.

Third, the global context significantly influences the prospects for industrialisation, shaped by rapid technological progress, demographic changes, climate change, green development, and the volatility and uncertainty that disproportionately affect the Global South. Accelerated technological advancement, the blurring of sector boundaries, increased mechanisation of agriculture, the growing importance of high-value tradable services, and their vital role in high-tech industries, along with the roles of digital and green technologies, are key features of the ongoing global shifts.

3 Amsden's the Rise of the Rest

The post–World War II period, especially the last four decades, has been characterised by the rise of the Global South and the strengthening of South–South cooperation. The world faces significant challenges in global development, maintaining a multipolar order, and upholding multilateralism, at a time when leading industrialised economies are abandoning and retreating from commitments such as the Paris Climate Action and net-zero targets.[3] Technological progress is shaping our world, presenting both challenges and opportunities. The Global South has emerged as a driver of the global economy, a manufacturing powerhouse, a champion of multilateralism and rule-based trading systems, and a leader in global green development. In the view of the prominent development economist Alice Amsden, this indeed signifies *The Rise of the "Rest"* (2001).

The primacy of productive transformation underpins Amsden's framework. This visualisation powerfully illustrates the dramatic shift in global economic power over the past seven decades, with Asia's rise exemplifying not a novelty but a historic resurgence of the Global South that Alice Amsden presciently analysed in her seminal 2001 work.

Innovation Leadership Has Shifted East or the "Rest"

Perhaps most significant for future competitiveness, Panel B of Chart 1 reveals Asia's dominance in patent applications (70% by 2024). The annotation marking China's 2010 overtaking of the United States is pivotal—this represents not just manufacturing capacity but innovation capacity, echoing the technological sophistication that characterised Asian economies in earlier centuries. This shift demonstrates what Amsden called "late industrialisation," where countries "industrialised without proprietary

[3] United Nations (2025a, b).

innovations" initially but through "pure learning" eventually built their own technological capabilities.

The East Asian Tigers pioneered this pathway in the 1960s–1980s, followed by China's massive resurgence from the 1980s onwards. While North America and Europe each held roughly 35% of patents in 1980, they've declined to under 20% each, confirming that the Global South is no longer merely producing goods but generating the intellectual property and technological advances that will define the twenty-first century.

Manufacturing as the Foundation of Productive Transformation

Panel C shows that Asia will account for 55% of global manufacturing value added by 2024, approaching the dominance it held before industrialisation (see Fig. 1.1). The "Manufacturing Surge Era" and China's accession to the WTO in 2010 mark key turning points in this revival. Amsden documented how China, India, Korea, and Taiwan "built their own national manufacturing enterprises that were investing heavily in R&D" with "developmental states that transformed themselves into champions of science and technology." The East Asian Tigers demonstrated that late industrialisers could catch up through disciplined industrial policy and technological learning. China then extended this model to an unprecedented scale, becoming the "workshop of the world" in the early twenty-first century—a position Britain held in the nineteenth century and that China itself had occupied for centuries before the Industrial Revolution. This manufacturing dominance provides both immediate economic benefits and the industrial foundation for technological leadership.

North America and Europe have experienced a significant decline in their combined share across all metrics. North America's GDP share has decreased from approximately 40% to 20%, and Europe has fallen by a similar amount. This realignment, mainly driven by the East Asian Tigers and greatly accelerated by China, signals the Global South's reclaiming of economic prominence after two centuries of Western dominance following the Industrial Revolution. The post-WWII period therefore marks a significant historical correction—the reassertion of economic power in the Global South, which had characterised most of recorded history until the eighteenth century.

Amsden's work highlights—as shown in Fig. 1.1 demonstrated through Asia's example—that economic performance is not a fixed outcome of geography, endowment, or institutions as prerequisites.

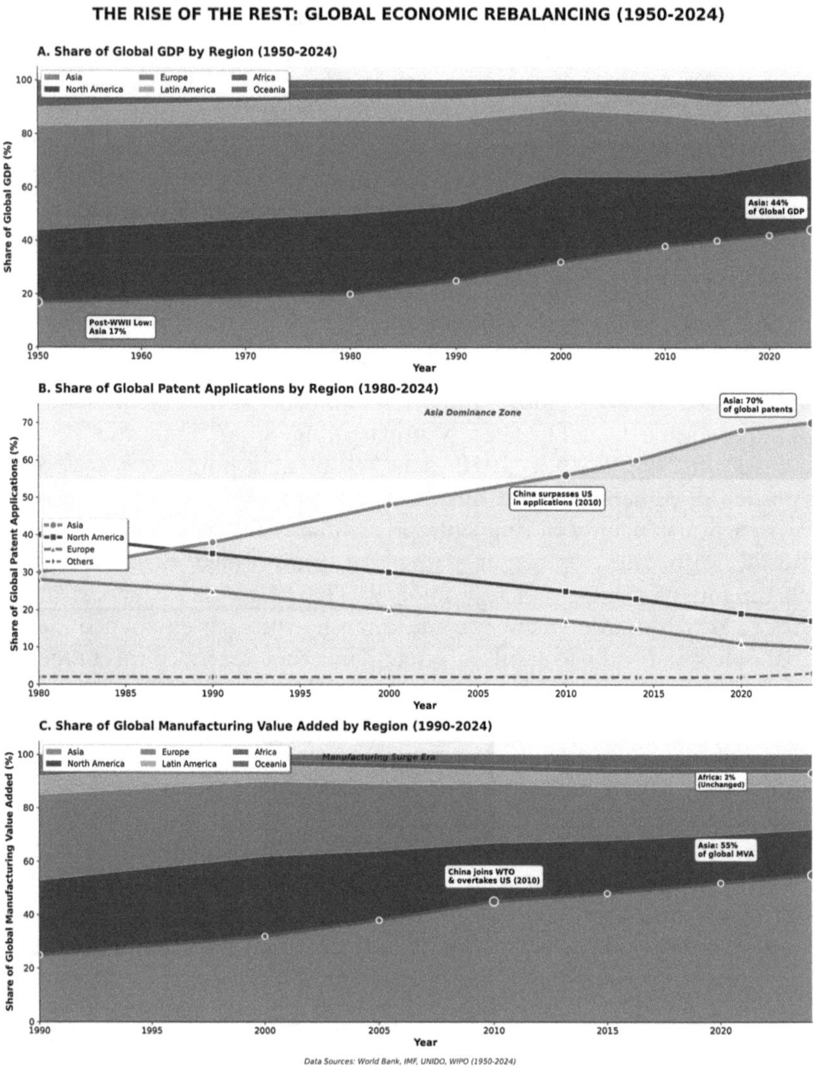

Fig. 1.1 The Rise of the Rest, GDP, MVA, Patent Application. (Source: Computed from various sources)

4 Organisation of the Book

This book is structured in three thematic parts—*Perspectives*, *Practices*, and *Prospects*—comprising eight chapters that systematically examine the key drivers, strategic shifts, and challenges of Africa's industrialisation. The analysis explicitly frames Africa's experience as one of late industrialisation, positioning this as the core of its structural transformation. The chapters progress from a broad historical analysis to detailed sectoral diagnostics and strategic foresight, effectively linking macro-level themes with meso- and micro-level observations. Part I, *Perspectives* (Chaps. 2 and 3), establishes the historical and theoretical context; Part II, *Practices* (Chaps. 4, 5, and 6), presents empirical case studies and policy applications; and Part III, *Prospects* (Chaps. 7 and 8), explores future pathways and strategic implications.

Chapter 2: Perspectives on Productive Transformation

This chapter establishes a conceptual framework for analysing industrial policy and productive transformation, arguing for their necessity in driving Africa's industrialisation. It posits that targeted policies are essential to catalyse structural change, directing resources towards manufacturing and other high-productivity sectors characterised by significant technological spillovers and linkages. A core theme is the strategic role of exports, not merely for revenue but as a critical channel for international learning and for alleviating persistent balance-of-payments constraints. The analysis further conceptualises industrial policy as a dynamic conduit for technological catch-up, emphasising that sustained growth depends on the development of technological and innovation capabilities (Oqubay 2015, 2025). Drawing on structuralist and evolutionary economics to provide a foundation for subsequent empirical analysis of country experiences and building on the importance of latecomer advantages, it highlights the key opportunities shaping the future of African transformation.[4]

[4] See Pasinetti (1981).

Chapter 3: The History and Performance of Industrialisation and Industrial Policy in Africa

This chapter explores the historical development of Africa's industrialisation, focusing on the stages of progress since the post-independence period (1960 onwards for most African nations). This chapter establishes the historical and theoretical foundation. It examines the evolution of African industrial policy, challenges the ideas of Afro-pessimism and African misrepresentation, and analyses the persistent and complex challenges of structural transformation from a long-term perspective. It investigates productive transformation with a particular emphasis on structural comparison, manufacturing value-added, export growth and composition, and the development of productive capability. It also considers demographic dynamics as a critical aspect of productive transformation. The chapter highlights low productive capacities and weak institutional frameworks, situating these issues within the broader context of global economic integration and technological progress.[5]

Chapter 4: Challenges of Industrial Development in Africa: A Policy Diagnosis

Chapter 4 examines the challenges faced in industrial development and the policies adopted by African governments, offering valuable insights for designing effective industrial strategies. Focusing on the development approaches and policies of African nations, the chapter provides policy-relevant analysis of the main obstacles and barriers to progress in Africa's industrial sector. It highlights policy areas of strategic importance for accelerating industrialisation—such as increasing productive capacity, establishing productive linkages, and developing the industrial workforce—rather than merely listing obstacles and objectives. Not all policy measures have the same strategic influence on industrialisation and economic growth. It draws from extensive research and decades of experience in industrial policy. Industrialisation is viewed within a broader context that places manufacturing at the centre, but also includes high-technology and export-oriented services, as well as high-value and industrial-scale agriculture.

[5] See Jerven (2011, 2013).

Chapter 5: The Anatomy of Industrial Chains: A Cross-Sectoral Diagnosis

Chapter 5 explores challenges and constraints by focusing on key sectors crucial to Africa's industrialisation through selected case studies of industries that substantially contribute to economic diversification, exports, and industrial growth. These include pharmaceuticals, cement, fertilisers, petrochemicals, light manufacturing (notably textiles and apparel), agro-processing, and the automotive sector. Understanding the industrial structure of each sector, considering political economy issues, gaining deeper insights into productive linkage effects, and continuously adjusting based on policy outcomes and implementation are vital components of an active industrial policy. The productive role of the state varies across sectors, timelines, and sub-national contexts. While some productive activities are concentrated around emerging technologies and the blurred boundaries of industries, sectoral approaches are essential to industrial policy and form the basis for promoting production linkages, sector-specific industrial ecosystems, and capabilities.[6]

Chapter 6: Productive Transformation in Africa: Comparative Case Studies

This chapter provides a comparative review of two African national economies from the perspective of productive transformation. It challenges Afro-pessimistic narratives by analysing the successful economic transformations of Mauritius and Morocco. Framed within structuralist development economics, it argues that these achievements were not mere "miracles" or solely the result of market liberalisation. Instead, they stemmed from deliberate, pragmatic, and adaptable industrial policies guided by strategic state intervention. The analysis contrasts Mauritius's long-term, phased diversification from a sugar-based economy with Morocco's more recent, state-led shift from import substitution to export-oriented growth in sectors such as automotive and aerospace. Despite differing contexts and pathways, both cases demonstrate the vital importance of productive state-business partnerships and policy learning. The chapter also emphasises that productive transformation is an ongoing process; both nations now face challenges related to maturity, including the

[6] See Oqubay and Lin (2019, 2020).

middle-income trap, skills gaps, and the need for innovation-driven growth. The final discussion draws essential lessons for African industrialisation, highlighting that strategic industrial policy and the capacity for continuous strategic renewal are crucial for sustainable economic catch-up. It emphasises that development paths are unique to each nation and involve diverse strategies.

Chapter 7: Productive Transformation: An Engine of Africa's Economic Integration and the AfCFTA

This chapter presents the AfCFTA analytically as the primary driver of Africa's productive transformation, extending its benefits beyond mere trade liberalisation. Its strategic significance lies in its clear aim to dismantle the colonial legacy of small, fragmented economies and to foster production within regionally integrated value chains. This serves as a vital correction to the continent's reliance on commodity exports and its marginal position in global trade. However, the chapter soberly assesses the substantial obstacles to this transformative agenda. The development of meaningful intra-African trade and competitive manufacturing is impeded not only by infrastructure deficits but also by political challenges, such as rising protectionism and the need for effective continental governance. Consequently, a single industrial policy is deemed unfeasible. The chapter concludes that the success of the AfCFTA is fundamentally political; its ability to promote productive transformation depends on establishing a unified political effort that can overcome internal divisions and coordinate a series of complementary national industrial strategies coherently. The chapter provides detailed accounts of African economic integration, its challenges, and key priorities.

Chapter 8: The Future of African Industrialisation

The chapter explores Africa's industrial future and concludes the book. This forward-looking section consolidates the findings and connects to broader issues regarding Africa's prospects for industrial transformation and expanding global partnerships, both in the Global South and the Global North. China remains a key player due to the progress made over the past 25 years and the resilience of the Forum on China-Africa Cooperation (FOCAC), an institutional innovation that has contributed to Africa's economic transformation. It offers insights into productive transformation, emphasising the importance of green and sustainable industrialisation, and China's advancement in green development as a potential contributor to green transition. Moreover, it offers strategic lessons for Africa and the broader Global South, underscoring the importance of agency, experimentation, and geopolitical rebalancing in shaping future pathways. Carbon-neutral industrialisation and low-carbon options could play a significant role in shaping future developments.[7]

Productive Transformation in Africa highlights that it remains the main challenge on the continent: *slow industrialisatio*n, *weak exports*, limited *productive capacity*, and minimal economic diversification. A key reason is the lack of political ambition, industrial policy, and state activism, as observed across various stages of development, industrial sectors, country cases, and policy areas in African countries, a legacy shaped by colonial dependency and external global factors. Furthermore, heterogeneity, diversity, and variation define the continent's performance. Africa's goal for economic transformation is rooted in industrialisation, which leverages emerging opportunities—including demographic shifts that drive markets and productive capacity, economic integration that consolidates scale and supply chains, and diversification with the Global South as a catalyst. Carbon-neutral industrialisation provides latecomer advantages rather than legacy burdens. The potential for industrialisation and latecomer benefits necessitates an active role for the state, pursuing industrial policy from a strategic viewpoint. Scholarly analysis of African industrialisation has address key methodological challenges, including data scarcity and a historical bias towards an "Afro-pessimist" narrative that viewed the continent as homogeneous. A more nuanced, heterodox perspective reveals a complex and uneven process, rather than a single failure, characterised by distinct historical phases and structural constraints.

References

Akyüz, Y. (2017) *Playing with fire: Deepened financial integration and changing vulnerabilities of the global south.* Oxford University Press.

Amsden, Alice. 1989. *Asia's Next Giant: South Korea and Late Industrialization.* New York: Oxford University Press.

Amsden, Alice. 2001. *The Rise of the "Rest": Challenges to the West from Late-Industrializing Economies.* Oxford: Oxford University Press.

[7] See CIKD (2023, 2025).

Centre for International Knowledge on Development (CIKD). 2023. *China's Progress Report. China's Progress Report on Implementation of the 2030 Agenda for Sustainable Development.* Beijing: Centre for International Knowledge on Development.

Centre for International Knowledge on Development (CIKD). 2025. *Global Development Report 2024. A World of Turbulence and Change: Cooperation to Address Global Common Languages.* Beijing: Foreign Language Press and China Development Press.

Centre for International Knowledge on Development CIKD. 2024. *A World of Turbulence and Change: Cooperation to Address Global Common Challenges.* China Development Press.

Chang, Ha-Joon. 1994. *The Political Economy of Industrial Policy.* Basingstoke: Macmillan.

Chang, Ha-Joon. 2002. *Kicking Away the Ladder: Development Strategy in Historical Perspective.* London: Anthem Press.

Cramer, Christopher, John Sender, and Arkebe Oqubay. 2020. *African Economic Development: Evidence, Theory, Policy.* Oxford: Oxford University Press.

Gerschenkron, Alexander. 1962. *Economic Backwardness in Historical Perspective.* Cambridge, MA: Harvard University Press.

Hirschman, Albert. 1958. *The Strategy of Economic Development.* New Haven: Yale University Press.

Jerven, Morten. 2011. *Africa: Why economists get it wrong.* London: Zed Publishers.

Jerven, Morten. 2013. *Poor Numbers: How We Are Misled by African Development Statistics and What to Do About It.* Cornell: Cornell University Press.

Kaldor, N. (1967) *Strategic factors in economic development.* New York State School of Industrial and Labour Relations, Cornell University.

Kaldor, N. (1980) *Essays on economic stability and growth* (2nd ed.). Holmes & Meier Publishers.

Lee, Keun. 2019. *The Art of Economic Catch-Up.* Cambridge: Cambridge University Press.

List, Frederick. [1841] 1856. *The National System of Political Economy.* Vol. I–IV. Memphis: Lippincott.

Oqubay, Arkebe. 2015. *Made in Africa: Industrial Policy in Ethiopia.* Oxford: Oxford University Press.

Oqubay, Arkebe. 2025. *Industrial Policy and Economic Development: Theory, Strategy, and Practice.* London: Palgrave Macmillan.

Oqubay, Arkebe, and Justin Yifu Lin. 2019. The Future of China–Africa Economic Ties: New Trajectory and Possibilities. In *China–Africa and an Economic Transformation*, ed. Arkebe Oqubay and Justin Yifu Lin, 367–383. Oxford: Oxford University Press.

Oqubay, Arkebe, and Justin Yifu Lin, eds. 2020. *The Oxford Handbook of Industrial Hubs and Economic Development*. Oxford: Oxford University Press.

Oqubay, Arkebe, Christopher Cramer, Ha-Joon Chang, and Richard Kozul-Wright. 2020. *The Oxford Handbook of Industrial Policy*. Oxford: Oxford University Press.

Pasinetti, Luigi. 1981. *Structural Change and Economic Growth: A Theoretical Essay on the Dynamics of the Wealth of Nations*. Cambridge: Cambridge University Press.

Thirlwall, Anthony. 2013. *Economic Growth in an Open Developing Economy: The Role of Structure and Demand*. Cheltenham: Edward Elgar.

United Nations. 2025a. Agenda 2030. https://sdgs.un.org/2030agenda.

United Nations. 2025b. Climate Action. The Paris Agreement. https://www.un.org/en/climatechange/paris-agreement.

CHAPTER 2

Perspectives on Productive Transformation

1 Structural Transformation and Industrial Policy

Industrial Policy and Structural Transformation

The conceptual framework for industrial policy fundamentally centres on its role as an active driver of structural transformation and economic catching-up. This view defines industrial policy not as an arbitrary set of interventions, but as a coherent strategy comprising explicit and implicit policy actions selectively directed at strategic sectors and emerging activities. Its core purpose, or "essence," is to steer structural change in line with a broader national vision, setting it apart from other economic policies. This long-term perspective requires strong synergies among macroeconomic policy, human capital development, and physical infrastructure, forming an integrated approach to promote productive investment and reshape the political economy. A key feature of this framework is its pragmatic, yet strategic, approach; it requires ongoing adaptation to evolving global and domestic circumstances, including limitations imposed by multilateral trade rules and the increasing significance of environmental considerations and sustainability. This pragmatic approach enables a trial-and-error method grounded in policy learning through experimentation and adjustment, which is typical of effective industrial policies in East Asia and China, where replacing failed instruments with new ones is a

A. Oqubay, *Productive Transformation in Africa*,
https://doi.org/10.1007/978-3-032-23941-9_2

valued, inherent feature of industrial policymaking. In many African countries, such as in Morocco's automotive industry (2000s–2010s) and Ethiopia's textile and leather Industries (2000s–2010s), the targeted productive investment and integrated industrial parks with subsidised infrastructure and power, but early productivity remained low due to skill gaps and supply chain weaknesses—illustrating the trial-and-error nature of learning.

Structural transformation—the ultimate aim of which is an "irreversible" shift seen not as a temporary change but as a fundamental and lasting shift in an economy's structure—highlights the long-term aspect and sets it apart from non-structural changes (Pasinetti 1981, 1993; Ocampo et al. 2009). It involves sectoral shifts from low- to high-productivity activities, driven by persistent productivity growth, technological spillovers, and changes in demand and institutions (Ocampo 2017).

South Korea's heavy and chemical industry drive (1970s and 1980s), despite initial imbalances and excess capacity in steel and petrochemicals, led to a persistent focus on building capabilities in these sectors, creating irreversible structural change and making them pillars of export by the 1980s and 1990s (Amsden 1989; Chang 1994). Similarly, Mauritius underwent economic transformation through diversification and industrialisation, shifting from a sugar mono-crop economy in the 1970s to having a significant share of the apparel and textile industry in the 1980s and 1990s (Oqubay 2025).

A *production-centric framework* is essential, as this transformation depends on developing a country's productive capacity and acquiring key capabilities. Historically, manufacturing has been seen as a vital driver of growth. This structuralist perspective, reflected in Kaldor's growth laws, indicates that manufacturing output growth directly leads to GDP growth, enhances its own productivity through both static and dynamic returns to scale (Verdoorn's Law), and boosts productivity in other sectors by transferring labour from diminishing-returns activities, such as subsistence agriculture.[1]

This technological dynamism arises from the sector's close connections to new knowledge, continuous improvements in production methods, and the realisation of increasing returns through specialisation and learning-by-doing (Kaldor 1967, 1980). Moreover, manufacturing is characterised by strong inter-sectoral linkages—supporting agriculture by providing a market for surplus produce and fostering the growth of productive services via outsourcing.

[1] Young (1928), UNCTAD (2006, 2013, 2016, 2019), UNCTAD-UNIDO, (2011).

However, conceptual boundaries are shifting, with phenomena such as "servicification" and the "industrialisation of freshness" blurring traditional sector boundaries, thereby expanding the scope for industrial policy and demanding its adaptation to these emerging trends. This is a nod to the global changes that create scope for the same features Kaldor et al. associate with manufacturing in some services and some agriculture nowadays.

Exports as a Vital Driver of Productive Transformation

The strategic importance of exports is a fundamental part of this transformational framework. From a structuralist point of view, exports are not just a result of liberalisation but a vital tool for deliberate positioning in global markets. Their significance is threefold. First, they serve as a primary source of international learning, pushing firms to meet global standards of quality, cost, and delivery, and acting as a focus for technological advancement. As Pasinetti (1981) argued, the spread of knowledge gained through international competition is a more crucial source of gain than the movement of goods itself.

Second, exports offer the most sustainable way to address balance-of-payments constraints that often impede growth and cause macroeconomic crises in developing economies. Third, they enable countries to expand markets for surplus production, overcoming the limits of domestic demand. This view sees export-led industrialisation (ELI) and import-substitution industrialisation (ISI) as complementary, sequential strategies, with ISI often laying the groundwork for a successful export drive.[2]

Taiwan's electronics sector (1970s–1990s) evolved from an initial ISI phase focused on protected domestic assembly and component manufacturing. As capabilities matured, firms such as Acer and Foxconn shifted towards export-oriented strategies, utilising prior knowledge to compete on a global scale—ISI and ELI occurred sequentially, not as stand-offs. Vietnam's electronics assembly (2010s–2020s): Samsung's substantial investment in smartphone manufacturing, accounting for 21% of Vietnam's exports by 2019 (COMTRADE 2025) introduced advanced production technology but offered limited development of local suppliers and transfer of R&D. Vietnam advanced into high-value electronics assembly but remained reliant on imported components and foreign design, exemplifying the latecomer advantage in manufacturing without fully assimilating technological capabilities, in contrast to Taiwan's TSMC model.

[2] Thirlwall (2002, 2011), Hirschman (1967, 1968).

The role of foreign direct investment (FDI) in this process is highly debated; its contribution to learning and spillovers is not automatic but depends on a deliberate host-country policy that regulates FDI through performance requirements, targets specific industries, and, most importantly, builds local capacity to realise the full potential benefits.

These perspectives on structural transformation directly inform industrial policy practice across several key areas. First, they reinforce the strategic importance of manufacturing-led industrialisation and exports, even for economies with large domestic markets. Second, they justify a sectoral approach in which priorities are set based on technological intensity, the strength of linkage effects, and demand elasticity. Third, they require policy instruments aligned with sector-specific structures that promote the transition to high-productivity activities. A critical principle here is linking state support and incentives to performance standards, particularly export performance, thereby creating a reciprocal monitoring system that disciplines firms to achieve international competitiveness.

Developing Productive Capability

At the core of this entire framework lies the enduring theory of nurturing productive capability, often linked to infant industry protection and known by alternative terms such as "productive power" or "productive forces" in classical political economy. This theory has been a pillar of industrial policy thought since the classical works of Alexander Hamilton and Friedrich List (Hamilton 1934; List 1856). It challenges static ideas of comparative advantage, arguing instead that nations actively develop their productive power. Its main principles hold that manufacturing is vital to wealth and power; that countries should focus on building national production systems; that sectors with higher value addition and knowledge intensity should be selectively targeted; and that temporary protection is necessary to give domestic industries time to learn and gather experience until they can compete on the international stage.

A modern and plausible synthesis of this view suggests that successful catch-up strategies involve a dynamic interaction between conforming to and defying comparative advantage. Initially, a country may adopt a Ricardian approach, exploiting latent advantages in areas like agricultural exports or light manufacturing. However, sustained structural transformation and escape from the middle-income trap require a deliberate shift to a Kaldorian strategy that actively creates new comparative advantage by focusing on manufacturing exports, concentrated investment, and learning, thereby enabling a nation to progress along the development ladder (Nolan 2014; Best 2018; Amsden and Chu 2003). Ultimately, the ability to shape comparative advantage, rather than solely exploit it, determines long-term success in economic catch-up and deepens the process of structural transformation.

The evolution of thinking on industrial policy is profoundly shaped by the challenges of technological learning and economic catch-up in the twenty-first century. This perspective is anchored in an evolutionary or Schumpeterian economic tradition, which posits technical change as the central driver of capitalism, with learning and capability development being critical for firm competitiveness (Schumpeter 1934, 1950). This view stands in stark contrast to neoclassical economics, which often treats innovation as an exogenous factor. The evolutionary tradition, supported by classical political economy, emphasises that the application of science to economic production is the epochal innovation of the modern age. Technical change is understood as a path-dependent process, fundamental to improving economic performance, and is characterised by uncertainty and duality. Schumpeter's concept of "creative destruction" captures the cyclical nature of this progress, where innovation—whether incremental or radical—constantly rejuvenates the industrial landscape. For latecomer economies, this process involves mastering and implementing new designs and production processes. This journey progresses from learning by doing and imitation to ultimately fostering domestic R&D capability.[3]

Malaysia's semiconductor industry (1970s–2010s) initially saw multinationals' assembly operations involve simple, labour-intensive tasks. Over decades, learning-by-doing and targeted training programmes enabled local firms to advance into wafer fabrication and design services—showing the shift from imitation to incremental innovation, although full R&D capability remained limited compared to Taiwan or South Korea.

Amsden presents a dynamic framework for understanding the staged yet interconnected process of productive transformation involving technological learning in late-industrialising firms. Amsden uses a broader concept of productive capability, which incorporates three core capabilities that firms progressively develop: production capability (optimising existing processes and machinery), investment capability (efficiently expanding capacity through new projects), and innovation capability (creating novel products and processes). These capabilities are interrelated and essential for technological catch-up. Innovation capability, without embodied

[3] See Schwartz (2010), Reinert (2008), Chandler (2004).

production facilities and investment capacity, cannot lead to genuine productive transformation. This interconnected progression emphasises that late industrialisation is not about pioneering radical inventions but about a disciplined, cumulative learning process. The ability to manage and engineer production effectively is a prerequisite for successful investment, which in turn provides the basis for authentic innovation.[4]

Amsden (1997) emphasises the importance of "bringing production back in" by arguing that the core economic role of successful late-industrialising governments is to actively collaborate with the private sector to develop firm-level "competitive assets" and technological capabilities. She asserts that industrialisation in this context is not driven by pioneering inventions but through a distinct process of "pure learning"—mastering and adapting already commercialised foreign technologies to produce tradable goods and implementing them across various industries. This requires states to go beyond macroeconomic management and directly support the development of large-scale, professionally managed firms and their entry into mid- or high-technology sectors. Through micro-level collaboration, the state and firms jointly acquire the necessary physical and knowledge-based assets, such as firm-specific skills and proprietary processes, to achieve international competitiveness. Ultimately, Amsden contends that the state's financial stability depends on the success of these specific industrial ventures, creating a symbiotic relationship where government policy is judged by its ability to foster productive, competitive firms. Production-centric approaches, firm capabilities, and economies of scale and scope are identified as central to industrial capitalism (Penrose 1959; Chandler 1990; Andreoni and Chang 2017, 2019).

China's high-speed rail development in the 2000s and 2010s involved technology transfer agreements with Siemens, Alstom, and Kawasaki. Chinese firms such as CRRC have mastered manufacturing and have gradually developed their own designs. Moreover, state funding, pilot projects, and performance goals sped up learning—highlighting how state-firm collaboration built competitive assets in mid- to high-tech sectors. Chinese railway technology firms have emerged as global leaders in the high-speed rail system.

Amsden (1997) emphasises that productive transformation concentrates on firm capabilities, strategy, and "competitive assets," as well as whether state support can generate genuine economic growth.

[4] See Cherif (2019), Akyüz (2017).

> "With respect to production, latecomer governments in postwar capitalist countries have assisted the private sector in building professionally managed, large-scale modern corporations and in entering mid-technology industries (471). [...] the prior process whereby factories, capital equipment, infrastructure, and firm-specific technological capabilities are amassed to produce tradables for any market" (p472) "[...] Micro-level studies of "the rest's" major export industries attest to extensive joint business-government collaboration in constructing the assets necessary to enter export activity, even in the case of industries based on natural resources and cheap labor." (p473) "[...] One must examine the state (or lack thereof) of development toward specific industries and firms. "For it is the success or failure of such ventures that ultimately determines the state's financial soundness (p474)."

Crucially, Amsden contends that this capability-building is not a natural market outcome but are actively orchestrated by the state. Industrial policies aim to push firms up this technological ladder, mainly through *reciprocal control mechanisms* (RCMs). Here, state support—such as subsidies or protection—is explicitly linked to firm performance, creating a disciplined, results-oriented partnership. This dynamic is strongly reinforced by an *export-led industrialisation* (ELI) strategy. By tying firm success to international competitiveness, ELI offers an objective, external benchmark that complements state-led RCMs. It compels firms to continually improve their production efficiency and product quality to remain competitive globally, thereby speeding up the entire learning cycle and making the catch-up process dynamic and sustainable.[5]

Kenya and Ethiopia's cut flower exports from the 1990s to the 2020s, along with strict European phytosanitary and social compliance standards (external benchmarks), compelled Kenyan and Ethiopian exporters to implement cold chains, traceability systems, and labour standards. Government support—covering infrastructure, research, and, in Ethiopia's case, land leases and duty-free inputs—was conditional on export performance. RCMs and ELI strengthened each other, establishing both countries as global leaders despite having minimal domestic flower markets. Ethiopia's rapid growth after 2005, driven by lower costs and government-backed investment in air cargo capacity, demonstrated how late entrants can penetrate even established export sectors when reciprocal mechanisms encourage learning and external market benchmarks provide measurable performance standards.

[5] See Amsden & Chu (2003), Chang (2003), Cramer et al. (2020).

Countries have historically pursued industrial policies to catch up, including Britain, the USA, and continental Europe; the Meiji Restoration; and, more recently, the East Tigers and China, as evidenced by classic works by Alexander Hamilton and Frederick List that illustrate the paths taken by the USA and continental Europe. The modern rediscovery of industrial policy has become popularised in mainstream economic discourse, as shown by scholars such as Charif and Hasanov at the IMF (The Return of the Policy That Shall Not Be Named: Principles of Industrial Policy, 2019). West European and US policymakers, including Germany's Angela Merkel, France's Emmanuel Macron, the New Deal of Franklin Roosevelt in the 1930s–1950s, and, more recently, Joe Biden and Donald Trump in the USA, have pursued industrial policy vigorously, with remarkable scale and renewed energy.

2 Technological Learning and Economic Catch-Up

A critical theoretical underpinning of this catch-up process is the concept of "the advantages of backwardness," as advanced by Gerschenkron (1962). This hypothesis suggests that latecomer economies, despite their disadvantages, can leverage their position to achieve rapid, discontinuous spurts of industrial development. Catch-up is defined as narrowing the gap between latecomers and frontrunners, with the potential for faster productivity gains, as new capital can embody the frontier of knowledge. However, this potential is not automatic; it requires a deliberate strategy and active state intervention.

Vietnam's smartphone and tablet production built and expanded in the 2010s and 2020s, considerable investment by Samsung's substantial investment introduced cutting-edge technology directly to Vietnam, enabling the country to leapfrog several stages of industrialisation. However, limited integration of local suppliers and R&D meant that Vietnam gained assembly value but not in design or component innovation—realising a latecomer advantage in production but not yet in full technological capability.

As Abramovitz (1986) noted, the growth potential weakens as productivity levels converge, making the latter stages of catch-up particularly challenging. Learning is the hallmark of this entire process, necessitating strategies that evolve through different phases. In early industrialisation, insertion into global value chains and imitation are essential. Still, sustained catch-up requires a different path to avoid the "catch-up paradox," in which latecomers advance faster than forerunners. This often involves "leapfrogging" into short-cycle technologies and gradually building R&D capabilities to move into innovation leadership (Lee 2019).

The difficulty of this transition is encapsulated in the concept of the "middle-income trap" (MIT). A plausible explanation for this phenomenon is not a set of static conditions, but a failure to invest adequately in the dynamic factors of productive and technological capabilities, which are the key drivers of productivity growth. The transition from a middle-income to a high-income economy hinges on a productive transformation into higher-value-added, knowledge-intensive activities. Thus, escaping the trap depends on the nature of the industrialisation trajectory—whether it leads to catch-up, stalled industrialisation, or premature deindustrialisation.

South Africa's mining sector (1990s–2020s), despite its high middle-income status and the production of sophisticated mining equipment, has suffered from a lack of diversification into higher-tech manufacturing and weak investment in innovation. This kept the economy reliant on commodities and energy, particularly coal. Its employment capacity has been limited, and premature deindustrialisation in manufacturing, combined with resource dependence, illustrates a middle-income trap driven by insufficient capability upgrading.

From this catch-up perspective, learning is the prime feature of late development, encompassing both technological learning within firms and policy learning by governments. This learning is embedded in practice, such as learning by doing, and requires an open system, contact with foreign knowledge, and strong absorptive capacity (Oqubay and Ohno 2019).[6] The experiences of successful East Asian economies highlight the importance of pragmatism—adopting what works and constantly adapting to international and domestic realities while adhering to a long-term vision. A key driver is the coherence and complementarity between productive capacity, export orientation, and innovation. Exports serve not only as a driver of growth through economies of scale but also as a disciplining device that promotes international learning and attests to competitiveness.

[6] *How Nations Learn: Technological Learning, Industrial Policy, and Catch-Up* (2019) illustrates that learning has been core to economic catch-up, policy learning by governments, and technological learning by firms.

The framework for fostering this learning is the national innovation system (NIS), which provides a holistic view of the conditions supporting innovative activities. This system encompasses firms, industries, and institutional networks, and has become increasingly open to external knowledge flows through trade, FDI, and technical alliances. The ability to exploit this external knowledge is a critical component of innovative capabilities. This premise has several essential implications for industrial policy. First, while NIS operates at a national level, augmented by sectoral innovation systems, as the drivers of agglomeration and technological learning are often industry-specific. Second, the evolving institutional structure balances the role of big businesses, which are crucial to global market exploitation and R&D, with support for new technology start-ups that continuously reinvigorate the innovation ecosystem. Third, collaboration among industrial firms, academia, and research centres is critical, with strong industry-university linkages being a vital element.

Finally, the distinction between innovation stages has significant policy implications. The mechanisms and instruments of industrial policy vary with the context and stage of industrialisation. In early stages, policies may focus on reverse engineering, licensing, and insertion into global value chains. In the middle stages, the focus shifts to technological institutes and targeted talent circulation. Ultimately, building an innovation-driven economy requires a focus on leapfrogging, massive investment in R&D, and the development of domestic capabilities, often illustrated by the transition from original equipment manufacturing (OEM) to own-design and manufacturing (ODM) and, finally, to own-brand manufacturing (OBM). This entire commitment to structural transformation and technological capability development underscores the necessity of state support and a creative state-market interaction, deeply embedded in the political economy. Taiwan's semiconductor industry (1980s–2020s): Evolved from OEM chip packaging (1980s) to ODM wafer fabrication (1990s via TSMC) and subsequently to OBM design leadership (2000s–2020s via MediaTek, TSMC advanced nodes). Extensive R&D investments, public research at ITRI, and talent returning from Silicon Valley propelled this shift—highlighting the OEM-ODM-OBM progression and emphasising the importance of innovation capability for advancing to a high-income economy.

3 The State and Political Economy

The state's role in economic development, particularly through industrial policy, is a subject of intense theoretical and practical debate, fundamentally challenging the myth of the self-regulating market. As Polanyi (1944) highlighted, the idea of a self-adjusting market is a "stark utopia," an institution that would inevitably annihilate the social and natural fabric without active state management. This reality underscores that market societies require the state not as a mere technical administrator but as a political actor making strategic decisions. This perspective forms the critical foundation for understanding industrial policy, revealing a spectrum of state-market relationships. At one extreme lies market fundamentalism, which idolises the free market and rejects state intervention, advocating privatisation and liberalisation, as seen in the Washington Consensus. A more moderate view is the market failure approach, which accepts selective state intervention to correct specific inefficiencies, such as in infrastructure or human capital, but confines the state to a facilitative role that replicates the conditions of a hypothetical perfect market without pursuing strategic transformation.

In contrast, the state activism perspective, central to this analysis, posits that the state actively shape and create markets to drive structural transformation and technological catch-up. This view sees the state as a daring partner and often a leader relative to the private sector, willing to undertake risks that businesses avoid. The critical question, as Chalmers Johnson (1982) noted, is not *if* the state intervenes, but *how* and *for what purpose*. This activist stance is embodied in the concept of the developmental state, which should not be understood as a static, pure prototype. Instead, it is a dynamic entity whose purpose and mechanisms evolve through different stages of industrialisation and across sectors. A dynamic perspective locates the state on a predatory-developmental continuum, shaped by its deliberate pursuit of developmental goals and its interaction with society. It is crucial to recognise that industrial policy does not operate in a political or institutional vacuum; policies that succeed in one context may fail in another due to differing political and institutional landscapes. The state's essential role is particularly pronounced for latecomer and late-latecomer economies navigating the challenges of catch-up development.[7]

[7] Hall (1987), Hirschman (1967, 1968).

Botswana's diamond-led development from the 1970s to the 2020s involved the state actively participating through a joint venture with De Beers (Debswana), capturing rents and investing in infrastructure, education, and economic diversification. Despite its resource wealth, disciplined fiscal management and long-term planning helped avoid the "resource curse"—demonstrating that developmental state principles can succeed even in resource-rich contexts. However, the Botswana government's engagement with De Beers has shown tensions, placing the country at a crossroads of economic diversification amid the artificial development of diamonds.

The political economy within which industrial policy is embedded is, therefore, not a secondary concern but a primary variable shaping its design, execution, and ultimate outcomes. Power relations and political variables are constitutive of economic policy, a profoundly political process conditioned by struggles between competing parties, ideologies, and social classes. Industrial policy itself actively shapes the market structure and the direction of private-sector growth. A policy focused on productive transformation and international trade positioning will cultivate a politically influential, manufacturing- and export-oriented private sector, which, in turn, will influence future policy. Conversely, a policy oriented towards extractive industries or finance will engender a different, often less dynamic, political-economic equilibrium. The cohesion, shared intellectual formation, and historical experiences of the political elite are significant factors. While complete consensus may be elusive, a basic agreement among ruling elites is necessary to secure the power needed to pursue industrial objectives.

A critical political economy test for an activist state is its capacity to discipline the private sector through the principle of reciprocity. The stark contrast between the success of East Asian industrial policies and the weaker performance in regions such as Latin America and Africa is often attributed to this variable. The state's ability to provide "productive rents" or incentives depends on its political capacity to demand performance in return. Managing rents for technology acquisition is constrained not just by state capacity but by political constraints that can render potentially growth-enhancing rents into growth-reducing ones if the state lacks the political strength to manage them effectively.

South Korea's Chaebols (1960s–1980s) emerged as national champions in the 1960s–1990s, and the state provided cheap credit, import protection, and subsidies to firms like Hyundai and Samsung but strictly enforced export targets and withdrew support from non-performers (for example, firms that failed to meet benchmarks lost privileges). The political capacity to discipline ensured that rents drove capability-building rather than just profit-taking. China's National Champions (1990s–2020s): Similarly, state banks channelled credit to firms like Huawei, BYD, and SMIC with clear technology acquisition and global market share targets; non-performing SOEs were restructured or allowed to fail. Singapore's Temasek Holdings (1970s–2020s), state ownership through Temasek in Singapore Airlines, Singapore Technologies, and Singtel was disciplined by commercial performance metrics and international competitiveness benchmarks, avoiding the inefficiency trap of typical SOEs. Ethiopian Airlines (1960s–2020s): remained state-owned but operated with commercial autonomy, reinvesting profits into fleet expansion and African hub strategy, disciplined by fierce regional and global competition—demonstrating that ownership form matters less than performance discipline. Morocco's OCP Group (1920s–2020s): The state phosphate monopoly was transformed into a globally competitive, innovation-driven firm through deliberate corporatisation, R&D investment, and downstream integration into fertilisers, with performance judged by export competitiveness and technological upgrading rather than mere rent extraction.

Kenya's import-substitution policy during the 1970s and 1980s, along with state protection and credit to manufacturing firms, lacked performance requirements or export discipline. Protected firms remained inefficient and uncompetitive; rents were consumed without upgrading capabilities. The absence of reciprocity turned growth-promoting potential into growth-reducing rent-seeking. This contrast shows that the key political economy variable is not state ownership versus private ownership, nor the provision of rents itself, but the state's political ability to enforce reciprocity—linking support to clear performance outcomes such as export targets, productivity improvements, or technological milestones. Successful cases (Korea, China, Singapore, Ethiopia, Morocco) share government discipline and bureaucratic capacity that are protected from capture, explicit performance benchmarks tied to international competitiveness, and a credible threat of withdrawal or restructuring for non-performers. Failed cases lack these enforcement mechanisms, enabling politically connected firms to claim rents without generating productivity or capability gains. The political economy lesson is that developmental state capacity lies not in intervention itself but in the ability to discipline recipients of state support—turning potential growth-enhancing rents into actual capability development rather than just profit-taking or rent-seeking.

Therefore, linking incentives to performance—such as export targets or productivity gains—is essential for improving developmental outcomes and guaranteeing a meaningful contribution from the private sector. It is not merely about having these incentives or reciprocal mechanisms but about utilising the most effective instruments (such as export performance) and consistently enforcing and adjusting them. This political context is inherently shaped by history and path dependency; for example, land reforms in East Asia created a political economy favourable to export-led industrialisation, while the different trajectory of land reform in Latin America created a constraining political dynamic.[8]

Inherent to the process of economic transformation is conflict. The rules of capitalism and the outcomes of industrial policies inevitably produce winners and losers, generating distributional conflicts across classes, sectors, and regions. As Hirschman (1977, 1991, 1995) argued, conflict is a persistent characteristic of a pluralist market society, and the most a society can aspire to is to "muddle through" from one conflict to the next.

From this perspective, political stability is a more complex issue than portrayed in conventional "business climate" indices. While a degree of stability and security is a minimum condition for attracting long-term investment and talent, it is insufficient on its own. What ultimately matters is a focus on productive transformation and technological capability. History shows that industrial growth and technical change have, in many instances, thrived even amidst significant instability and warfare, suggesting that the quality and focus of policy can sometimes transcend imperfect conditions.

Finally, a clear understanding of industrial policy requires dispelling several pervasive myths. The most common is reducing industrial policy to simply "picking winners," ignoring its broader role in shaping market dynamics and building systemic capabilities. Another is the false ideological dichotomy between state and market, when in reality every market has been shaped by some form of state intervention. Similarly, a vigorous industrial policy is not about a dominant state in a command economy, but about building a dynamic private sector. False dichotomies also persist between export-led and import-substitution industrialisation, which in

[8] See Mazzucato (2011).

practice are often complementary, and regarding FDI, which can be strategically directed to support domestic firms rather than operating as an isolated enclave. As Wade (2004) argues, the failure of neoclassical economics to guide effective industrial policy stems from its tendency to think in terms of curves rather than step changes and from its inability to distinguish between economic activities with different growth potentials.

In contrast, successful catch-up countries have consistently nurtured "superior" activities through strategic protection and subsidies, buffering them from—but not insulating them from—competitive pressures. Ultimately, industrial policy remains essential for structural transformation in the twenty-first century. It is inseparable from politics and political economy, and its success depends on a continuous process of learning from both international and local experience, supported by rigorous research, to constantly adapt to a changing domestic and global environment.

4 Industrial Policy in Practice: Navigating an Evolving Landscape

The Practice of Industrial Policies

A comprehensive understanding of industrial policy is intrinsically linked to the overarching objective of structural transformation, drawing on foundational concepts such as infant-industry protection and the intricate state-market mechanism. Far from being abstract declarations, these policies are purposeful instruments designed to drive structural change, generate employment, and advance national strategic interests. While predominantly designed and implemented at the national level, industrial policy also operates at regional and subnational levels. The practice of successful industrial policy is thus a dynamic and adaptive process, centred on principles that foster dynamism, coherence, and complementarity to achieve technological catch-up and productive transformation.

Central to this practice is the concept of linkage dynamics, as pioneered by Hirschman (1958). Linkage effects provide a conceptual tool for identifying how one productive activity can induce investment in others, creating a compelling sequence of development decisions. For latecomer economies, correctly identifying sectors with strong backward and forward linkages is crucial for accelerating structural change. This approach shifts the focus from perceived resource scarcity to the strategic ability to catalyse investment and unlock latent potential.

Complementing this is the idea of *latitude for performance*, a variable across different industries that involves these features, enabling leverage of performance depending on the inherent technological and economic characteristics within a sector's industrial structure. For instance, according to Hirschman, the aviation or air industry's narrow latitude for performance enables many developing countries to succeed in it. The same applies to the cement industry, which operates a continuous production process despite its capital intensity.

In African aviation services (1990s–2020s), which employs over 50,000 direct and indirect workers and generates about US$8 billion in exports in 2024, Ethiopian Airlines succeeded by exploiting aviation's "narrow latitude"—standardised global maintenance, safety, and service protocols leave little room for variation, enabling latecomer airlines to compete quickly once these standards are met. This contrasts with auto manufacturing's "wide latitude," where incremental process innovations and supplier ecosystems matter greatly, making catch-up more difficult. However, narrow latitude does not translate into industrial competitiveness without the right corporate strategy and significant investment in technological capability, fleet, infrastructure, and skills that build economies of scale in such a highly competitive global industry.[9]

A production-centric perspective highlights the dynamism of export-led industrialisation, which boosts productivity, opens access to larger markets, and acts as a key source of international learning and foreign exchange. However, this does not exclude strategic import substitution. Additionally, there is a vital interdependence between manufacturing and agriculture. As Nicholas Kaldor (1967) argued, productive, commercialised agriculture is not a rival to industry but a necessity, creating initial demand for manufactured goods and supplying surplus for industrial growth.

A third crucial balance is between foreign direct investment (FDI) and domestic firms. While FDI can provide essential capital and technology in globalised production networks, building an innovation-driven economy also requires focusing on developing domestic technological capabilities, as demonstrated by the different paths of East Asian economies. Nonetheless, these patterns are not always balanced, and the linkages and growth dynamics often occur in unconventional forms, with imbalances and tensions. For such complementarity to develop, policies and

[9] See UNECA (2016), Oqubay (2015), Oqubay and Lin (2020).

strategies focused on managing imbalances and strengthening linkages, which vary across industries, geographic spaces, political economies, and timeframes.

Beyond sectoral linkages, the deliberate cultivation of industrial ecosystems and cluster dynamics is a fundamental feature of modern industrial policy. Agglomeration economies foster specialisation, increase returns to scale, and act as catalysts for innovation and learning. While industrial districts can form organically, successful latecomer strategies involve their deliberate development as dynamic, evolving entities rather than static collections of firms (Marshall 1920). As Michael Best argues, dynamic districts continuously upgrade and reconfigure their production chains, unlike static districts that lack an internal growth dynamic. The vitality of these hubs is shaped by an open culture of learning and a network of interconnected institutions—including universities, research centres, and government bodies—that promote knowledge exchange, collective efficiency, and a blend of cooperation and competition. Effective policies for such clusters involve talent attraction, support for start-ups and spin-outs, and strategies tailored to the cluster's specific stage of development, from initial formation to maturity.

The design and execution of industrial policy are invariably fraught with inherent tensions that is strategically managed. A primary challenge is ensuring strategic compatibility and coherence. Instruments align with a grand national vision and focus on developing productive capacity and technological learning. Sustained productivity growth requires a combination of learning-by-doing and major "true" innovations. Achieving coherence across multiple policy instruments and between short-term actions and long-term goals is challenging but critical, as inconsistency in execution undermines effectiveness and learning.

Furthermore, industrial policy does not exist in a vacuum; its success is contingent on complementing other policy domains. Human capital development is essential, evolving from basic education for agricultural growth to advanced technical training and university-industry linkages in an innovation-driven economy. Similarly, physical infrastructure—from basic connectivity to advanced logistics—that evolve with the development stage, requiring long-term planning and capital commitment. Macroeconomic policy has to be complementary, ensuring that exchange rates, taxation, and fiscal policy support the production-centric pathway rather than undermining it through instability or misaligned incentives.

A vital principle for navigating these tensions is enforcing competitiveness and discipline. Drawing on East Asian experiences, support and incentives for firms are contingent on performance standards, such as export targets or productivity gains, and adhere to a principle of reciprocity. As Alice Amsden (1989, 2001) noted, the most effective industrial policies "give nothing away for free." This requires a capable bureaucracy insulated from rent-seeking interests, along with tools such as export discipline and fostering domestic rivalry to incentivise international competitiveness and continuous innovation. The incentive structure should also accelerate "creative destruction," support vibrant new entrants while allowing non-competitive firms to exit. Ultimately, the practice of industrial policy is a complex balancing act that thrives not by eliminating tensions, but by leveraging them as a source of dynamism.

Adapting Industrial Policies to Emerging Issues

A critical aspect of industrial policy is to adapt to emerging issues that define its contemporary practice in a rapidly evolving global landscape. That industrial policy is inherently dynamic; its success depends on constant adaptation to both external shifts and local conditions. Empirical evidence underscores that outcomes are markedly uneven across sectors, a variation primarily driven by three interconnected factors: the distinct industrial structure of each industry, the prevailing politics and political economy, and the density of linkage effects that can be harnessed. This triumvirate explains why uniform policy prescriptions fail and why a nuanced, sector-specific approach is essential for effective design and implementation.

The context for this struggle is fundamentally shaped by changing patterns of global production and the world economy. The dominant feature of the last half-century has been the internationalisation of production through global value chains (GVCs), also featured as "global business revolution" (GBR) and the dominance of multinational corporations (MNCs) (Nolan 2014). This new architecture, coupled with a shifting international governance system marked by WTO rules, the TRIPS agreement, and a Sino-centric economic order, has significantly constrained the policy space available to developing nations. As Wade argues, the mobility of capital in the GVC era has tipped the balance of power decisively in favour of MNCs, allowing them to readily shift production in response to host-country policies or labour costs, thereby creating a regime of "slow or no long-run convergence" for many developing economies. The post-2008 global political economy reflects contradictory tendencies, including the simultaneous advocacy by emerging powers for a pro-WTO multilateral trading system, a backlash favouring bilateralism, and the continued integration of regional markets, creating a complex and fragmented governance environment.

Simultaneously, accelerated technological advancement presents both unprecedented opportunities and profound challenges. The fusion of technologies such as AI, automation, and digitisation—often referred to as the Fourth Industrial Revolution—is disrupting every industry. However, this process is accompanied by the risk of "technological romanticising," a deterministic hype that ignores the need for technology to serve social well-being and transformation. The unrestrained power accrued by leading technology MNCs can undermine state capacity and citizen rights. Critically, the impact of these technologies is not uniform across sectors, necessitating that industrial policies develop a sophisticated, sector-level understanding to effectively mitigate disruptions and harness opportunities, particularly in human capital development, innovative infrastructure, and R&D.

Finally, the imperative of sustainability now demands a central place in industrial policy discourse. The historical neglect of environmental costs during earlier periods of industrialisation is no longer tenable. While corporate stance varies with economic interest, and consumer awareness has grown, market forces alone have proven insufficient to drive the necessary ecological transition. An emerging and critical perspective holds that economic growth and environmental sustainability are not mutually exclusive but can be mutually reinforcing. Achieving sustainable development requires the deliberate integration of green objectives at the very core of industrial policy. This involves crafting a regulatory regime that penalises polluters, designing industrial incentives that reward resource efficiency and sustainability, and fostering innovation in environmental technologies to simultaneously drive job creation, economic growth, and ecological preservation. In conclusion, the practice of industrial policy in the twenty-first century have to strategically adapted to navigate the intersecting challenges of the middle-income trap, a constraining global production system, disruptive technological change, and the existential imperative of environmental sustainability.[10]

[10] See Mathews (2017), Mathews and Oqubay (2025).

5 Conceptual Framework of Productive Transformation

The book's conceptual framework, rooted in structuralist development economics perspectives, is built on three pillars of the industrial policy framework: the development of productive capacity, the political economy of industrialisation, and strategies shaped by latecomer advantages. The research design on which the book develops its analysis and its arguments integrates extensive comparative research based on selected case studies, employing mixed-methods research that draws on long-term historical evidence, sector- and nation-specific case studies, and future-oriented analysis to outline opportunities for Africa's industrial trajectory.

Productive Capability

Structural transformation is viewed as a shift towards production-centred strategies, based on Amsden's focus on production capability, Hirschman's production linkages, and Kaldor's sector-oriented approach. Key arguments from Thirlwall (2013) and Kaldor (1967) highlight export and manufacturing growth as central to production-driven interventions, with technology and innovation serving as the engines of dynamic comparative advantage. Firm-level capabilities, as discussed by Amsden (1989) and Penrose (1959), are crucial for embedding innovation and productivity within industrial structures and firm capacities.

China's industrial transformation from the 1980s to the 2020s shifted from labour-intensive exports like textiles and toys to strategic development in machinery, electronics, and high-speed rail. This progression culminated in leadership in innovation sectors such as 5G (Huawei), electric vehicles (BYD), and solar panels (LONGi, JinkoSolar). Major R&D investment (2.6% of GDP by 2025) and over 6.5 million R&D staff, along with strategic SOE reforms with performance discipline and leveraging latecomer advantages through technology acquisition and indigenous innovation, transformed China into a global manufacturing and innovation power. This entire process demonstrates the evolution from simple production capacity to advanced innovation capability embedded in firm-level competencies and the creation of dynamic comparative advantages. This perspective challenges pessimistic views of Africa's prospects for industrialisation through manufacturing and export-led strategies, asserting that production-oriented approaches remain crucial.[11]

[11] See Lin (2012, 2016).

Industrialisation Strategy

The framework promotes an activist industrial policy in which the state plays an active role, going beyond mere facilitation, by adapting interventions across various sectors, development stages, and institutional contexts. Sectoral targeting is key—acknowledging that industrial structure influences outcomes—aligning with findings that Africa's successful industrialisation depends on clear long-term plans, sector-specific support, and strong institutional coordination. Strategies should also foster productive power by applying a reciprocal-monitoring mechanism, promoting developmental partnerships among government, the private sector, academia, the scientific community, and labour, ensuring that subsidies and coordination mechanisms lead to sustained structural transformation.

Latecomer Advantages and Opportunities

Building on Gerschenkron's idea of the advantage of backwardness (latecomer advantage) and Amsden's concept of late development, Africa's position as a latecomer offers potential to leap into new economic areas by harnessing irreversible global shifts. The key prospects focus on adopting carbon-neutral industrial pathways as drivers of Africa's carbon-neutral industrialisation, engaging productively with the Global South to catalyse Africa's economic transformation through promoting productive investment, trade diversification, development financing, and using technology for learning and creating a supportive policy environment.

Latecomer advantages in the twenty-first century, with technological advances in green energy—such as falling costs of solar power and batteries—and digital platforms enable latecomers to bypass traditional, carbon-intensive industrial paths that earlier nations faced. China's leadership in electric vehicles, solar panels, and digital payments—like Alipay and WeChat Pay—illustrates how latecomers can benefit from rapid technology cycles and decreasing capital costs. At the same time, diversification of economic cooperation beyond traditional Western powers—via China's BRI infrastructure financing, India's digital public infrastructure models, and South–South trade networks—broadens policy options and funding sources for African latecomers. This reshaped global landscape provides unmatched opportunities to blend green industrialisation with digital transformation, supported by alternative development finance and technology partnerships that earlier industrialisers lacked due to Western-dominated institutions and reliance on fossil fuels.

Opportunities for Africa also arise from demographic shifts and urbanisation, which are primary drivers of socio-economic transformation, as well as from the development of the continent-wide single market under the AfCFTA and Africa's deep economic integration. The framework acknowledges Africa's heterogeneity, diverse development paths, and the "possibilist" perspective that industrialisation trajectories are not fixed but can be strategically shaped.

References

Abramovitz, Moses. 1986. Catching Up, Forging Ahead, and Falling Behind. *The Journal of Economic History* 46 (2): 385–406.

Akyüz, Yilmaz. 2017. *Playing with Fire: Deepened Financial Integration and Changing Vulnerabilities of the Global South*. Oxford: Oxford University Press.

Amsden, Alice. 1989. *Asia's Next Giant: South Korea and Late Industrialization*. Oxford: Oxford University Press.

Amsden, Alice. 1997. Editorial: Bringing Production Back in—Understanding Government's Economic Role in Late Industrialization. *World Development* 25 (4): 469–480.

Amsden, Alice. 2001. *The 'Rise of the Rest': Challenges to the West from Late-Industrializing Economies*. Oxford: Oxford University Press.

Amsden, A. and Chu, W.-W. (2003) *Beyond Late Development" Taiwan's Upgrading Policies*. MIT Press.

Amsden, Alice, and Wan-wen Chu. 2003. *Beyond Late Development: Taiwan's Upgrading Policies*. Cambridge, MA: MIT Press.

Andreoni, Antonio, and Ha-Joon Chang. 2017. Bringing Production and Employment Back into Development: Alice Amsden's Legacy for a New Developmentalist Agenda. *Cambridge Journal of Regions, Economy and Society* 10 (1): 173–187.

Andreoni, Antonio, and Ha-Joon Chang. 2019. The Political Economy of Industrial Policy: Structural Interdependencies, Policy Alignment and Conflict Management. *Structural Change and Economic Dynamics* 48:136–150.

Best, Michael. 2018. *How Growth Really Happens: The Making of Economic Miracles Through Production, Governance, and Skills*. Princeton: Princeton University Press.

Chandler, A. (1990) *Scale and scope: The dynamics of industrial capitalism*. Harvard University Press.

Chandler, Alfred. 2004. *Scale and Scope: The Dynamics of Industrial Capitalism*. Cambridge, MA: Harvard University Press.

Chang, Ha-Joon. 1994. *The Political Economy of Industrial Policy*. London: Macmillan.

Chang, Ha-Joon. 2003. *Kicking Away the Ladder: Development Strategy in Historical Perspective*. London: Anthem Press.

Cherif, Reda, and Fuad Hasanov. 2019. *The Return of the Policy That Shall Not Be Named: Principles of Industrial Policy*. IMF Working Paper WP/19/74. March.

COMTRADE (2025) *Data on Trade and Export Goods*. Geneva.

Cramer, Christopher, and John Sender. 2019. Oranges Are Not Only Fruit: The Industrialization of Freshness and the Quality of Growth. In *The Quality of Growth in Africa*, ed. Ravi Kanbur, Akbar Noman, and Joseph Stiglitz, 209–233. New York: Columbia University Press.

Cramer, Christopher, John Sender, and Arkebe Oqubay. 2020. *African Economic Development: Evidence, Theory, Policy*. Oxford: Oxford University Press.

Gerschenkron, Alexander. 1962. *Economic Backwardness in Historical Perspective*. Cambridge, MA: Harvard University Press.

Hall, Peter. 1987. *Governing the Economy: The Politics of State Intervention in Britain and France*. Cambridge: Polity Press.

Hamilton, Alexander. 1934. *Papers on Public Credit, Commerce and Finance*, ed. Samuel McKee. New York: Columbia University Press.

Hirschman, Albert. 1958. *The Strategy of Economic Development*. New Haven: Yale University Press.

Hirschman, Albert O. 1967. *Development Projects Observed*. Washington, DC: The Brookings Institution.

Hirschman, Albert O. 1968. The Political Economy of Import-substitution Industrialization in Latin America. *Quarterly Journal of Economics* 82 (1): 2–32.

Hirschman, Albert. 1977. *The Passions and the Interests: Political Arguments for Capitalism Before Its Triumph*. Princeton: Princeton University Press.

Hirschman, Albert. 1991. *The Rhetoric of Reaction: Perversity, Futility, Jeopardy*. Cambridge, MA: The Belknap Press of Harvard University Press.

Hirschman, Albert. 1995. *A Propensity to Self-Subversion*. Cambridge, MA: Harvard University Press.

Johnson, Chalmers. 1982. *MITI and the Japanese Miracle: The Growth of Industrial Policy, 1925–1975*. Stanford: Stanford University Press.

Kaldor, Nicholas. 1967. *Strategic Factors in Economic Development*. Ithaca: New York State School of Industrial and Labour Relations, Cornell University.

Kaldor, Nicholas. 1980. *Essays on Economic Stability and Growth*. 2nd ed. New York: Holmes & Meier Publishers.

Lee, Keun. 2019. *The Art of Economic Catch-Up: Barriers, Detours and Leapfrogging in Innovation Systems*. Cambridge: Cambridge University Press.

Lin, Justin, and Volker Treichel. 2012. *Learning from China's Rise to Escape the Middle-Income Trap: A New Structural Economics Approach to Latin America*. Policy Research Working Paper, 6165. August.

Lin, Justin. 2016. The Latecomer Advantages and Disadvantages: A New Structural Economics Perspective. In *Diverse Development Paths and Structural Transformation in Escape from Poverty*, ed. Martin Andersson and Tobias Axelsson, 43–67. Oxford: University Press.

List, Friedrich. 1856. *National System of Political Economy*. Vol. I–IV. Memphis: Lippincott.

Marshall, Alfred. 1920. *Principles of Economics*. London: Palgrave Macmillan.

Mathews, John. 2017. *Global Green Shift: When Ceres Meets Gai*. London: Anthem Press.

Mathews, John, and Arkebe Oqubay, eds. 2025. *The Oxford Handbook on the Greening of Economic Development*. Oxford: Oxford University Press.

Mazzucato, Mariana. 2011. *The Entrepreneurial State: Debunking Public vs. Private Sector Myths*. London: Anthem Press.

Nolan, Peter. 2014. *Chinese Firms, Global Firms: Industrial Policy in the Age of Globalization*. New York: Routledge.

Ocampo, J. Antonio. 2017. Dynamic Efficiency: Structural Dynamics and Structural Change in Developing Countries. In *Efficiency, Finance, and Varieties of Industrial Policy*, ed. A. Noman and J. E. Stiglitz. New York: Columbia University Press, Chapter 3.

Ocampo, José Antonio, Cordina Rada, and Lance Taylor. 2009. *Growth and Policy in Developing Countries: A Structuralist Approach*. New York: Columbia University Press.

Oqubay, Arkebe. 2015. *Made in Africa: Industrial Policy in Ethiopia*. Oxford: Oxford University Press.

Oqubay, Arkebe, and Justin Yifu Lin, eds. 2020. *The Oxford Handbook of Industrial Hubs and Economic Development*. Oxford: Oxford University Press.

Oqubay, Arkebe, and Kenichi Ohno, eds. 2019. *How Nations Learn: Technological Learning, Industrial Policy, and Catch-Up*. Oxford: Oxford University Press.

Oqubay, A. (2025) *Industrial Policy and Economic Development: Theory, Strategy, and Practice*. Palgrave Macmillan.

Pasinetti, Luigi. 1981. *Structural Change and Economic Growth: A Theoretical Essay on the Dynamics of the Wealth of Nations*. Cambridge: Cambridge University Press.

Pasinetti, Luigi. 1993. *Structural Economic Dynamics: A Theory of the Economic Consequences of Human Learning*. Cambridge: Cambridge University Press.

Penrose, Edith. 1959. *The Theory of the Growth of the Firm*. Oxford: Oxford University Press.

Polanyi, Karl (1944) The Great Transformation: The Political and Economic Origin of Our Time. New York: Farrar & Rinehart.

Reinert, Erik. 2008. *How Rich Countries Get Rich and Why Poor Countries Stay Poor*. London: Constable.

Schumpeter, Joseph. [1934] 2017. *The Theory of Economic Development*. New York: Routledge.

Schumpeter, Joseph. 1950. *Capitalism, Socialism, and Democracy*. 3rd ed. New York: Harper and Brothers.

Schwartz, Herman. 2010. *States Versus Markets: The Emergence of a Global Economy*. 3rd ed. New York: Palgrave.

Thirlwall, Anthony. 2002. *The Nature of Economic Growth: An Alternative Framework for Understanding the Performance of Nations*. Cheltenham: Edward Elgar.

Thirlwall, Anthony. 2011. Balance of Payments Constrained Growth Models: History and Overview. *PSL Quarterly Review* 64 (259): 307–351.

Thirlwall, Anthony. 2013. *Economic Growth in an Open Developing Economy: The Role of Structure and Demand*. Cheltenham: Edward Elgar.

Tregenna, F. 2009. Characterising Deindustrialisation: An Analysis of Changes in Manufacturing Employment and Output Internationally. *Cambridge Journal of Economics* 33 (3): 433–466.

Tregenna, Fiona. 2013. Deindustrialization and Reindustrialization. In *Pathways to Industrialization in the Twenty-First Century: New Challenges and Emerging Paradigms*, ed. Adam Szirmai, Wim Naudé, and Ludvico Alcorta. Oxford: Oxford University Press.

UNCTAD. 2006. *Developing Productive Capacities. The Least Developed Countries Report 2006*. Geneva: United Nations.

UNCTAD. 2013. *Global Value Chains: Investment and Trade for Development. World Investment Report*. Geneva: United Nations.

UNCTAD. 2016. *Structural Transformation for Inclusive and Sustained Growth. Trade and Development Report*. Geneva: United Nations.

UNCTAD. 2019. *World Investment Report, WIR 2019*. Geneva: UNCTAD.

UNCTAD-UNIDO. 2011. *Fostering Industrial Development in Africa in the New Global Environment. Economic Development in Africa Report 2011*. Geneva/New York: United Nations Industrial Development Organization and United Nations Conference on Trade and Development.

UNECA. 2016. *Greening Africa's Industrialization. Economic Report on Africa*. Addis Ababa: United Nations Economic Commission for Africa.

Wade, Robert. 2004. *Governing the Market: Economic Theory and the Role of the Government in East Asian Industrialization*. Princeton: Princeton University Press.

Young, Allyn. 1928. Increasing Returns and Economic Progress. *Economic Journal* 38 (152): 527–542.

CHAPTER 3

The History and Performance of Industrialisation and Industrial Policy in Africa

1 Evolution of African Industrialisation (1960–2025)

Evidence on African Industrialisation

Research on African industrialisation faces significant challenges regarding methodologies. Firstly, there is a notable lack of reliable evidence at the national level, across industries, and over an extended time frame. Data are not consistently available at the continental level, as international organisations, including the UN and the World Bank, employ regional classifications such as sub-Saharan Africa (SSA) and the Middle East and North Africa (MENA). The time series datasets do not extend from 1960 to the present, and the evidence for the earlier decades is meagre and incomplete. If governments and scholars are truly to take industrialisation seriously, they need to pay more attention to this critical issue. It is a major policy challenge that reflects ideas, interests, and institutions that all need to change. Not all African governments conduct yearly manufacturing surveys, and those that do often reveal substantial weaknesses and are susceptible to political interference that can affect their outcomes (Oqubay 2015; Cramer et al. 2020).

Second, the evidence and analysis have been influenced by the misperception of *Afro-pessimism*, which claims that Africa's future does not rest on industrialisation or export-led industrialisation in the twenty-first

A. Oqubay, *Productive Transformation in Africa*,
https://doi.org/10.1007/978-3-032-23941-9_3

century and that Africa lacks the capacity and prospects for industrialisation, without offering empirical evidence grounded in original research to support this view. Third, much of the academic work and research output regards Africa as a homogeneous entity, sometimes referred to as the *African Dummy*, neglecting the continent's diversity and the various socio-political contexts in countries such as Nigeria and Ethiopia (Jerven 2011, 2013). Lastly, the literature is predominantly shaped by Eurocentric or dominant Western philosophical values examined from a mainstream perspective.

However, alternative perspectives on African economic development and industrialisation have emerged over the past two decades, highlighting the importance of pluralism and heterodox views, alongside interdisciplinary and comparative studies that utilise mixed methods and orientations. The emerging literature emphasises the significance of diversity, heterogeneity, variation, and unevenness as promising avenues for understanding African industrialisation. Structuralist perspectives and political economy dimensions have received increased focus in examining African industrialisation from a long-term viewpoint, considering industrialisation as a driver of structural transformation and manufacturing as an engine of economic growth.

Africa's industrial transformation path differs significantly from that of Asia. While China and India dominated global manufacturing until the mid-nineteenth century—accounting for half of the world's GDP and industrial output—Africa's industrialisation mainly expanded after decolonisation in the 1960s. Furthermore, this initial industrialisation was largely limited to extractive industries that supplied raw materials to European manufacturers rather than to the development of domestic productive capacity. African industrialisation has since progressed through four distinct stages, shaped by the interaction of industrial development strategies, domestic political economy factors, and changes in the international economic environment.

The origins of industrialisation before the 1950s are poorly documented. Colonial patterns dominated this period, with significant differences between settler and non-settler colonies, such as those in the South African settler economy and those in Kenya and Morocco (El Aynaoui and Oqubay 2026).[1] As shown below, Africa's industrialisation after

[1] See Bekele (2019), Jerven (2017), Clapham (1988, 2019), Chan (2025), Zartman (2026), Zewde (2002), Pankhurst (1996), Oualalou (2026).

independence can be divided into four stages: the first stage, from the early 1960s to the late 1970s; the second stage, from the early 1980s to the late 1990s; and the third stage, from the early 2000s to the mid-2020s.

Industrialisation During Pre-Independence Africa (Before the 1960s)

Evidence about pre-1960 industrialisation remains limited and incomplete. Austin, Frankema, and Jerven (2017: 348) note that "any long-term analysis of African economic development suffers data-availability constraints," with long manufacturing output series available only for a few countries. Nevertheless, African handicraft and cottage industries—especially high-quality textile weaving and iron smelting—existed long before colonial rule, providing essential farm tools and fabrics for local consumption. Green (2019) documents that by 500–700 CE, copper artefacts in the Upper Senegal River Valley were traded for cloth produced on spindle-looms, demonstrating early West African manufacturing capacity. However, these indigenous industries declined during the nineteenth and early twentieth centuries as European Industrial Revolution products flooded African markets, particularly in Ghana and Nigeria. Green's research further reveals how transformations in West and West-Central African cloth production contributed to the continent's economic marginalisation alongside the rise of the export slave trade.

Colonial rule severely constrained African industrialisation. Manufacturing was deliberately limited to extractive industries (mining and cash-crop processing) and basic consumer goods (textiles, beverages, cigarettes, soap) that served settler populations without competing with European manufacturers. Significant industrial development occurred only in settler colonies like South Africa (independent within the British Empire by 1910) and Southern Rhodesia (autonomous by 1923), where white minority governments could direct investment towards manufacturing. The British Treasury actively rejected promoting African manufacturing after World War II, viewing colonial development primarily as a mechanism to assist British economic recovery rather than foster potential competitors (Austin et al. 2017). Colonial trade policies, coercive cultivation schemes, and free-trade regulations systematically pre-empted economic diversification and eroded indigenous handicrafts (Frankema et al. 2018). Although some import-substitution industrialisation (ISI) occurred for bulky intermediate goods like cement, rails, and sacks that benefitted from natural protection, colonial powers deliberately restricted advanced manufacturing (Clarence-Smith 2016). This extractive model maintained Africa as a supplier of raw materials and captive market for European goods, producing deindustrialisation patterns similar to colonial India.

By the late 1950s, some manufacturing growth had occurred in consumer goods, food and beverages, and cash-crop processing. Zimbabwe and the DRC registered manufacturing outputs of 16% and 14% respectively in 1960 (Austin et al. 2017: 353). Patterns differed significantly between settler colonies (South Africa, Kenya) and non-settler territories due to variations in government systems and investment priorities. South Africa's settler rulers developed extensive mining operations with sustained state investment in major economic sectors throughout the twentieth century until apartheid's end. Ethiopia presents an exceptional case, having remained independent and maintained its handicraft and cottage industries as major producers for rural areas, while the central government established local banks, Ethiopian Airlines, and telecommunications from the early twentieth century (Oqubay 2015, 2019a, b; Shiferaw and Söderbom 2019).

Import-Substitution and State-Led Industrialisation (1960s–1970s): The "Golden Era"?

Africa's economic performance clearly demonstrates that African countries achieved the highest economic growth during the early industrialisation period, with commendable growth rates of 4.5% in the 1960s and 4.2% in the 1970s (see Fig. 3.1 and Table 3.1). This performance exceeded the world's average growth of 3.9% and approached Asia's 5.2%. Furthermore, it was accompanied by a significant increase in manufacturing value added, averaging 6.2% during the 1960s and 1970s. South Africa accounted for a substantial share of sub-Saharan Africa's manufacturing output, representing more than half, primarily due to its large mining-industrial complex. Meanwhile, Northern Africa emerged as a significant industrial sub-region, alongside coastal areas in other sub-regions. Landlocked countries lagged in their industrialisation efforts, hindered by high transport and logistics costs, which constituted 35–50%.[2]

[2] World Bank (2023).

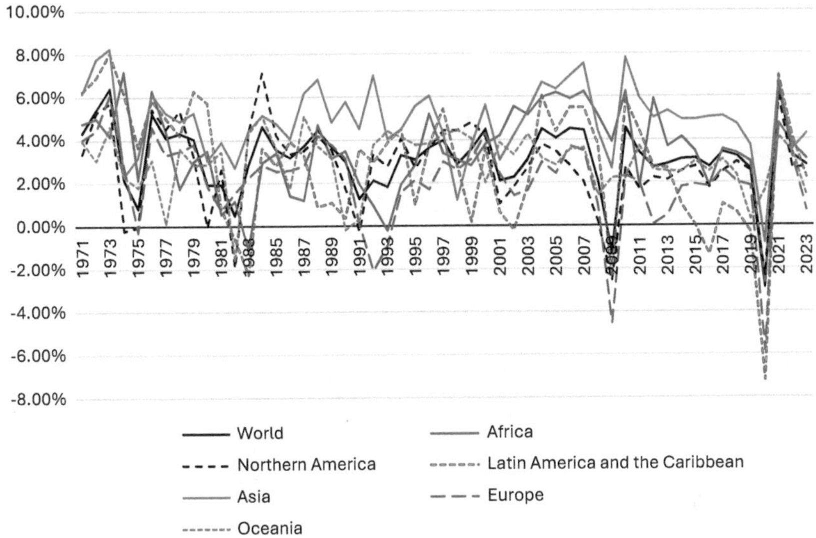

Fig. 3.1 GDP growth rate in Africa compared to other regions, 1971 to 2024. (Source: Computed by author using GDP data (constant 2015 US$, millions) from UNCTAD Data Centre)

Africa's industrialisation during this period featured several key aspects. Firstly, it was characterised by import-substitution industrialisation aimed at the domestic market, with significant investments in light manufacturing and basic industries. Second, most African countries relied on a planned economy and state-led industrialisation, investing in major industrial projects overseen by the government. The prevailing policy perspective viewed industrialisation and manufacturing as promising paths for Africa, emphasising the necessity of a strategic role for the state. However, industrialisation at this stage was constrained by limited human capital development, weak institutional strength of the state, underdeveloped infrastructure, and restricted access to development financing. Many researchers consider this period arguably as Africa's "golden age," with the field of development economics during this era favouring industrialisation and the state's role in economic development (Cramer et al. 2020).

Table 3.1 Average GDP growth rate from 1971 to 2024 by world regions

Region	*1971–1980*	*1981–1990*	*1991–2000*	*2001–2010*	*2011–2020*	*2021–2023*	*1971–2023*
World	3.88%	3.15%	3.01%	3.03%	2.43%	4.16%	3.16%
Africa	4.23%	2.08%	2.56%	5.44%	2.80%	3.86%	3.45%
Northern America	3.26%	3.28%	3.40%	1.79%	1.87%	3.79%	2.78%
Latin America and the Caribbean	5.82%	1.39%	3.17%	3.10%	0.35%	4.42%	2.86%
Asia	5.22%	4.86%	4.65%	5.50%	4.39%	4.86%	4.92%
Europe	3.41%	2.63%	1.54%	1.68%	0.87%	3.46%	2.11%
Oceania	2.81%	2.84%	3.50%	3.05%	2.41%	2.97%	2.93%

Source: Computed by author using GDP data (constant 2015 US$, millions) from UNCTAD Data Centre

The Lost Decades of Liberalisation (1980s–1990s)

This period was characterised by the slowest economic growth in Africa's eight-decade post-independence history. Economic growth declined to an average annual rate of 2.2% in the 1980s and 2.6% in the 1990s, nearly half of what it had been in previous decades. African economic growth was notably lower than Asia's 4.9% in the 1980s and 4.6% in the 1990s. Growth in Africa was accompanied by sluggish growth in manufacturing value added, causing the share of manufacturing value added (MVA) in African GDP to decrease from 17% in 1981 to 11–13% in 1999 (see Fig. 3.1). The poor performance during Africa's lost decades was primarily attributed to the Washington Consensus and Structural Adjustment Programs (SAP), which advocated for economic liberalisation, privatisation, and the dismantling of state apparatus and industrial policies across the continent.

However, many African governments faced economic crises as the import-substitution strategy was poorly managed and executed, leading to excessive external borrowing, high inflation, and falling incomes. To make matters worse, the first major oil crisis happened at the end of the 1970s, which was the final straw for numerous African nations. By the early 1980s, many countries had no alternative but to turn to the IMF—an organisation that does not lend money without conditions. Conditionalities were part of the package. Unlike Asian countries, the implementation of the import-substitution strategy in immediate post-colonial Africa was flawed, lacking foresight and a clear purpose, unlike the approach seen in Asia.

Furthermore, the IMF stepped in with its prescription for economic management when African countries had reached a point of no return and most had exhausted their options. The question remains: how many of these countries have learned from the painful experience of subjecting themselves to IMF conditionalities? Policy learning is essential, and there is much that African countries can learn from their earlier experiments with industrialisation based on the import-substitution industrialisation strategy.

Furthermore, this period was characterised by a decline and stagnation in manufacturing, with the share of global manufacturing output decreasing from 0.6% to below 0.3%. Many African countries experienced a debt burden, resulting in insufficient investment in infrastructure. Numerous productive investments made by African governments were privatised, including factories and utilities. The repercussions of this era had a damaging impact on African industrialisation. During these two decades, the Asian Tigers and China expanded their industrial capacity. They became closely integrated into global value chains, attracting substantial foreign direct investment (FDI) and exporting competitively at low prices, making it difficult for African goods to compete in international markets. Finally, it is essential to emphasise that the figures above are somewhat problematic because they rely on averages across a broad, though not entire, part of the continent, and even during this period, there was noticeable variation. During this period, Mauritius progressed in export-led industrialisation, sustaining momentum from the 1990s and achieving the highest growth in the textile sector. The South African economy experienced a significant slowdown, primarily due to international sanctions, which resulted in a decline in its share of African manufacturing. The Nigerian manufacturing sector dwindled from 14% in 1980 to 6% in 1995. Due to the wave of neo-liberalisation, African countries reduced average industrial tariffs from 34% in the late 1970s to 11% in the late 1990s. Local industrial goods, including footwear and textile products, struggled to compete effectively in the domestic market. Numerous domestic manufacturers closed in the 1990s, leading to substantial unemployment in the manufacturing sector.

New Growth Paths and Diversification (2000s–2020s)

By the late 1990s, researchers and policymakers could see that the promises of the Washington Consensus prescriptions were unlikely to drive economic growth and create jobs, as GDP growth lagged behind population growth during the lost decades of the 1980s and 1990s. In the 2000s, some African leaders challenged the prevailing wave of neo-liberalisation. For instance, Ethiopian Prime Minister Meles Zenawi opposed the IMF's recommendation to open the banking sector to foreign banks, which led to sanctions against Ethiopia (Stiglitz 2003). African leaders sought to foster an African Renaissance by embracing initiatives such as the New Partnership for Africa's Development (NEPAD).

The economic successes of the Asian Tigers and China inspired the exploration of alternative paths and strategies, a movement accelerated by the establishment of the Forum on China-Africa Cooperation (FOCAC) in 2000. Many governments promoted economic diversification and robust growth, supported by additional factors, including a prolonged commodity boom cycle, which, with slightly different timings, helped improve economic governance. Numerous African countries diversified their trade with Asia, particularly with China, and gained access to development finance for vital infrastructure projects, thereby revitalising the African construction sector and the booming cement industry. Several African governments, including Ethiopia, Kenya, Côte d'Ivoire, and Morocco, pursued an industrial ecosystems strategy to support industrialisation, with slightly different timings. In many African nations, the debt burden was alleviated by the Heavily Indebted Poor Countries (HIPC) initiative, resulting in improvements in human capital and public governance.

In the 2000s, Africa experienced notable growth of 5.4%, comparable to Asia's 5.5%. However, the external environment of the 2010s was less favourable for Africa than for other regions. This decade was marked by the repercussions of the Global Financial Crisis, the global commodity price crash, and the COVID-19 pandemic, which precipitated an economic recession. Economic growth slowed to 3.1% during the 2010s, underscoring the vulnerability of African economies, ongoing structural transformation challenges, sluggish industrialisation, and limited economic diversification. The continent experienced a recession for the first time in 25 years, since the mid-1990s. This period was also characterised by accelerated technological advancements, a sluggish and volatile global economy, and geopolitical tensions, with food and energy insecurity significantly affecting the continent due to climate change.

2 Structural Transformation and Industrialisation in Africa

Marginal Contribution of Manufacturing

Africa's lagging structural transformation displays three critical features. First, regarding economic growth, African countries recorded a modest increase of 3.5% between 1970 and 2025, significantly lower than the average growth rate of 4.9% in Asia. For economic growth to support structural transformation, it has to be considerably higher and comparable to the catch-up economies in East Asia and China over several decades. Second, African countries are overdependent on commodities such as oil, gas, and mineral resources, characterised by minimal value addition and limited diversification into other sectors. This issue is directly linked to the absence of policies promoting economic diversification and industrialisation.

Third, manufacturing, which is considered an engine of structural transformation and growth, has a low level and weak contribution of manufacturing value added (MVA) in terms of its average share of GDP and employment, approximately 10.3% and 7.6%, respectively, in 2023. This reflects the limited role of the manufacturing sector (see Fig. 3.2). However, manufacturing jobs increased by 5.2% in the same year, underscoring the potential for dynamic growth. The average growth rate of African manufacturing value added was 2.4%, and African MVA accounts

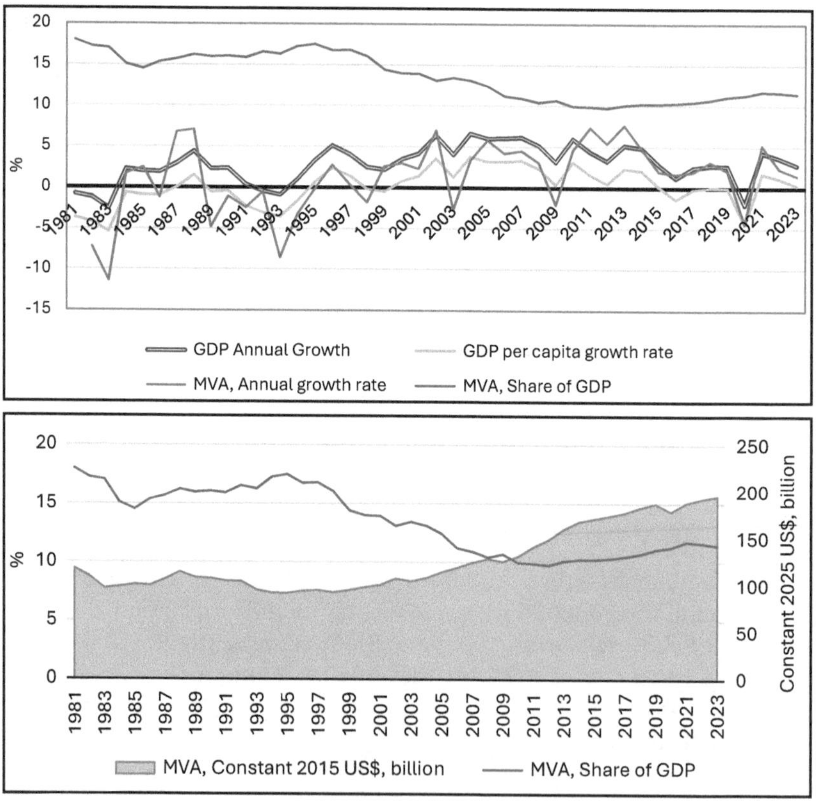

Fig. 3.2 Manufacturing and GDP growth dynamics, sub-Saharan Africa (1981–2024). (Source of data: World Bank World Development Indicators)

for only 2% of global MVA, considerably lower than the continent's 3.2% share of global GDP (World Bank 2025; UNIDO 2025). Furthermore, the share of manufacturing exports in overall exports is even lower, accounting for 1.3% in 2023. Africa faces a persistent trade deficit in manufactured goods.

Regarding employment, the female-to-male workforce participation ratio is 40:60, indicating a significant gender imbalance, although we should approach such figures with caution. With respect to sectoral composition, the primary contributors to most African economies are food and beverage products, along with other non-metallic mineral products (such as cement). At the same time, the contribution of medium-high and high technology (MHT) industries remains minimal.

Given mixed outcomes, it is crucial to note that African countries significantly lag behind in industrialisation and structural transformation, underscoring the need for accelerated industrial development and the urgent need to address the structural changes and demands arising from Africa's demographic pressures.

However, it is notable that the performance of industrial development and mixed policy outcomes varies across different nations. The successes of Mauritius's textile and apparel sector from the 1970s to the 1990s, along with the expansion of Morocco's automotive industry in the 2000s and 2010s, demonstrate that industrialisation in Africa is indeed achievable. Secondly, the MVA has grown steadily since the mid-1990s, indicating that claims in the premature de-industrialisation literature warrant scrutiny. While recognising mixed outcomes, it is vital to note that African countries substantially lag behind in industrialisation and structural transformation, underscoring the need for accelerated industrial development and the urgent need to address the structural changes and demands arising from Africa's demographic pressures.

Africa's slow industrialisation and weak manufacturing sector should not necessarily lead to a pessimistic conclusion or premature deindustrialisation.[3] Instead, policymakers and researchers need to focus on conducting in-depth research to identify the drivers and root causes of the relatively poor performance and to devise strategies and policies to address the gaps.

[3] See Rodrik (2015, 2018), Lee (2019).

Unevenness and Structural Heterogeneity in African Industrialisation

It is noteworthy that the progress of industrialisation in Africa differs markedly between countries. A key characteristic of African manufacturing is the unevenness and heterogeneity observed across national economies and industries. Northern Africa has the largest share of MVA in GDP, followed by Western Africa, which showed improvement in the 2010s, whereas the Southern region experienced a relative decline. Eastern and Central Africa have a relatively low MVA-to-GDP ratio, but this has been increasing in recent years.

Selecting specific countries helps compare and shows the variety of African industrialisation paths (see Fig. 3.3). Ethiopia and Kenya, two East African economies sharing a border and many structural similarities, provide a particularly useful comparison (see Fig. 3.3). Kenya started its industrialisation journey earlier than Ethiopia, marked by large European investments in manufacturing and horticulture over a long period. As a result, Kenya's manufacturing value added (MVA) as a share of GDP has consistently been higher than Ethiopia's from 1981 to 2023, although it has declined since 2011. In contrast, Ethiopia has seen strong GDP growth at about twice Kenya's average since the 2000s, with much higher

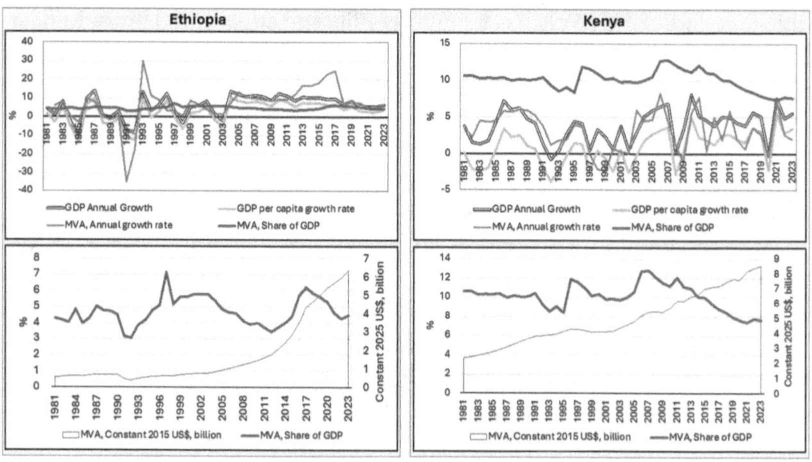

Fig. 3.3 Manufacturing and GDP growth dynamics, Ethiopia and Kenya. (Source: Author's computation based on data from World Bank World Development Indicators)

MVA growth rates. These different paths reflect variations in industrial policy and political-economy between the two nations. Kenya has higher MVA per person than Ethiopia, although Ethiopia's faster growth hints at a possible convergence.

Mauritius and Morocco have implemented industrial policies that have led to a sustained shift in the share of manufacturing value added, increasing from 10% to 20% over an extended period. However, the composition of the MVA differs (see Fig. 3.4). While textiles and apparel contribute a significant share in both countries, Morocco's automotive industry is experiencing substantial growth.

The industrialisation patterns of Nigeria and South Africa are divergent; GDP growth in South Africa has remained low for an extended period, accompanied by a sluggish increase in MVA (see Fig. 3.5). This has resulted in a declining share of manufacturing, which fell from 25% in 1981 to 12.5% in 2023, reflecting the deindustrialisation that occurred during the 2000s and 2010s. Nigeria experienced a similar decrease in MVA from 2000 to 2015, but has recently shown gradual positive growth. The GDP growth rate has been modest, and the economy relies heavily on oil and gas, the primary contributors to exports and government revenues. Nigeria and South Africa have significant MVA figures, totalling $50 billion and $40 billion, respectively, in 2023.

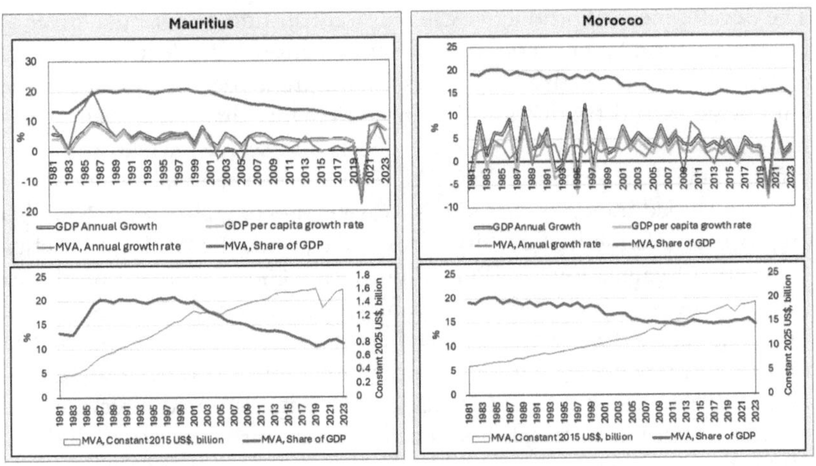

Fig. 3.4 Manufacturing and GDP growth dynamics, Mauritius and Morocco. (Source: Author's computation based on data from World Bank World Development Indicators)

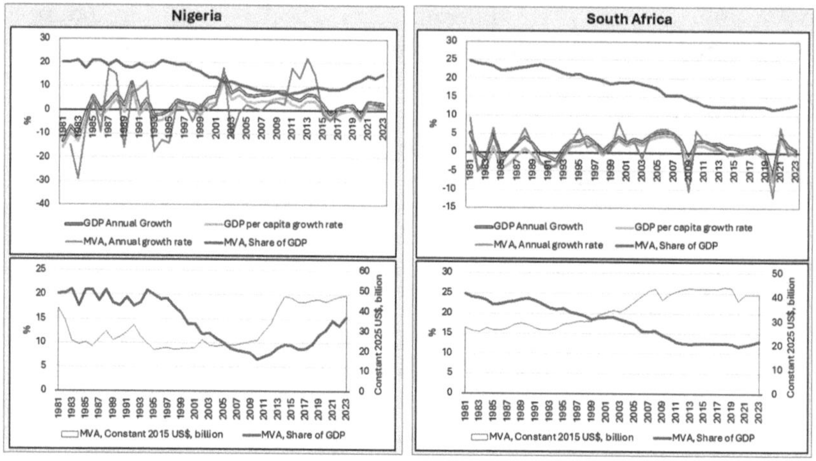

Fig. 3.5 Manufacturing and GDP growth dynamics. (Source: Author's computation based on data from World Bank World Development Indicators)

3 Productive Capability and Economic Transformation

Productive Capacity

The development of productive capability constitutes an essential driver of industrialisation and economic transformation. Productive capacity encompasses productive resources, entrepreneurial skills, industrial employment, and production linkages—elements that collectively determine a country's ability to produce goods and services while sustaining growth and development (UNCTAD 2006). International organisations have developed standardised metrics to assess these capabilities: UNCTAD employs the Productive Capacity Index (PCI), while the World Intellectual Property Organization (WIPO) utilises the Global Innovation Index (GII) to measure technological capability (see Tables 3.2 and 3.3). The PCI aggregates 46 indicators across eight categories, providing policymakers and researchers with a comprehensive framework to analyse economic structure, identify bottlenecks, and design targeted interventions. Africa's performance reveals both challenges and progress. From 2001 to 2022, the continent's average PCI of 28.21 remained significantly below both the global average and Asia's 45%. Nevertheless, Africa demonstrated modest but consistent improvement, rising from 23% to 32% over this

Table 3.2 Frontier Technology Readiness Index 2022

	Total score	*2022 rank*	*Score group*	*ICT rank*	*Skills rank*	*R&D rank*	*Industry rank*	*Finance rank*
South Africa	0.61	56	Upper middle	71	77	36	67	25
Morocco	0.55	70	Upper middle	73	113	53	55	33
Mauritius	0.54	73	Upper middle	96	57	82	74	34
Nigeria	0.32	119	Low	119	108	68	157	153
Ethiopia	0.15	155	Low	162	161	80	106	137

Source of data: (UNCTAD 2023a, b, c)

period (Fig. 3.6), suggesting gradual strengthening of productive foundations despite persistent gaps relative to other regions.

Furthermore, the frontier technology readiness index measures countries' positioning in 17 green and digital technologies, highlighting that most African countries lag, making it challenging to reverse this trend. It evaluates ICT, skills, R&D, industry, and finance rankings to assess overall technological capability (see Table 3.3). The message is that Africa's industrialisation is determined by productive capacity and progress in innovation.

FDI inflows to Africa totalled $54 billion and $53 billion in 2022 and 2023 respectively, considerably lower than the $83 billion in 2021 and $72 billion in 2008, although investment in critical minerals has increased. By comparison, Asia attracted over $0.62 trillion while global FDI reached $1.3 trillion in 2023, significantly lower than the 2007 peak of $2 trillion (UNCTAD 2023a). Key trends include long-term FDI stagnation, rising flows to services, slowing manufacturing FDI outflows (mainly concentrated within domestic markets), and a diminishing role of FDI in China. These patterns underscore that FDI flows predominantly to countries already demonstrating large and growing markets, reinforcing existing disparities in global capital allocation.

Africa has 50 million micro, small, and medium enterprises, with an annual loan requirement of $416 billion (UNCTAD 2022). According to surveys across multiple countries, the challenging business environment has posed a significant obstacle for African firms. Approximately 32% identified access to finance as a binding constraint. In comparison, another 26% pointed out government services, including political instability, access

Table 3.3 Global Innovation Index, 2023

Country	*Overall*	*Institutions*	*Human capital and research*	*Infrastructure*	*Market sophistication*	*Business sophistication*	*Knowledge and technology outputs*	*Creative outputs*
Country	Overall GII rank	Rank	Rank	Rank	Rank	Rank	Rank	Rank
Mauritius	57	26	64	74	24	91	90	57
South Africa	59	88	84	68	45	61	56	63
Morocco	70	83	86	94	80	107	65	55
Nigeria	109	115	80	123	127	82	124	84
Ethiopia	125	116	131	132	114	130	84	126

Source of data: World Intellectual Property Organisation 2023

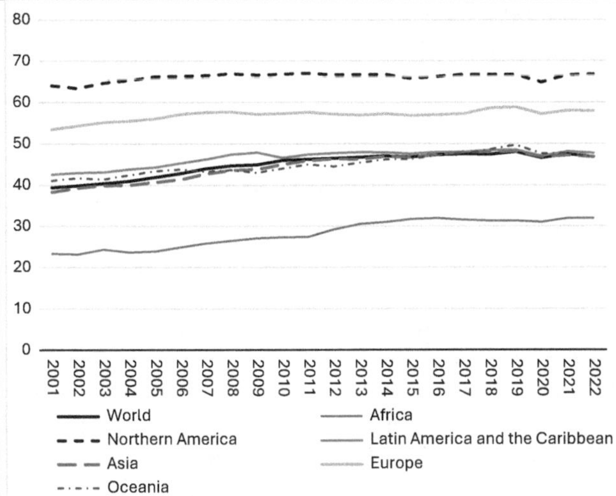

Region	PCI Average (2001 - 2022)
World	44.97
Africa	28.21
Northern America	66.09
Latin America and the Caribbean	46.56
Asia	44.49
Europe	56.89
Oceania	45.01

Fig. 3.6 Productive Capacities Index by region, Africa and others, 2001 to 2022. (Source of data: UNCTAD, Productive Capacities Index (PCI) 2023)

to land, business licensing and permits, corruption, courts, customs and trade regulations, and crime and theft. Furthermore, 14% emphasised access to land, electricity, and transport; 11% referred to tax rates and transport administration; and 9% mentioned an inadequately educated workforce and labour regulation (World Bank 2023).[4]

Industrial Employment

Employment in industrial sectors as a share of total employment reflects the contributions and levels of industrialisation, serving as a crucial measure of the economy's productivity and structural change. In Africa, employment in industrial sectors and the quality of manufacturing jobs have been limited, remaining significantly lower than in many Asian countries. There are concerns that industrial employment in Africa is arguably underreported for various reasons (Cramer et al. 2020). However, performance has not been static and shows considerable variation among African countries, as illustrated in the chart below (Fig. 3.7). Industrial

[4] Electricity and transport: 11% referred to tax rates and transport administration, and 9% mentioned an inadequately educated workforce and labour regulation (World Bank).

employment has been lower in Ethiopia and Nigeria, although recent positive progress has been made. In contrast, industrial employment has been higher in Mauritius, Morocco, and South Africa, although it has declined over the past 25 years.[5]

Gross Capital Formation and Savings

The level of gross capital formation and savings indicates the growth potential in productive investment. Asian countries are recognised for their high gross savings and gross capital formation as a share of GDP, with China and South Korea as typical examples. In Africa, both parameters are relatively lower than in Asia, contributing to a slower pace of industrialisation. However, performance among African countries is heterogeneous. For instance, Ethiopia and Morocco exhibited high levels of gross capital formation, exceeding 30%, and approximately 29% of gross savings between 2011 and 2022 (see Figs. 3.8 and 3.9). These figures were lower for South Africa and Mauritius (see Tables 3.4 and 3.5).

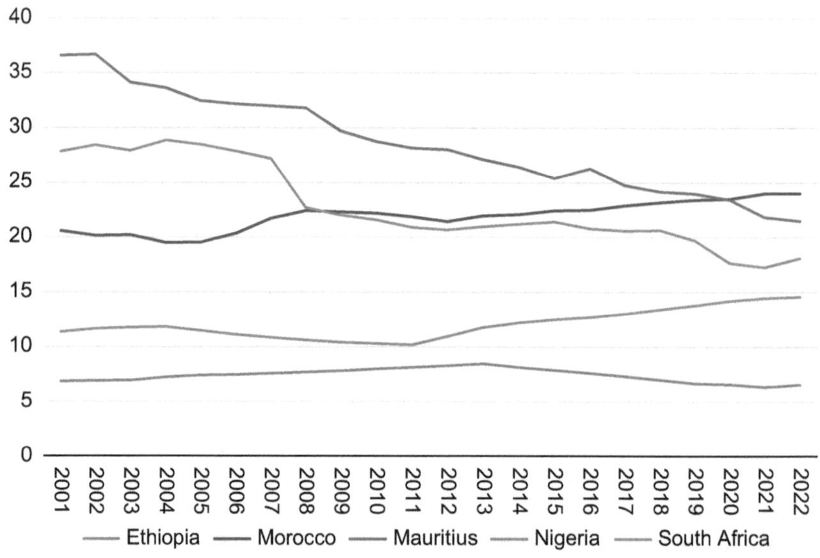

Fig. 3.7 Employment in industry (% of total employment), selected countries, 2001 to 2022. (Source of data: World Bank WDI)

[5] See Oqubay et al. (2021).

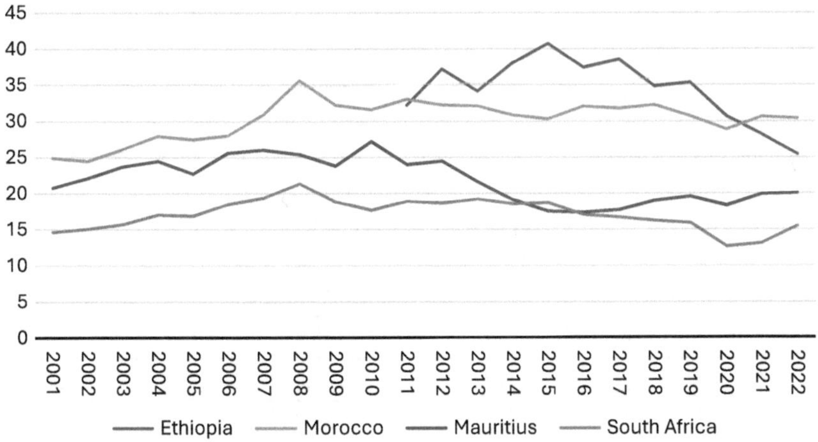

Fig. 3.8 Gross Capital formation (% of GDP), selected African countries, 2001 to 2022

Regarding capital accumulation and industrialisation experiences, UNCTAD's work highlights that the "profit-investment nexus" was crucial for the rapid industrialisation of the Asian Tigers (UNCTAD 1996). Evidence from East Asian industrialisation shows that, besides high savings levels enabling significant Gross Capital Formation, a key form of private sector investment was reinvestment of retained profits (earnings). In the 1960s, 1970s, and 1980s, a notable portion (over 60%) of investment—by both domestic and foreign firms came from retained profits, with companies reinvesting their earnings to fund expansion or start new ventures. This indicates that investment is not solely driven by existing savings, as is often assumed. It also suggests that this type of investment can support low-income countries, where traditional savings-based models may be inadequate due to low income and a limited tax base. Clearly, such a self-sustaining profit-investment cycle doesn't develop spontaneously; it requires deliberate policy measures (Akyuz and Gore 1996).[6]

[6] For more details and analysis of the East Asian experience, see Trade and Development Report (1996), Chapter 2, "Export, Capital Formation and Growth" (p. 108), and "The Investment-Profit Nexus in East Asian Industrialisation", World Development, 24(3).

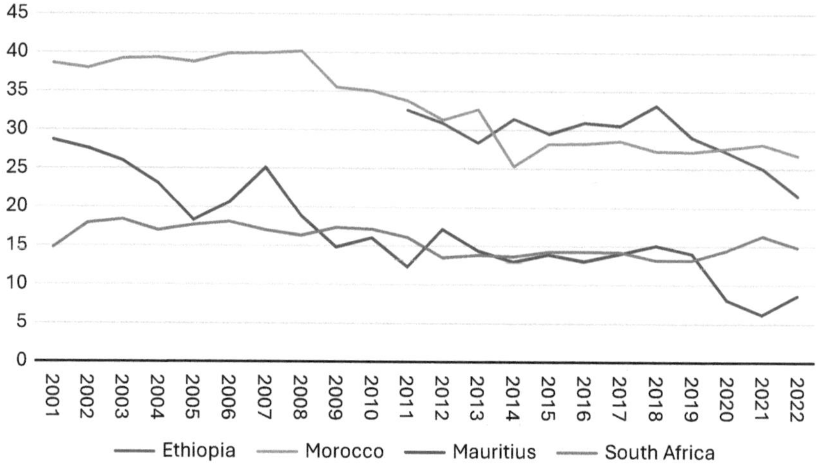

Fig. 3.9 Gross savings (% of GDP), selected African countries, 2001 to 2022

Table 3.4 Average capital formation of 2001–2010 and 2011–2022

	Average (2001–2010)	*Average (2011–2022)*
Ethiopia		34.3
Morocco	28.9	31.2
Mauritius	24.1	19.8
South Africa	17.5	16.7

Source of data: World Bank WDI

Table 3.5 Average gross savings of 2001–2010 and 2011–2022

	Average (2001–2010)	*Average (2011–2022)*
Ethiopia		29.2
Morocco	38.5	28.8
Mauritius	21.9	12.5
South Africa	17.2	14.3

Source of data: World Bank WDI

Export Capability and Commodity Overdependence

Africa remains vulnerable to a global economy characterised by volatility and uncertainty, alongside significant shocks, particularly in trade and investment—over 50% of African nations depend on oil, gas, or minerals. In contrast, only a third rely on intra-African trade for less than 1–6% of intermediate inputs, while integration into high-value-added supply chains remains limited. In 2014, the commodity crash resulted in a fiscal deficit of 2.0%. Low levels of connectivity and energy present key bottlenecks in intra-African trade. During the COVID-19 pandemic, trade-in-services exporters (such as Egypt and Morocco) were the most affected. The decline in African development assistance was abrupt, and borrowing costs surged to 11.6% in 2023 (UNCTAD 2024; see Table 3.6). Economic diversification to reduce dependency on commodities is the primary strategy for addressing economic shocks and building resilience.

Commodity exports have accounted for a significant share of total merchandise exports across African countries. Commodity-dependent countries are defined as countries that rely on commodities and raw materials for over 60% of their exports (Fig. 3.10). Export diversification will contribute to absorbing shocks, increasing the availability of inputs and services, enhancing employment, creating spillovers of technology and skills, and fostering the development of production networks, thereby accelerating structural change, productivity growth, and inclusive development (UNCTAD 2022).

The composition and growth of exported manufactured value-added goods are directly linked to the level of development of productive capacity and industrialisation. African countries play a marginal role in global exports of goods and services, accounting for 2% and 4.5% of global exports in 2022, respectively. These countries experience trade deficits and

Table 3.6 Commodity exports as a share of total merchandise exports (2020)

Mining products in %		*Fossil fuels in %*		*Agricultural products in %*	
Ghana	Gold 94.9	Angola	Oil 96.4	Ethiopia	Coffee 75.3
Liberia	Gold 71.7	Nigeria	Oil and gas 95.7	Kenya	Tea & mate 71.8
Mali	Gold 93.3	Mozambique	Coal 95.6	Benin	Cotton 91.1
Zambia	Copper 89.8	Gabon	Oil 89.3	CDI	Cocoa 91.6
Namibia	Copper 80.6	Libya	98.7	Madagascar	Spices 72.8
Rwanda	Gold 91.7	Congo	91.6	Uganda	Coffee 85.0
Tanzania	Gold 78.3				

Source: UNCTAD (2022)

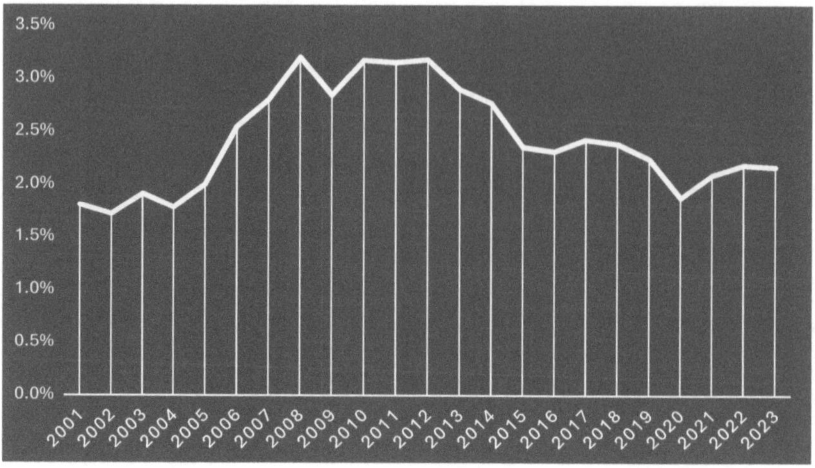

Fig. 3.10 Share of Africa in global commodity exports, 2001 to 2023. (Source: Computed by the author using data from UN Comtrade)

struggle with balance-of-payments constraints, contributing to foreign-exchange scarcity and the heavy burden of servicing external debt. Furthermore, performance from 2001 to 2022 shows significant variation over time and among countries. South Africa exhibits strong export performance; Ethiopia faces significant constraints in its balance of payments; and Nigeria is overly dependent on oil and gas. Most African countries rely on commodity exports with limited value addition.

The primary challenges facing Africa's export capacity include its minimal contribution to global exports, the prevalence of low-value products in the composition of merchandise exports and services, substantial trade imbalances in most African countries, and limited diversification of the export sector (see Table 3.6 and Fig. 3.11). However, as the data concerning sample countries illustrate, it is essential to recognise that the dynamics of export capability significantly vary among different African nations (Fig. 3.12). Low export capability—in terms of volume, export value, and composition—is a critical aspect of low productive capacity rather than trade openness.

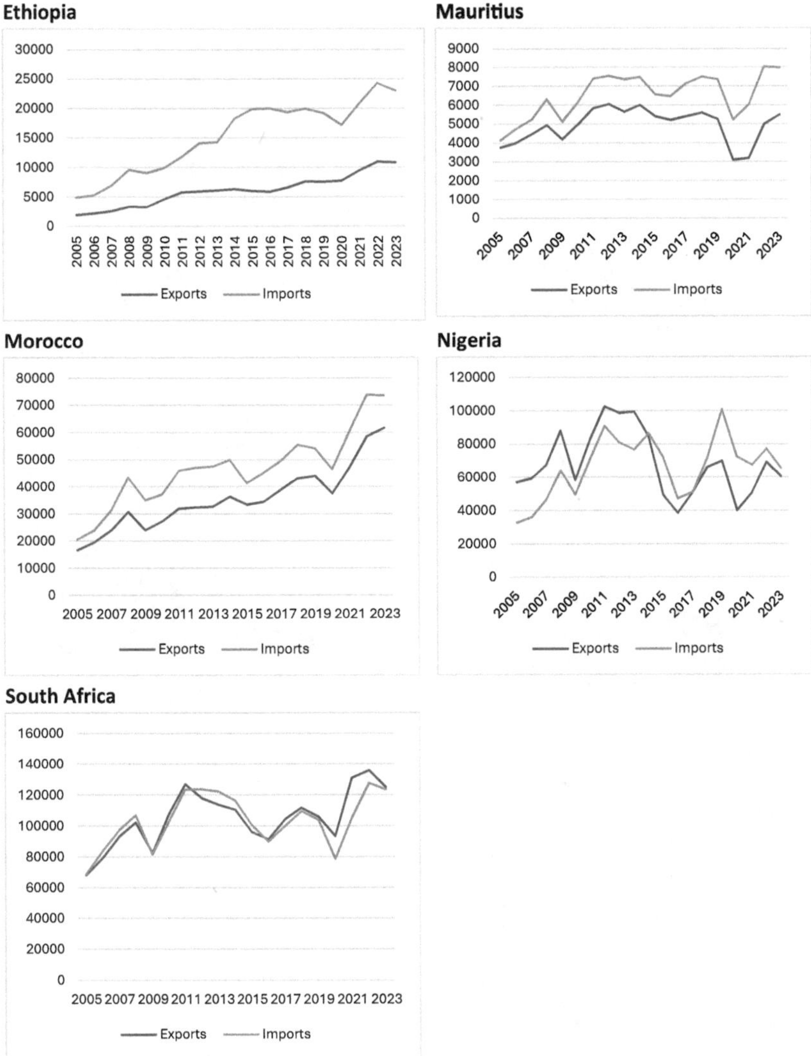

Fig. 3.11 Trade imbalance, exports and imports of goods and services, selected African countries, 2005–2023 (current prices, million US$). (Source of data: UNCTAD Data Hub)

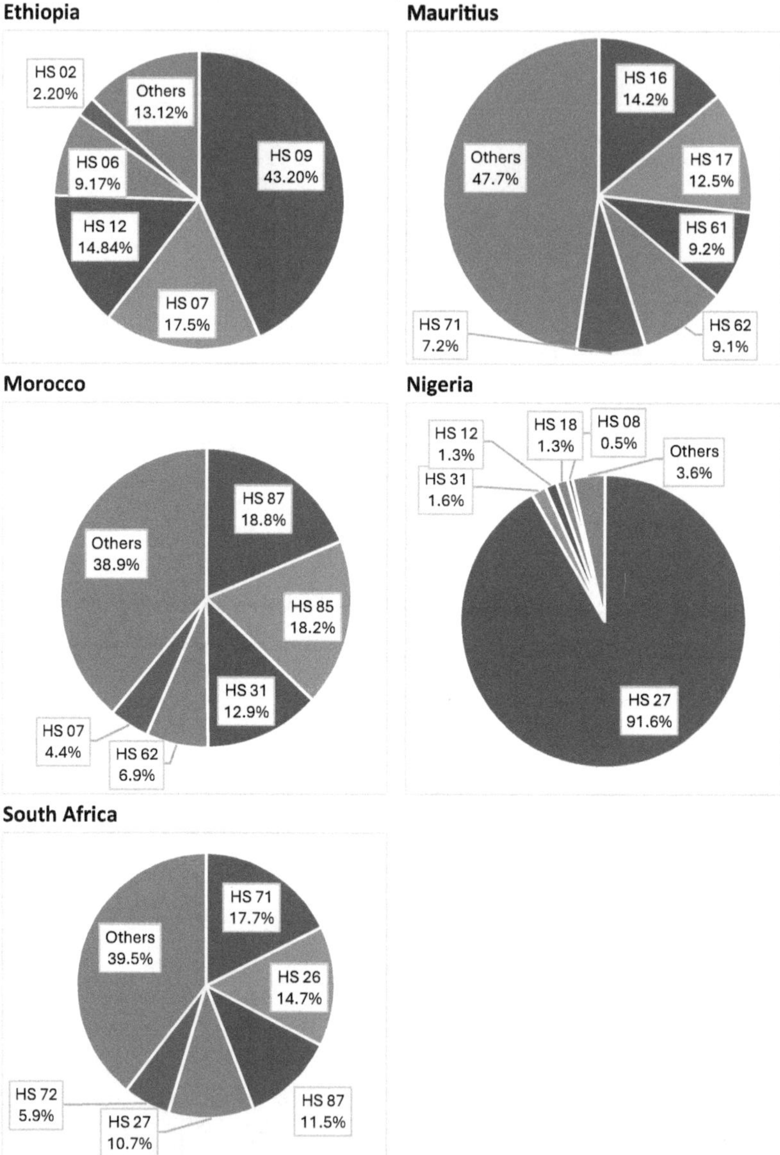

Fig. 3.12 Composition of exports, top five commodity exports (based on 2-digit HS codes) from selected African countries in 2023

HS 02	Meat and edible meat offal
HS 06	Trees and other plants, live; bulbs, roots and the like; cut flowers and ornamental foliage
HS 07	Vegetables and certain roots and tubers; edible
HS 08	Fruit and nuts, edible; peel of citrus fruit or melons
HS 09	Coffee, tea, mate and spices
HS 12	Oil seeds and oleaginous fruits; miscellaneous grains, seeds and fruit, industrial or medicinal plants; ...
HS 16	Meat, fish or crustaceans, molluscs or other aquatic invertebrates; preparations thereof
HS 17	Sugars and sugar confectionery
HS 18	Cocoa and cocoa preparations
HS 26	Ores, slag and ash
HS 27	Mineral fuels, mineral oils and products of their distillation; bituminous substances; mineral waxes
HS 31	Fertilizers
HS 61	Apparel and clothing accessories; knitted or crocheted
HS 62	Apparel and clothing accessories; not knitted or crocheted
HS 71	Natural, cultured pearls; precious, semi-precious stones; precious metals, metals clad with precious metal, ...
HS 72	Iron and steel
HS 85	Electrical machinery and equipment and parts thereof; sound recorders and reproducers; ...
HS 87	Vehicles; other than railway or tramway rolling stock, and parts and accessories thereof

Fig. 3.12 (continued)

4 African Demographic Dynamics and Urbanisation

At the continental level, Africa's demographic trends will be crucial in shaping the continent's prospects for growth and industrialisation, in light of global comparative dynamics. The African population is projected to grow over the coming decades, reaching 2.5 billion by 2050 (see Figs. 3.13 and 3.14) (UNDESA 2025). More importantly, a faster pace of urbanisation will result in 1.6 billion people residing in urban centres, accounting for two-thirds of the total population (see Fig. 3.15). Rapid urbanisation and accelerated industrialisation will create complementarity, foster economic agglomeration, and generate positive spillovers. The industrialisation strategies of African countries should be rooted in an understanding of these implications and in harnessing these forces to develop a growing market, expand productive capacity, and create substantial, well-paid jobs. Furthermore, establishing a single African market should be strategically incorporated into the industrial development strategies of African countries, with a concerted effort to achieve significant progress in intra-African trade and strengthen Africa's position in the global market.

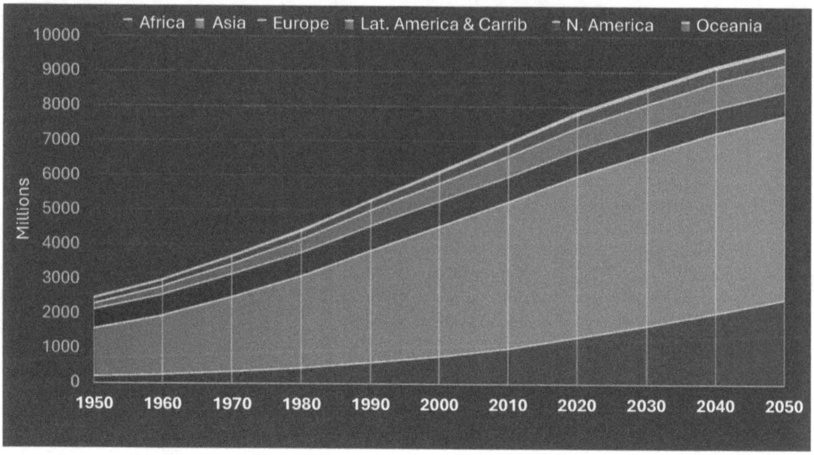

Fig. 3.13 Demographic dynamics of Africa and the world (1950–2050). (Source of data: UN DESA)

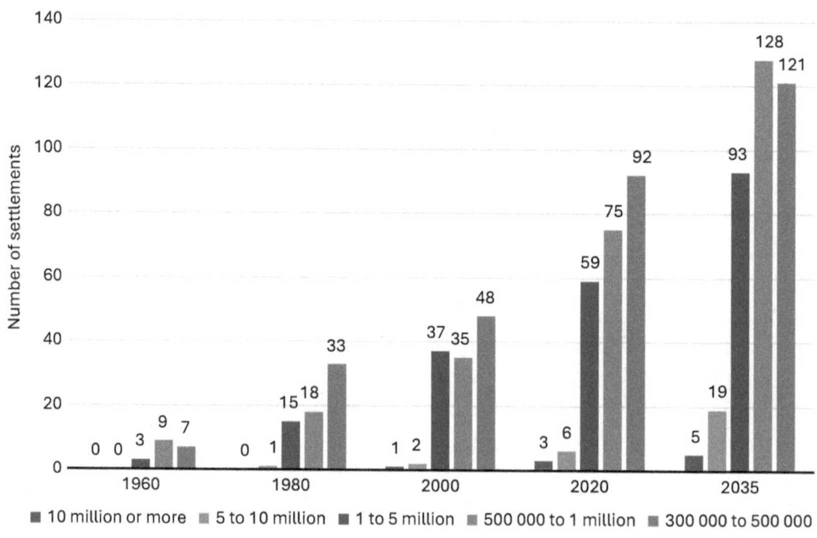

Fig. 3.14 Urban settlement and urbanisation in Africa (1960–2035). (Source of data: UN DESA)

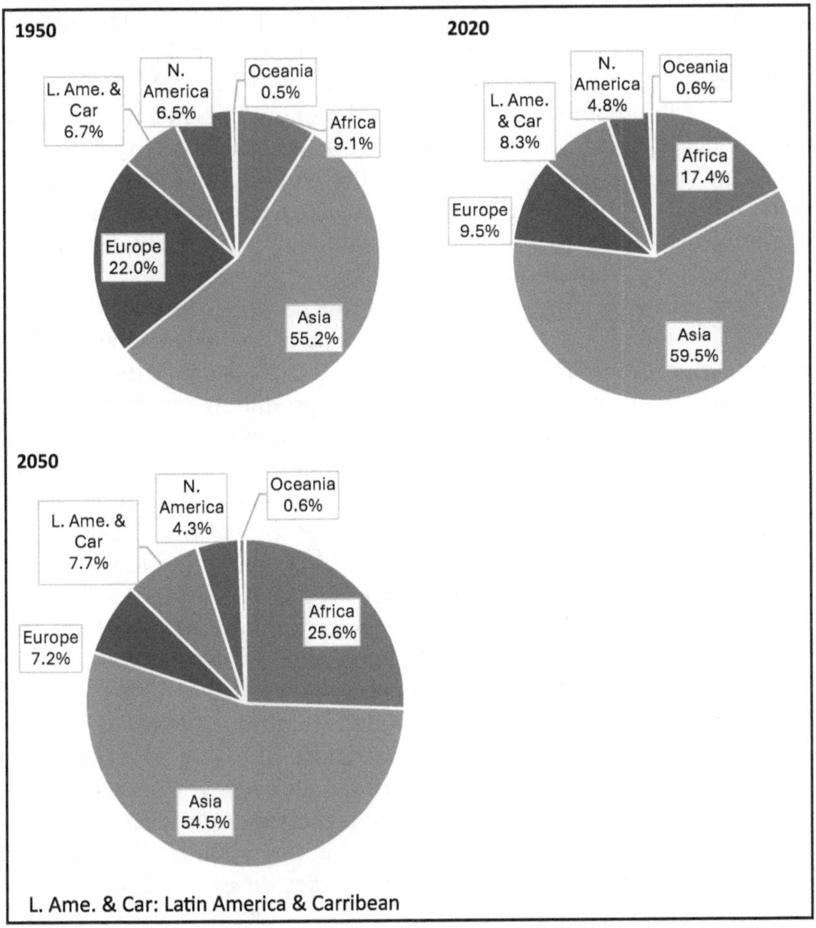

Fig. 3.15 Share of Africa and other regions (1950–2050). (Source of data: UN DESA)

5 Conclusions on Patterns of African Industrialisation

The evolutionary trajectory since independence reveals three distinct phases. The post-colonial "Golden Era" (1960s–1970s) was characterised by state-led import-substitution industrialisation (ISI), resulting in strong growth and expansion in manufacturing value added (MVA). However, it was hampered by poor decisions, weak institutions, limited human capital, and rising debt. The "Lost Decades" (1980s–1990s), driven by Structural Adjustment Programmes (SAPs), involved economic liberalisation and the dismantling of state capacity and industrial policy, which led to a decline in MVA and growth. The period after 2000 marked a shift towards pragmatic industrial policy and diversification, with rebounding growth but ongoing vulnerability to global shocks, highlighting the incomplete nature of structural transformation.[7]

Several analytical themes emerge from the economic history of African industrialisation. First, structural heterogeneity is fundamental; performance varies significantly across the continent, challenging the idea of a single 'Africa'. Second, a substantial deficit in productive capabilities serves as the primary constraint, as evidenced by low scores on indices such as the Productivity and Capabilities Index (PCI) and the Global Innovation Index (GII). Second, Africa's weak productive capabilities, as measured by the Productive Capacity Index (PCI) and the Global Innovation Index (GII), arise from, and simultaneously reinforce, limited industrialisation through cumulative causation mechanisms. This seems characterised by weak investment and savings, a challenging business environment, and limited technological capacity. Third, dependence on commodities and weak export capabilities persist, making economies vulnerable to shocks and marginalising them in global manufacturing trade (with just 1.3% of exports), thereby resulting in persistent balance-of-payments constraints.

Africa's future is at a crucial crossroads, shaped by a unique demographic transition and urbanisation. The projected population of 2.5 billion by 2050 and rapid urbanisation present a potential demographic dividend—a substantial labour force and market—if swift industrialisation drives job creation. Furthermore, the evidence advocates for adopting a stance of pragmatic realism rather than simplistic pessimism or optimism. Success relies on recognising continental heterogeneity, learning from historical policy lessons, and seizing opportunities, with a political commitment to high growth and industrialisation through the continuous development of productive capabilities and the implementation of context-specific industrial policies.

[7] See UNCTAD (2013, 2018, 2019), UNCTAD-UNIDO (2011), UNECA (2016).

References

Akyuz, Yilma, And Charles Gore (1996) 'The Investment-Profit Nexus in East-Asian Industrialisation'. World Development 24(3), pp. 461–470.

Austin, Gareth Austin, Ewout Frankema, and Morten Jerven. 2017. Patterns of Manufacturing Growth in Sub-Saharan Africa. In *The Spread of Modern Industry to the Periphery Since 1871*, ed. Kevin H. O'Rourke and Jeffrey G. Williamson, 345–374. Oxford: Oxford University Press.

Bekele, Shiferaw. 2019. Ethiopia's Transition from a Traditional to a Developing Economy, 1890s–1960. In *The Oxford Handbook of the Ethiopian Economy*, ed. Fantu Cheru, Christopher Cramer, and Arkebe Oqubay. Oxford University Press.

Chan, Stephen. 2025. *The Economic Transformation and Political Economy of Zambia: The Search for Modernity, Equity and Principle*. London: Palgrave Macmillan.

Clapham, Christopher. 1988. *Transformation and Continuity in Revolutionary Ethiopia*. Cambridge University Press.

Clapham, Christopher. 2019. The Political Economy of Ethiopia: From the Imperial Period to the Present. In *The Oxford Handbook of the Ethiopian Economy*, ed. Cheru Fantu, Cramer Christopher, and Oqubay Arkebe, 51–65. Oxford University Press.

Clarence-Smith, William Gervase. 2016. Colonial Industrialisation, 1840s–1960s. In *The Cambridge History of Capitalism, Volume 2: The Spread of Capitalism: From 1848 to the Present*, ed. Larry Neal and Jeffrey G. Williamson, 405–428. Cambridge: Cambridge University Press.

Cramer, Christopher, John Sender, and Arkebe Oqubay. 2020. *African Economic Development: Evidence, Theory, Policy*. Oxford: Oxford University Press.

El Aynaoui, Karim, and Arkebe Oqubay, eds. 2026. *The Oxford Handbook of the Moroccan Economy*. Oxford: Oxford University Press.

Frankema, Ewout, Jeffrey G. Williamson, and Pieter Woltjer. 2018. An Economic Rationale for the African Scramble: The Commercial Transition and the Commodity Price Boom of 1845–1885. *The Journal of Economic History* 78 (2): 231–267.

Green, Toby. 2019. *A Fistful of Shells: West Africa from the Rise of the Slave Trade to the Age of Revolution*. Chicago/London: University of Chicago Press/Allen Lane/Penguin.

Jerven, Morten. 2011. *Africa: Why Economists Get It Wrong*. London: Zed Publishers.

Jerven, Morten. 2013. *Poor Numbers: How We Are Misled by African Development Statistics and What to Do About It*. Cornell: Cornell University Press.

Jerven, M. (ed) (2017) Measuring African Development: Past and Present. Routledge.

Lee, Keun. 2019. *The Art of Economic Catch-Up*. Cambridge: Cambridge University Press.

Oqubay, Arkebe. 2015. *Made in Africa: Industrial Policy in Ethiopia*. Oxford: Oxford University Press.

Oqubay, Arkebe. 2019a. Industrial Policy and Late Industrialization in Ethiopia. In *The Oxford Handbook of the Ethiopian Economy*, ed. Fantu Cheru, Christopher Cramer, and Arkebe Oqubay, 724–746. Oxford: Oxford University Press.

Oqubay, Arkebe. 2019b. The Structure and Performance of the Ethiopian Manufacturing Sector. In *The Oxford Handbook of the Ethiopian Economy*, ed. F. Cheru, C. Cramer, and A. Oqubay, 747–768. Oxford: Oxford University Press.

Oqubay, Arkebe, Fiona Tregenna, and Imraan Valodia, eds. 2021. *The Oxford Handbook of the South African Economy*. Oxford: Oxford University Press.

Oualalou, Fathallah. 2026. Economic History of Morocco. In *The Oxford Handbook of the Moroccan Economy*, ed. Karim El Aynaoui and Arkebe Oqubay. Oxford: Oxford University Press.

Pankhurst, Richard. 1996. *The History of Famine and Epidemics in Ethiopia: From Early Times to the Twentieth Century*. Addis Ababa: Haile Selassie I University Press.

Rodrik, Dani. 2015. Premature Deindustrialization. Paper Number 107, January.

Rodrik, Dani. 2018. *New Technologies, Global Value Chains, and the Developing Economies*, NBER Working Paper 25164. https://www.nber.org/system/files/working_papers/w25164/w25164.pdf.

Shiferaw, Admasu, and M. Söderbom. 2019. The Ethiopian Manufacturing Sector: Productivity, Export, and Competitiveness. In *The Oxford Handbook of the Ethiopian Economy*, ed. Fantu Cheru, Christopher Cramer, and Arkebe Oqubay, 747–770. Oxford: Oxford University Press.

Stiglitz, Joseph E. 2003. *Globalization and Its Discontents*. New York: Penguin.

UNCTAD. 1996. Chapter 2, Export, Capital Formation and Growth. In *Trade and Development Report 1996*, 108. Geneva: UNCTAD.

UNCTAD. 2006. *"Developing Productive Capacities" the Least Developed Countries report*. Geneva: UN Conference on Trade and Development.

UNCTAD. 2013. *World Investment Report 2013. Global Value Chains: Investment and Trade for Development*. Geneva: UN Conference on Trade and Development.

UNCTAD. 2018. *World Investment Report: FDI and the Sustainable Development Goals*. Geneva: UN Conference on Trade and Development.

UNCTAD. 2019. *World Investment Report 2019. Special Economic Zones*. Geneva: UN Conference on Trade and Development.

UNCTAD. 2022. *Rethinking the Foundations of Export Diversification in Africa: The Catalytic Role of Business and Financial Services. Economic Development in Africa Report 2022*. Geneva: UNCTAD.

UNCTAD. 2023a. *Productive Capacity Index*. Geneva: United Nations.

UNCTAD. 2023b. *Trade and Development Report 2023. Growth, Debt and Climate: Realigning the Global Financial Architecture*. Geneva: UN Conference on Trade and Development.

UNCTAD. 2023c. *Technology and Innovation Report 2023. Opening Green Windows: Technological Opportunities for a Low-Carbon World*. Geneva: United Nations.

UNCTAD. 2024. *World Investment Report 2024. Investment Facilitation and Digital Government*. Geneva: UN Conference on Trade and Development.

UNCTAD-UNIDO. 2011. *Economic Development in Africa Report 2011: Fostering Industrial Development in Africa in the New Global Environment*. New York/Geneva: United Nations Industrial Development Organization and United Nations Conference on Trade and Development.

UNECA. 2016. *Transformative Industrial Policy*. Addis Ababa: United Nations Economic Commission for Africa.

UNIDO. 2025. *Industrial Dataset*. September. Available at https://stat.unido.org/data/table?dataset=indstat&revision=4#data-browser (accessed on 15 December 2025).

United Nations Department of Economic and Social Affairs. 2025. *World Population Prospects 2024. Data Portal*. New York: United Nations.

World Bank. 2023. *Enterprise Survey Database*. Washington, DC: The World Bank Group.

World Bank. 2025. *Development Indicators Database*. Washington, DC: World Bank.

World Intellectual Property Organisation (2023) Global Innovation Index. Available at https://www.wipo.int/en/web/global-innovation-index/2023/index (Accessed on 15 December 2025).

Zartman, I. William. 2026. Political Economy in Morocco. In *The Oxford Handbook of the Moroccan Economy*, ed. Karim El Aynaoui and Arkebe Oqubay. Oxford: Oxford University Press.

Zewde, Bahru. 2002. *A History of Modern Ethiopia: 1855–1991*. James Currey.

PART II

Practices and Strategies

CHAPTER 4

Challenges of Industrial Development in Africa: A Policy Diagnosis

The challenges and constraints of industrialisation in Africa vary from country to country and across sectors. For this book, it is essential to focus selectively on key challenges that hold strategic and policymaking significance, ensuring a sound diagnosis rather than providing an extensive list. The book will examine five strategic challenges of Africa's industrialisation: (i) political stability and policy uncertainty; (ii) workforce development; (iii) industrial hubs and corridor development; (iv) industrial financing; (v) productive investment and linkages. Additionally, conducting a diagnosis and review of sectors is relevant, as policy challenges differ among them. This sectoral dimension is presented in Chap. 5, highlighting diverse industries of great importance to various national contexts.

1 Political Stability and Policy Uncertainty

Industrial development requires prioritising its role in the development strategies of African countries, focusing on resource allocation and carefully designing and implementing policy instruments over extended periods, even in resource-constrained contexts. Nevertheless, it remains one of the core challenges faced by many African nations. Political constraints manifest in various forms. For example, in many countries, political stability has been a key factor influencing the success of industrial policies. Ethiopia managed to sustain the highest economic growth and rate of

A. Oqubay, *Productive Transformation in Africa*,
https://doi.org/10.1007/978-3-032-23941-9_4

industrialisation for over two decades. Political stability was crucial for economic development and attracting productive investment between 2004 and 2019. Côte d'Ivoire experienced some of the continent's highest economic growth rates and significant expansion of its manufacturing sectors but was hampered by political instability and civil war. In Ethiopia's case, the conflict in the Northern region in the early 2020s led to slower economic growth, reduced productive investment, and a misallocation of resources away from development priorities, as well as the destruction of the country's human and material resources. African national governments have to prioritise peace, development, and the peaceful resolution of political conflicts.

The second major challenge is the lack of political commitment to the industrial development strategy, as well as a significant gap between the design and implementation of industrial policy. This gap is often threatened by frequent policy changes due to national election cycles or shifts in prioritisation, even when the ruling party remains the same. Such instability creates considerable uncertainty for investors who need to make long-term investments.

Third, poor coordination among government agencies at the national level further aggravates the challenge, as various ministries prioritise their specific mandates. For example, the Ministry of Finance and Revenue prioritises revenue generation, while the Ministry of Industry may focus on supporting investors and industrial development. Coordination further declines between national and local government levels, especially when ethnicity significantly influences the political landscape. These problems occur when national goals are neither shared nor used to guide priorities across government agencies. Overall coordination of industrial development should not rest with a single ministry, such as the Ministry of Industry; instead, it should be led by the respective Prime Ministers or Presidents to ensure all government institutions work together effectively and address strategic issues. This model works best when there is a deliberate effort to establish centres of excellence or lead agencies. Many countries have tried this approach, with varying success. A common issue in many African governments is that too many cabinet ministries are created for political reasons rather than to form an effective cabinet for optimal policy performance. For strategic areas like investment and export promotion, lead agencies or statutory boards, such as the Economic Development Board of Singapore, could be the most suitable and effective approach.

Fourth, in many cases, macroeconomic realities and sectoral policies do not align with or support industrial policies due to inadequate planning and a failure to resolve the inherent tensions among the relevant public entities, which weakens outcomes and overall impact. Notably, macroeconomic stability is a vital factor that can either hinder or facilitate productive investment, creating conditions to boost firms' productivity. High inflation, high bank interest rates, a shortage of foreign exchange, and significant currency devaluation can be barriers to manufacturers' performance and investment flows. We also showed that overvalued exchange rates are a more common problem, undermining competitiveness especially (Cramer et al. 2020). In countries struggling to compete on low wages, developing a macroeconomic environment conducive to industrialisation and supporting industrial policies should be central to enhancing policy predictability.

Fifth, various studies on manufacturing firms indicate that red tape and corruption significantly undermine performance and increase production costs, as observed in tax and customs authorities, as well as other regulatory bodies (Oqubay 2015). African governments should continually work to reform government agencies and promote a corruption-free business environment. Several measures could be employed to reduce corruption and improve the business climate by focusing on lead agencies, digitisation, and a comprehensive strategy to streamline the regulatory framework. Learning from international best practices, such as Singapore's efforts to reduce corruption and foster a business-friendly environment, as well as those on the continent from countries like Mauritius and Rwanda, could offer valuable insights.

In a nutshell, the lack of political commitment, political stability, policy predictability, and weak coordination are critical issues that require strategic responses and consistently adhered. Without progress in the political frontier, industrial development is unlikely to succeed.

2 Industrial Financing and Industrialisation

Development economics and economic catch-up experiences demonstrate that development banks are the flagships of developmental states and critical conduits for industrialisation in late-developing economies, as seen in the East Asian Tigers, China, and Brazil (Amsden 1989, 2001). Amsden's seminal analysis of South Korea's transformation reveals four fundamental principles that distinguish effective development banking from failed experiments elsewhere—principles directly relevant to Africa's productive transformation agenda. First, development banks served as strategic channels for directing subsidised long-term finance to priority sectors, particularly heavy and chemical industries, through policy loans allocated at preferential interest rates to support strategic industrial transformation. Second, and most critically, these subsidies were not dispensed as giveaways but rather "on the principle of reciprocity," whereby the state imposed strict performance standards on all subsidy recipients: firms receiving long-term capital at negative real interest rates were required to use borrowed capital productively rather than speculatively, and those allowed to sell in protected domestic markets were obligated to produce and sell in export markets (Amsden 1989). This performance-based monitoring mechanism distinguished successful East Asian development banks from their counterparts in Turkey and India, where subsidies became giveaways without adequate discipline. Third, late industrialisation based on learning rather than innovation necessitated developing deep sectoral and financial expertise within development banks, as "salaried managers responsible for exploiting borrowed technology" emerged as gatekeepers of foreign technology transfers and champions of building in-house technological capabilities (Amsden 1989). Fourth, effectiveness depended fundamentally on the state's institutional capacity to monitor firm performance, enforce compliance with performance standards, and withdraw support from underperforming recipients—a capacity requiring sophisticated technical expertise in both finance and industrial sectors.

The broader history of development banks highlights their crucial role across various contexts and periods. Gerschenkron's (1962) influential work on economic backwardness established that in moderately backward countries, banks played a leading role in industrialisation, whereas in highly backward countries, the state initially took on this role, with development banks acting as vital institutional innovations to address capital market failures. Diamond's (1957) foundational study offered early systematic analysis of development banking practices across multiple nations, documenting how specialised financial institutions mobilised long-term capital for industrial enterprises when conventional banking systems proved insufficient. Yasuda's (1993) examination of Japanese development banks, particularly the Industrial Bank of Japan and the Japan Development Bank, illustrated how these institutions fostered Japan's post-war economic growth through targeted long-term financing and policy coordination. More recently, Griffith-Jones and Ocampo's (2018) comprehensive analysis in *The Future of National Development Banks* demonstrates the continued relevance of these institutions, examining their roles in innovation, structural change, sustainable infrastructure financing, and financial inclusion across both developed and developing economies. Di John's (2020) chapter on "The Political Economy of Development Banking" in *The Oxford Handbook of Industrial Policy* offers critical perspectives on governance, political economy constraints, and institutional design features that determine the effectiveness of development banks as instruments of industrial policy. Zalk (2021) emphasises the urgent need to scale up African development banks, arguing that institutions like Germany's KfW, Brazil's BNDES, and China's policy banks offer important lessons for facilitating long-term investment, de-risking projects, and crowding in private capital for structural transformation and green industrialisation.

A significant challenge for Africa's productive transformation is the inability to provide adequate financing with subsidised interest rates and long repayment periods for strategic priority industries and innovative activities. The lack of financing for industrialisation is a complex, structural challenge shaped by the historical evolution of particular countries and intensified by the dismantling of state institutions and public banks driven by economic liberalisation under the Washington Consensus. While a few exceptions exist where development financing has been crucial—such as the Development Bank of Mauritius (DBM) and the South African Industrial Development Corporation (IDC, founded in 1940)—many state-led development banks have been unable to fully perform their productive roles. This contrasts sharply with successful models such as BNDES in Brazil (founded in 1952) and China Development Bank (CDB), which have made significant contributions to industrialisation and economic catch-up.

Several constraints hinder effective development banking in Africa. First, access to development and industrial financing remains a major obstacle, especially for small and medium enterprises facing higher interest rates and bureaucratic barriers, as confirmed by IFC Enterprise Surveys (2025). Second, banks often lack the necessary resources, governance systems, and creditworthiness to mobilise funds and demonstrate strong performance because they cannot comply with industrial policy frameworks. This issue is worsened by a lack of specialisation and expertise. Di John (2009) emphasises that significant African capital exists but remains offshore and uninvested in "bankable projects," with insufficient effort to attract capital and create favourable conditions. Unlike Asia, where capital flight is partly offset by round-tripping—investors hiding money offshore but reinvesting domestically—Africa experiences net capital outflows, a critical political economy issue. Third, development financing's reliance on lending instruments rather than equity participation or co-ownership causes entities to prioritise risk aversion over acting as stakeholders and active contributors to project success. Moreover, there is a notable disconnection in utilising public funds, such as pension schemes, for productive activities that support industrial development. The lack of coordination among various state-owned banks and financial institutions presents a significant barrier to pooling funds, and development banks have not fully mobilised additional resources alongside multilateral development finance institutions. Additional constraints include insufficient foreign exchange for borrowers, limited experience in venture capital financing, and inadequate domestic resource mobilisation—essential given the strategic importance of development financing and the risks associated with external financing. In many African countries, commercial banks are less willing to target priority industries and interest rates are high.

However, essential lessons exist from successful development banks in the Global South, particularly China's specialised policy banks (China Development Bank, Industrial and Commercial Bank of China, Agricultural Bank of China) and Brazil's BNDES, which have resulted in significant capabilities and decades of successful development financing. Similar lessons can be drawn from the Development Bank of Mauritius and South Africa's IDC, which have financed various industrial projects and green transitions, although some argue the IDC has not done enough. Multilateral development finance institutions, such as the International Finance Corporation (IFC), British International Investment (BII), the European Investment Bank (EIB), and the African Development Bank (AfDB), have supported critical industrial projects, though they remain inadequate in scale and resources necessary for industrialisation. Development financing from the Global South, especially China, has greatly supported African industrialisation with approximately US$200 billion allocated to energy (34%), transportation (30%), and ICT (10%). However, this faces challenges from new macroeconomic conditions, including rising external debt and global interest rates, while industrial financing for domestic manufacturing firms remains a key obstacle.

African governments should establish credible national development banks that act as channels for industrialisation, applying the reciprocity principle and performance-based monitoring mechanisms that distinguished successful East Asian development banks. Joint financing from development finance institutions in the Global South, like the Asian Infrastructure Investment Bank (AIIB) and the New Development Bank (NDB), plays a vital role in bridging financing gaps for member countries. Given financing limitations, governments need to create attractive and targeted incentives for productive foreign direct investment (FDI) and encourage foreign manufacturers to bring their own funding to prevent crowding out domestic firms. Complementary approaches include industrial hubs that decrease financing needs by providing targeted industrial infrastructure—such as factory buildings and facilities for leasing—and equipment leasing systems tailored to specific industries. However, the scale and complexity of the challenge underscore the need for a strategic approach to adequate development financing that incorporates the four fundamental principles from successful development banking experiences: targeted finance to priority sectors, reciprocity-based performance standards, deep sectoral and financial expertise, and robust institutional capacity for monitoring and enforcement.

3 Development of Industrial Hubs and Economic Corridors

Industrial hubs—from industrial clusters to corridor development—generate a strong impetus for industrialisation and innovation in various ways, as witnessed worldwide and particularly in the Asian experience (Oqubay and Lin 2020).[1] First, industrial hubs contribute to significant collective efficiency and inter-firm learning, promoting specialisation and division of labour among firms, as well as strengthening production linkages. Second, industrial hubs provide effective industrial and innovation ecosystems, which require constant upgrading, revitalisation, and adaptation. Third, given the constraints—budget, financing, bureaucratic barriers, infrastructure limitations, and political economy—focusing on industrial hubs allows for the privatisation of priority industries. Fourth, as evidenced by the experiences of the COVID-19 global pandemic, industrial hubs have contributed to the resilience of firms facing various shocks. Ultimately, the development of industrial hubs facilitates industrial upgrading, promotes

[1] *The Oxford Handbook of Industrial Hubs and Economic Development* (2020) provides over a dozen chapters on Asian industrial hubs which could offer relevant lessons.

carbon-neutral pathways, and integrates with urban development. In the case of China, industrial hubs have served as institutional innovations to accelerate economic catch-up and transformation.

The development of industrial hubs has emerged as one of the most widely adopted industrial development strategies in many African countries, with Mauritius being an early pioneer in the 1970s.[2] In 2025, it was estimated that there were 250 industrial parks across Africa, each with distinct features, but they were also concentrated in a limited number of countries. However, the actual design and execution reveal significant disparities, and the outcomes have been mixed. Unlike the results of Asia's rapid industrialisation, the overall assessment indicates that the outcomes have been uneven. Various research outputs highlight several challenges and constraints that contribute to low performance.[3]

First, the primary and most significant challenge was that the industrial hubs were developed without integration into the country's development strategy and industrial policy framework, resulting in a limited impact on industrialisation. Pursuing the development of industrial hubs as a critical component of the industrial development strategy involves the political will to prioritise resources and efforts for successful execution, which requires multidimensional reforms. The development of industrial hubs has often taken an extended period, has not been accompanied by investment reforms, and has lacked accompanying industrial policy interventions. There is also an illusion that investing in complex infrastructure hardware will bring about miraculous changes without incorporating the knowledge and lessons from both local and international experiences to ensure positive outcomes.

Second, numerous shortcomings arise at both the design and execution levels. One common drawback has been in location decisions, which should be based on productive criteria to ensure the success of industrial clusters. However, failures arise when these decisions are made based on political considerations rather than productive criteria, along with inadequate studies that consider various determinants, including site technical studies, economic and financial feasibility, and environmental and social safeguards. The lack of access to land and high lease prices poses a significant hurdle that carries political sensitivity in many African countries. The

[2] Stiglitz (2011), Rodrik (2012), Oya, Ramtohul, and Tandrayen-Ragoobur (2025), Oqubay (2025).

[3] UNIDO (2023), Stein (2020), Lin and Xu (2019).

wrong selection of locations may also contribute to difficulties in ensuring a supply of industrial labour or talent, which is usually not given adequate consideration.

Third, a significant challenge is the country's insufficient investment in infrastructure, especially in power and connectivity, which hampers firms' performance and growth potential. The lack of adequate infrastructure also hinders the functionality of industrial parks, leading to power interruptions and blackouts. Substantial support from local governments is crucial to ensure that the services and utilities necessary for factories and their employees, including housing, are in place.

Fourth, the lack of financing to develop industrial hubs poses a significant challenge for many African countries, particularly in light of the post-COVID-19 financial squeeze. However, this challenge can be effectively addressed by implementing government policies to attract and engage private developers, who possess the expertise to develop and operate them, and by providing adequate government support and incentives, including profit tax holidays. The government should aim to give land and utilities for industrial hubs, and in situations where this is not feasible, alternative packages should be implemented.

Fifth, a significant challenge in many African countries has been that many industrial hubs lack one-stop government services, including customs, and the operation and management of industrial parks fall below internationally compliant standards. Adequate preparation and development of the required capability are essential and necessitate a long-term approach. In this sphere, numerous solutions have been introduced in various Asian industrial hubs that can be adapted to Africa's specific context.

In summary, it is crucial to recognise that developing industrial hubs and corridors is essential for accelerating industrial growth, and a strategic approach in designing an industrial policy framework is necessary. A one-size-fits-all solution is unlikely to be effective, but learning from existing lessons and maximising insights from practical and targeted experiences through piloting and experimenting with a phased approach can improve performance. In addition to experiences from Asia, countries like Morocco offer significant insights. However, the specific modalities and strategies tailored to accommodate the unique circumstances of individual African countries.

4 Promoting Productive Investment and Linkages

Productive Investment

A central priority for economic catch-up in developing countries lies in mobilising and directing underdeveloped, scattered, and underutilised resources to stimulate productive investment for accelerated industrialisation. Development economics and economic history indicate that all developing countries possess opportunities for economic development despite resource constraints, with no absolute prerequisites for industrial and economic catch-up. Hirschman (1958) characterises this process as the enrolment of "resources and abilities that are hidden, scattered, and badly utilised" for development purposes, while Gerschenkron (1962) demonstrates that countries can catch up by building on the advantages of backwardness—or latecomer advantages—despite lacking the prerequisites that earlier industrialisers possessed. This dynamic is evident in the economic catch-up experiences of East Asia and China, where development banks emerged as critical institutions for mobilising scattered resources and channelling them toward strategic industrial priorities. However, the prospects for African industrialisation and the respective development trajectories of individual countries remain divergent, reflecting the distinctive domestic, continental, and external realities that shape each nation's capacity to mobilise resources, build institutional capabilities, and implement effective industrial policies. The challenge for Africa, therefore, is not merely accessing finance but instead establishing the institutional frameworks—particularly credible development banks operating on reciprocity principles—that can transform scattered resources into strategic productive investment capable of driving structural transformation.

The private sector is a driving force behind African industrialisation, and it is the government's responsibility to promote policies that channel resources to strategic priority sectors and enable productive transformation. Depending on the chosen approach to local productive transformation, as well as macroeconomic factors and fluctuations in the international capital market, African governments can tap into various sources of investment. From a long-term perspective, African governments should strategically emphasise promoting domestic investment by utilising mechanisms that encourage firms to invest in productive sectors, supporting development banks, and implementing specific policies to assist different categories of firms, including small, medium-sized, and large companies. The challenges faced by each category of firms are significantly different.

What are the primary challenges in promoting productive investment? First, due to the prevailing political economy, private investors tend to invest in industries or economic activities that seem lucrative while avoiding the risks associated with manufacturing or industrialisation. Local firms prefer to invest in manufacturing for local markets rather than focusing on exports, considering the intensity of international competition and the related risks. To encourage firms to transition into productive sectors, policies should provide more effective incentives that gradually foster a more productive political economy. However, even those local firms that express interest face significant obstacles in building market and productive capabilities, as well as developing managerial skills that enhance their competitiveness in international markets. From this perspective, the government employ various mechanisms to support local firms, including offering subsidies and incentives, developing capabilities, and utilising industrial ecosystems to facilitate linkages and learning. The importance of foreign firms—those with a proven track record in production capacity and export competitiveness—lies in helping local firms to emulate and improve their competitiveness. The failure of many governments to adopt such policies—in essence, industrial policies—has resulted in limited success.

Second, promoting high-quality, productive investment on a massive scale requires reforming government institutions within the investment promotion sphere. Investment promotion should target industry specificity, types of firms, and their origins. One of the most effective ways to build productive capacity is to reform government agencies to ensure optimal support for firms. However, many governments fall short of this ideal. Firms face immense uncertainty and a lack of policy predictability due to frequent and haphazard policy changes. The rule of law and the protection of investors' property are significant concerns in many countries. The actions of various government agencies often lack effective coordination, forcing executives to spend their time navigating bureaucratic red tape. Many firms express concerns about corruption and a lack of transparency in tax and customs regulations. Reforming government institutions necessitates a comprehensive overhaul of the entire system to transform services, provide adequate support for businesses, and deepen transparency and reform. African governments could learn from positive experiences that can serve as valuable input. While it may be unrealistic to reform the civil service and all institutions, the government can select lead agencies that play distinct roles and focus on reforming these specific institutions. Given the strategic importance of investment as a source of productive capacity, such an initiative should be championed by the highest executive body, such as investment boards led by a prime minister or president, at the outset of making breakthroughs.

Third, in many cases, government efforts to promote export markets and address the constraints that firms face in accessing the African market and responding to the trade protectionism of various trading partners are inadequate. Few countries, such as Mauritius and Morocco, have been proactive in this area. Additionally, there is a significant gap in comprehensive support for industrial financing and the industrial ecosystem. Such support extends beyond institutional reforms and enhances the ability to develop firms' competitive advantage in the spirit of productive government–private sector partnership, focusing on priority sectors.

ELI and ISI Strategies

One of the primary questions often asked is whether to focus on export-led industrialisation (ELI) or import-substitution industrialisation (ISI), a question that is relevant from both conceptual and practical perspectives. It may be more useful to frame the question around how to ensure the complementary effects by integrating export-led and import-substitution industrialisation. There are fundamental reasons why exports have a strategic role in industrialisation. Exports provide a massive market opportunity that allows for benefitting from economies of scale and specialisation by expanding the limits of domestic markets. They play a critical role as a source of international learning, constantly enhancing the competitiveness of firms. Exports also significantly relieve constraints on the balance of payments, which is the limiting factor for high growth. Additionally, exports can open up avenues to develop natural resources that would otherwise be unfeasible due to the domestic market's size. An additional dimension emphasised by Hirschman (1958) is what he calls "import swallowing," where growth in imports could potentially lead to the development of a domestic industry.

Considering the strategic importance of exports, "ensuring complementarity" with import-substitution within the ELI framework was a challenging balancing act in the East Asian experience, involving careful management of ELI while pursuing strategic ISI to enhance local value addition and promote industrial upgrading, which requires skilful handling of industrial policy. The East Asian experience demonstrates that a strategic and pragmatic approach to industrial policy, managed by a capable state and guided by well-coordinated policies, was essential for a balanced and successful implementation of ELI alongside ISI.

New investments and expansions could have a greater developmental impact and generate additional investment through linkage effects or production linkages—particularly forward and backward linkages, as well as employment and fiscal linkages. Domestic value addition—creating economic value locally and enhancing manufacturing, technology, and know-how transfer—is a vital approach for developing domestic capacity. Linkage effects could be understood in terms of policymaking and policy learning, as highlighted by Hirschman's (1981: 80): "it is also possible, that the state, as a result of having intervened successfully in one sector of the economy, will acquire the capability and the appetite to tackle advances for other sectors or for the economy in general."

5 Workforce Development and Industrialisation

One of the primary constraints on Africa's industrialisation has been the difficulties and challenges of developing an industrial workforce, which remains a significant concern for both foreign and domestic firms. This issue is strategic for several reasons. First, firms have internationally competitive, and low productivity poses a substantial obstacle to their competitiveness. This is especially evident in production activities, where labour productivity is a major contributor to overall productivity. Second, considering the demographic dynamics in Africa and the pressure to generate large-scale employment, workforce development becomes vital due to the scale and urgency involved. Third, with the rapid pace of technological advancements, there is a need for new skills and reskilling to keep up with changing times. Fourth, throughout history, for all industrialising economies, building an industrial workforce has been a key strategic priority and a major driver of industrial transformation, as latecomer developers compete with initially low labour costs and improve technological capabilities at all stages of industrialisation (Gebrechristos 2025; ILO 2023).

Evidence from several African countries, including Côte d'Ivoire, Ethiopia, Mauritius, and Morocco, shows that the challenges of developing an industrial workforce are varied.[4] A key difficulty many companies face is an insufficient labour supply to operate multiple shifts and run at full capacity, a common problem among many Asian manufacturers. For example, numerous large firms in Ethiopia have encountered this issue despite the country's plentiful labour, which surpassed the expectations of both businesses and government policymakers. Various factors make it hard to secure an adequate labour supply, even when it appears available. Many African nations are still new to industrialisation, and the workforce often originates from rural villages and small towns. Newly hired workers frequently lack industrial experience or prior exposure to manufacturing, which demands a different set of industrial culture and work disciplines. Many firms also struggle with absenteeism and retention during the first 2 or 3 years.

Furthermore, obstacles to labour mobility, such as ethnic tensions and the effective functioning of labour market institutions, hindered labour supply and workforce development. In other cases, labour mobility has improved workforce supply, as demonstrated in Côte d'Ivoire. As economies diversify towards services, recruiting local workers becomes a major challenge, as seen in Mauritius. In various national contexts, the development of industrial hubs has played a key role in alleviating these issues and promoting the growth of industrial discipline.

A second challenge faced by the industrial workforce is the welfare and working conditions of workers, especially in labour-intensive industries and areas with concentrated production clusters. A major issue has been rising inflation and high living costs, such as housing, local transport, and food expenses in many African countries, which put considerable pressure on workers' low wages at a time when productivity improvements have not occurred. Experience indicates that collaboration between the government and firms is essential to enhance workers' welfare, which directly affects the productivity and competitiveness of firms and helps develop industrial capacity sustainably. Positive experiences show that various measures can be put in place to address housing supply, canteen services, medical care, and affordable public transport (Gebrechristos 2025).

A third significant issue is the slow growth of productivity and skill development, which are vital for building competitive industries. Skills development and ongoing productivity improvements require a strategic approach that ensures firms prioritise skills development as a key and

[4] Gebrechristos (2025), Oya (2019a, b).

continuous obligation. The government should introduce policy tools to motivate firms to invest in skills development. Skill development is complemented by performance-related payments (PRPs) to motivate workers and foster continual production management enhancements. Governments and industry should work together to ensure that technical schools and university education align with the evolving needs of industry. The talents required in the early stages of production, as well as rare expertise, motivated and incentivised, as they boost the productivity growth of local workers. Positive lessons from successful practices, as seen in the Moroccan automotive industry and Ethiopia's textile and apparel sector, show that firms have sent local workers to their Asian production facilities for skills and managerial development (Gebrechristos 2025).[5]

Labour productivity is essential for industrialisation and driving structural transformation. History shows that for any economy, increasing labour productivity is crucial for sustained economic growth and the rapid expansion of the manufacturing sector. When combined with rising employment, skill development, and technological progress, productivity raises real labour incomes and helps reduce extreme poverty. Without improvements in output per worker, governments can only control inflation and maintain competitiveness by suppressing and keeping real wages low, which can undermine efforts to reduce poverty. Conversely, higher productivity allows wages to grow, encourages enterprises to upgrade skills and technology, and results in the production of higher-value goods and services. This promotes more inclusive growth, supports human development and poverty alleviation, and helps curb inequality. As Paul Krugman (1994: 11), Nobel laureate in economics, aptly states: "Productivity isn't everything, but in the long run it is almost everything. A country's ability to improve its standard of living over time depends almost entirely on its ability to raise output per worker."

Therefore, a strategic approach to workforce development is crucial for sustained industrialisation, where the government, firms, and labour unions should collaborate. Without such strategic intervention, little progress can be achieved in Africa's industrialisation. As technological advancements accelerate, African governments should focus on

[5] See Nigisty Gebrechristos, *Industrialisation and Workforce Development in Africa: Policy Dynamics, Firms, and Industrial Ecosystems* (Palgrave Macmillan, 2025), which offers conceptual and empirical analysis grounded in extensive primary research.

strengthening their technical and vocational education and training (TVET) systems and reforming technology universities.

In conclusion, although these strategic issues remain the primary challenges for policymaking, the approaches differ to reflect the diversity of national contexts. Each sector and the various stages of industrialisation and investment demand distinct strategies to suit the specific local circumstances.

6 Conclusion on Strategic Policy Issues and Challenges

The chapter highlights five interconnected strategic challenges that impede Africa's industrialisation and productive transformation, going beyond a mere list to a diagnostic framework.

Success hinges on *political stability, policy predictability,* effective *state coordination,* and a strong *macroeconomic* environment that supports productive transformation. Evidence from several African countries suggests that stability is crucial for sustained growth and investment. The primary obstacle is the implementation gap, caused by a lack of long-term political commitment, frequent policy shifts, and poor inter-ministerial coordination (such as between finance and industry ministries). This necessitates decisive leadership from the presidency or the prime minister's office to align priorities. Moreover, macroeconomic instability (including high inflation and foreign exchange shortages) and corruption directly impede industrial performance, underscoring the need for a strategic, sustained effort to foster a predictable, favourable political and economic climate.

A key challenge is the *insufficient long-term development financing.* The dismantling of state institutions under the Washington Consensus created a gap, with many African development banks unable to act as catalysts. Issues include limited resources, poor governance, risk-averse lending practices (favouring equity), and a disconnect from national industrial policies. The successes of development banks in China (CDB), Brazil (BNDES), Mauritius (DBM), and South Africa (IDC) demonstrate the importance of credible, well-funded national institutions. Because of scale limitations, a strategic approach combining these with targeted FDI and innovative mechanisms like equipment leasing is essential.

Although industrial hubs are a widely adopted strategy to promote agglomeration economies and resilience, their outcomes have been inconsistent due to significant design flaws. The main issue is their disconnection from a comprehensive industrial policy framework. Success requires more than just infrastructure; it depends on location decisions based on productive—not political—criteria, sufficient investment in power and connectivity, and efficient on-site management with integrated services. Financing challenges can be addressed by involving private developers with government backing. A phased, customised approach that learns from international and continental best practices (e.g., Morocco, Mauritius) is essential.

The main challenge is mobilising scattered resources for productive investment. The analysis promotes a practical integration of *Export-Led Industrialisation (ELI)* and Import-Substitution Industrialisation (ISI) within a strategic framework. ELI offers scale, learning, and foreign currency, while strategic ISI improves local value addition. Major obstacles include a political economy that prefers low-risk non-industrial sectors, weak institutional support for firms, and a lack of targeted investment promotion. Reforming lead agencies to provide predictable, coordinated support and actively developing export markets are essential for fostering production linkages and domestic capacity.

Building a competitive *industrial workforce is a crucial bottleneck.* Challenges are not only numerical but also qualitative: a lack of industrial discipline and experience among new workers, poor retention, and welfare issues (low wages relative to high living costs) that hinder productivity. Notably, slow productivity growth poses a significant threat to long-term competitiveness and poverty reduction. A strategic, collaborative effort is essential among government, firms, and unions, focusing on skills development aligned with industry needs, performance-related incentives, and improvements in worker welfare to establish a sustainable industrial base.

In a nutshell, tackling these five strategic areas—political coherence, financing, hubs, investment, and workforce—through context-specific, learning-focused, and well-coordinated policies is essential for Africa's industrial transformation. However, depending on the level of economic development, political economy, and development strategies, the emerging strategic issues can vary significantly.

References

Amsden, Alice H. 1989. *Asia's Next Giant: South Korea and Late Industrialization.* New York: Oxford University Press.

Amsden, Alice H. 2001. *The Rise of "The Rest": Challenges to the West from Late-Industrializing Economies.* Oxford/New York: Oxford University Press.

Cramer, C., Sender, J., and Oqubay, A. (2020) *African Economic Development: Evidence, Theory, Policy.* Oxford University Press.

Di John, J. (2009) *From Windfall to Curse? Oil and Industrialization in Venezuela, 1920 to the Present.* Penn State University Press.

Di John, Jonathan. 2020. The Political Economy of Development Banking. In *The Oxford Handbook of Industrial Policy*, ed. Arkebe Oqubay, Christopher Cramer, Ha-Joon Chang, and Richard Kozul-Wright, 292–318. Oxford: Oxford University Press.

Diamond, William. 1957. *Development Banks.* Baltimore: The Johns Hopkins Press (for the Economic Development Institute, International Bank for Reconstruction and Development).

Gebrechristos, Nigisty. 2025. *Industrialisation and Workforce Development: Policy Dynamics, Firms, and Industrial Ecosystems.* London: Palgrave Macmillan.

Gerschenkron, Alexander. 1962. *Economic Backwardness in Historical Perspective: A Book of Essays.* Cambridge, MA: Harvard University Press.

Griffith-Jones, Stephany, and José Antonio Ocampo, eds. 2018. *The Future of National Development Banks.* Oxford: Oxford University Press.

Hirschman, Albert. 1958. *The Strategy of Economic Development.* New Haven: Yale University Press.

Hirschman's. 1981. *Essays in Trespassing: Economics to Politics and Beyond.* Cambridge: Cambridge University Press.

ILO. 2023. *Employment conditions in Ethiopia's garment and floriculture sectors.* Geneva: International Labour Organization.

Krugman, Paul. 1994. *The Age of Diminished Expectations.* Cambridge, MA: MIT Press.

Lin, Justin Yifu, and Jiajun Xu. 2019. China's Light Manufacturing and Africa's Industrialization. In *China-Africa and an Economic Transformation*, ed. Arkebe Oqubay and Justin Yifu Lin, 265–281. Oxford: Oxford University Press.

Oqubay, Arkebe. 2015. *Made in Africa: Industrial Policy in Ethiopia.* Oxford: Oxford University Press.

Oqubay, Arkebe. 2025. Learning from Mauritius' Economic Transformation: A Policymaker's Perspective. In *The Oxford Handbook of the Mauritian Economy*, ed. Carlos Oya, Ramola Ramtohul, and Verena Tandrayen-Ragoobur, 435–462. Oxford: Oxford University Press.

Oqubay, Arkebe, and Justin Yif Lin. 2020. Industrial Hubs and Economic Development: Conclusion and Pathways to the Future. In *The Oxford Handbook of Industrial Hubs and Economic Development*, ed. Arkebe Oqubay and Justin Yifu Lin. Oxford University Press.

Oya, Carlos. 2019a. Building an Industrial Workforce in Ethiopia. In *The Oxford Handbook of the Ethiopian Economy*, ed. Fantu Cheru, Christopher Cramer, and Arkebe Oqubay, 651–670. Oxford University Press.

Oya, Carlos. 2019b. Labour Regimes and Workplace Encounters Between China and Africa. In *China-Africa and an Economic Transformation*, ed. Arkebe Oqubay and Justin Yifu Lin, 239–264. Oxford: Oxford University Press.

Oya, Carlos, R. Ramtohul, and V. Tandrayen-Ragoobur, eds. 2025. *The Oxford Handbook of the Mauritian Economy.* Oxford: Oxford University Press.

Rodrik, Dani. 2012. *The Globalisation Paradox: Why Global Markets, States, and Democracy Can't Coexist.* Oxford: Oxford University Press.

Stein, Howard. 2020. Industrial Policy, Institutional Transformation, and the Development of Industrial Parks. In *The Oxford Handbook of Industrial Hubs and Economic Development*, ed. A. Oqubay and J. Y. Lin, 103–122. Oxford University Press.

Stiglitz, Joseph E. 2011. The Mauritius Miracle. *Project Syndicate.* Online. http://www.project-syndicate.org/commentary/the-mauritius-miracle.

United Nations Industrial Development Organization (UNIDO). 2023. *Industrial Parks and Sustainability: The Case of Hawassa Industrial Park, Ethiopia.* UNIDO.

Yasuda, Ayako. 1993. *The Performance and Roles of Japanese Development Banks*, Working Paper, May 1993.

Zalk, Nimrod. 2021. Africa's development banks: The urgent need for scale. *LSE Business Review*, November 17.

CHAPTER 5

The Anatomy of Industrial Chains: A Cross-Sectoral Diagnosis

1 The Rationale of Industrial Chains and Classification

This book explores seven key industries vital for Africa's industrialisation. Its aim is not to offer exhaustive sectoral analysis—an effort beyond its reach—but to highlight high-potential sectors, diagnose main constraints, and suggest necessary interventions. The analysis does not strictly adhere to the International Standard Industrial Classification (ISIC) system because this system is inadequate for capturing essential technological linkages, economic attributes, and industrial structures necessary for understanding productive transformation (UN 2008; Andreoni and Chang 2019; Oqubay et al. 2020).

ISIC classification obscures critical distinctions in three ways. First, it groups technologically heterogeneous activities: "non-metallic mineral products" (ISIC 23) conflates capital-intensive, scale-dependent cement production with ceramics or glass manufacturing, which have entirely different technological requirements and value chain structures; similarly, "fabricated metal products" (ISIC 25) encompasses both basic metal structures and precision engineering components requiring vastly different capabilities (Lall 2000).

Chandler's (1990) influential analysis of industrial capitalism illustrates that competitive advantage mainly depends on exploiting economies of scale and scope, which vary considerably across industries and influence

A. Oqubay, *Productive Transformation in Africa*,
https://doi.org/10.1007/978-3-032-23941-9_5

their structural characteristics. Economies of scale originate from high-volume, capital-intensive production requiring substantial investment in factories and distribution networks—examples include sectors like steel, cement, chemicals, and oil refining, where unit costs decline sharply as output grows, and firms attain minimum efficient scale to stay competitive. Economies of scope arise from leveraging organisational expertise across multiple product lines within related markets—such as machinery, pharmaceuticals, and branded consumer goods—where firms utilise shared technologies, distribution channels, or research facilities. Chandler notes that harnessing these economies necessitates three interconnected investments: in sufficiently large production facilities to benefit from scale, in national and international marketing and distribution networks, and in management structures to coordinate high-volume production and multi-product operations (Chandler 1990). Crucially, successful firms make these "three-pronged investments" simultaneously and employ salaried managers with specialised skills to coordinate production and distribution more effectively than market mechanisms can. Once these organisational capabilities are established, they serve as barriers to entry and sources of sustained competitive advantage—what Chandler refers to as "first-mover advantages" that enable pioneering firms to dominate industries for decades (Chandler and Hikino 1997). Second, ISIC considers distinct stages of the value chain as unified sectors: "textiles and apparel" (ISIC 13–14) merges capital-intensive textile production with labour-intensive garment assembly, despite these representing fundamentally different upgrading pathways and policy requirements (Gereffi 2018). Chandler's framework clarifies why: textile production exemplifies capital-intensive, throughput-dependent manufacturing requiring integrated spinning, weaving, and finishing processes managed by professional hierarchies—a classic scale-economies industry where first-movers like British and American textile firms succeeded through vertical integration and high-volume production. Conversely, garment assembly remains fragmented and labour-intensive, rarely achieving the throughput necessary for scale economies or the product diversity enabling scope economies, thus remaining vulnerable to low-cost rivals and reliant on brand-owners' marketing capacities. Third, ISIC overlooks coherent cross-sectoral activities: agro-processing spans multiple ISIC categories yet constitutes a unified industrial chain with shared technological features and opportunities for exploiting economies of scope through product diversification and by-product utilisation.

These ISIC limitations become more pronounced as technological advances blur sectoral boundaries (Andreoni and Chang 2019; Oqubay et al. 2020). The merging of information and communication technologies with manufacturing creates hybrid industries—such as advanced manufacturing and Industry 4.0—where digital services and physical production are indistinguishable. Likewise, biotechnology integrates with agriculture and pharmaceuticals, materials science combines with electronics, and software becomes embedded in traditional machinery, all challenging conventional ISIC classification. Electric vehicle manufacturing exemplifies this convergence: it includes automotive production (ISIC 29), battery technology (ISIC 20), electronics (ISIC 26), and software development (ISIC 62), yet it forms a cohesive technological ecosystem requiring integrated policy approaches and organisational capabilities that span traditional industry boundaries. Chandler and Hikino (1997) illustrate that such technological convergence has been a feature of industrial capitalism since the Second Industrial Revolution, when electrical and chemical technologies founded new hybrid industries. This trend intensified in late-twentieth-century capitalism, where competitive advantage increasingly hinges on "dynamic capabilities"—organisational skills to integrate, build, and reconfigure internal and external competences to adapt to rapidly changing environments. In this context, Chandler contends that national competitive advantage in industries relies less on natural resource endowments or labour costs and more on institutional frameworks that enable firms to develop the organisational capabilities necessary to exploit economies of scale and scope while coordinating across technological boundaries (Chandler 1990; Chandler and Hikino 1997). Focusing solely on ISIC-defined sectors thus risks overlooking inter-sectoral spillovers, cross-cutting organisational capabilities, and system-level innovations that are progressively key to competitiveness and structural transformation.

Therefore, this book adopts an industrial structure perspective that integrates value chain approaches, Nolan's global system approach, and a technological capability perspective that cuts across ISIC categories to identify industries where Africa can build competitive advantages, develop domestic linkages, and achieve structural transformation (Gereffi 2018; Lall 2000; Oqubay et al. 2020). This approach aligns with contemporary understanding—building directly on Chandler's insights about scale economies, scope economies, three-pronged investments, and organisational capabilities—that industrial policy targets not merely sectors but rather the technological capabilities, production systems, managerial competencies, and innovation ecosystems that transcend traditional industry boundaries (Andreoni and Chang 2019; Oqubay et al. 2020). For Africa's industrialisation, this means identifying industries where scale and scope characteristics match available resources and institutional capacities, supporting firms in making the coordinated investments necessary to exploit these economies, and building the organisational capabilities—including management hierarchies, technical expertise, and inter-firm coordination mechanisms—that Chandler's historical analysis demonstrates are essential for competitive success in modern industrial capitalism.

2 Sectoral Approach as a Key Feature of Industrial Policy

The sectoral review of various industries emphasises a fundamental premise: productive transformation is grounded in specific sectors. This imperative rests on multiple reinforcing arguments. Kaldor's (1967) insights establish that sectoral structure matters profoundly—a "sectoral approach" remains essential despite technological advances or blurred industry boundaries—because sectors exhibit distinct growth dynamics, productivity characteristics, employment effects, and spillover multipliers. Hirschman's production linkage effects and political economy considerations are intrinsically interconnected and display industry-specific traits, meaning that the backward and forward linkages, along with the political coalitions and resistance they generate, vary fundamentally across industries. Moreover, the technological and economic attributes of sectors—capital intensity, scale economies, learning curves, skill requirements—constitute crucial factors in shaping and executing industrial policies, as the experiences documented by Amsden (1989, 2001), Chang (1994, 2003), and Schwartz (2010) consistently demonstrate.

At the firm level, this sectoral specificity manifests concretely: firms specialise and develop capabilities within particular industries, and even when they diversify, their choices are driven by strategic considerations and thorough assessments of existing competence, accumulated capabilities, corporate strategy, and competitive advantages rather than by random expansion. Porter's (1990) insights on firm strategies are inextricably tied to industrial reviews of competitive forces precisely because competitive dynamics, entry barriers, supplier relationships, and buyer power vary systematically across sectors. Oqubay (2015) synthesises these insights by demonstrating that mixed outcomes of industrial policies arise from three interrelated drivers: variation in sectoral industrial structure (determining technological possibilities and scale requirements), the political economy within each sector (shaping feasible interventions and coalition dynamics), and the dynamics of linkage effects (creating spillovers or bottlenecks). These three drivers interact to create sector-specific policy challenges and opportunities.[1]

Consequently, developing industrial ecosystems, adopting strategies for industrial and technological upgrading, facilitating inter-firm learning, and enabling collective action all depend fundamentally on sector specificity. The rationale behind dynamic comparative advantage—whether latent or actively constructed—and competitive edge are necessarily sector-specific because they rest on accumulated capabilities, technological trajectories, and market structures that differ across industries. Similarly, global specialisation and regional value chains—examined through the analytical lenses of global value chains (GVCs), global production networks (GPNs), and global business revolutions (GBRs)—are rooted in specific sectors with distinct governance structures, upgrading possibilities, and entry requirements (Gereffi 2018; Schmitz 2007; Dicken 2015; Coe and Yeung 2015; Nolan 2001). However, recognising sectoral specificity does not imply that industries are rigid, isolated entities; rather, they exhibit various levels of association, cross-sectoral spillovers, and technological convergence that industrial policy to address.

The practical implications for designing and implementing industrial policies become evident when comparing sectoral characteristics. The cement industry and textile sector, for instance, have fundamentally different features that shape feasible strategies: cement is driven primarily by import-substitution industrialisation (ISI) logic, guided by domestic market demand, and produces an essentially non-tradable product constrained by transport costs, whereas textiles participate in globally fragmented value chains with tradable products at every stage. The seven industries examined in subsequent chapters—automotive, cement, textile and apparel, pharmaceuticals, fertilisers, agro-industry, and others—represent different linkage structures and industrial characteristics while remaining broadly interconnected with cross-cutting development challenges such as urbanisation, agricultural transformation, and sustainability transitions. Textiles and apparel, as light manufacturing sectors, maintain strong backward linkages to agriculture through cotton and natural fibre production.

[1] See Manyazewal and Shiferaw (2019).

The cement industry serves as a key driver of urbanisation and the construction sector, generating significant indirect employment through its forward linkages. Each sector thus embodies a distinct configuration of technological requirements, market structures, linkage effects, and policy challenges.

Across these seven sectors, the chapters highlight how drivers of and constraints on industrial development vary systematically, necessitating differentiated industrial policies tailored to sectoral realities. Targeting and reviewing sectors constitute crucial diagnostic tools because they reveal where binding constraints lie, what capabilities to build, and which policy instruments prove effective. Critically, within the same industry, challenges and appropriate diagnoses vary substantially at different development stages and between countries with different endowments, market sizes, and institutional capacities. This variation underscores why sectoral analysis is simultaneously industry-specific and context-sensitive, examining how universal sectoral characteristics interact with country-specific conditions to create unique policy spaces and transformation possibilities.

The selected industries are examined not in a hierarchical order but rather as representative cases illustrating diverse pathways for productive transformation across Africa's heterogeneous economies. The analysis heavily relies on background reports from "The Greening of African Economic Development," a British Academy research project led by the author, which systematically investigates industrial development trajectories in Ethiopia, Mauritius, Morocco, Nigeria, and South Africa—five countries that together account for half of Africa's GDP in purchasing power parity terms and a third of its population. These countries also have markedly different structural conditions, resource endowments, and stages of industrial development. This strategic country selection allows for an examination of how the six key productive sectors operate under different contexts: from resource-rich economies like Nigeria to manufacturing-focused economies like Morocco and Mauritius; from large domestic markets like Ethiopia to export-oriented platforms; and from middle-income South Africa to lower-income settings. By analysing these sectors across such diverse environments, the study identifies common constraints facing African industrialisation—such as inadequate development finance, weak technological capabilities, and limited domestic linkages—as well as country-specific bottlenecks that require tailored policy solutions. This comparative approach shows that although these six sectors are essential for Africa's structural transformation and green growth in all contexts, the order of interventions, institutional needs, and feasible upgrading paths vary significantly depending on each country's existing capacities, market structures, and policy frameworks.

3 Pharmaceutical Industry

Given Africa's demographic dynamics, the pharmaceutical industry remains strategically crucial for maintaining health services and managing pandemics. It is essential to develop a healthy, productive workforce, and, given the increase in average life expectancy and the need to address the current low level of healthcare, building the pharmaceutical industry and biotechnology research capacity is vital. However, the continent's pharmaceutical sector faces considerable challenges. Firstly, it relies heavily on imports, which account for 80% of its demand; the widespread presence of substandard, imported medicines and counterfeits exacerbates this dependence. Existing pharmaceutical companies are primarily involved in formulation, adding little value because they rely on importing active reagents, ingredients, and other inputs. This vulnerability hampers the continent's resilience against regional and global pandemics. Second, the absence of government policies prioritising the industry, coupled with high regulatory fragmentation and limited regulatory harmonisation, creates a significant bottleneck. Third, the African market remains highly fragmented and limited in size, further complicated by dependence on donor funding for procuring pharmaceutical goods in certain countries.

Fourth, underdeveloped pharmaceutical hubs and industrial ecosystems pose significant challenges, with Egypt and South Africa currently serving as the main pharmaceutical centres. Although Ethiopia has established a pharmaceutical industrial hub, it has made limited progress so far in attracting investment and starting production of pharmaceutical products. While creating a competitive pharmaceutical industry in most African countries may be difficult, a vital strategy should focus on establishing major regional pharmaceutical hubs that benefit from economies of scale, ensure logistical connectivity, develop the entire value chain, and encourage investment in research and development in medicine and biotechnology.

Pharmaceutical Sectors in Ethiopia, Egypt, and India (1970s–2020s): Ethiopia's firms started with basic tablet formulation (production capability) and then invested in sterile injectable plants (investment capability), but they lacked R&D and API synthesis. Consequently, innovation remained limited. Egypt followed a similar pattern—strong in production and investment capacity for generics manufacturing, yet minimal API production and R&D kept the sector in a middle capability trap, despite a large domestic market and regional exports. Conversely, India made progress across all three Amsden capabilities—moving from formulation (production) to large-scale plants (investment) and ultimately to API synthesis and bio-pharma R&D (innovation). A deliberate policy linking patent protection reversal to R&D incentives enabled firms like Ranbaxy and Dr. Reddy's to achieve full technological capability, transforming them into global innovation players. This demonstrates that investment capability alone is insufficient without concurrent innovation development and emphasises the interconnected progression essential for genuine catch-up.

India is among the countries that have emerged as a leading producer and exporter of generic medicines, leveraging the provisions of international agreements and targeted policies. In India's pharmaceutical industry (1970s–2000s), suspension of patent protection and domestic content requirements enabled local firms like Ranbaxy and Cipla to reverse-engineer and dominate generic drug production; later WTO compliance compelled capability enhancement, and India became a global generics powerhouse—infant protection proved effective when time-bound and performance-linked.

Similarly, African countries can learn from Bangladesh, which has developed a vibrant pharmaceutical industry that supplies 94% of local demand and exports to over 100 countries, including 27 LDCs (least developed countries) (Gay 2018; Gay and Gallagher 2020). How did Bangladesh succeed in growing its pharmaceutical sector? First, it capitalised on its LDC status and the WTO TRIPS waiver for LDCs, which allows it to produce generic medicines even if they are still under patent protection. LDCs are exempt from TRIPS obligations. Second, it attracted foreign investors to manufacture in Bangladesh and benefit from the TRIPS waiver. This helped local firms upgrade their capabilities through partnerships with foreign investors. Third, skill development received greater emphasis as part of the pharmaceutical industry development policy. In short, Bangladesh proved that even low-income and LDCs can develop the pharmaceutical industry with the right policies and by leveraging the TRIPS waiver. Out of 54 countries in Africa, 33 are LDCs and could learn from Bangladesh's example. Of course, some firms in Bangladesh are now concerned because graduation means losing LDC-specific international support measures, including the TRIPS waiver.

4 Cement Industry

The cement industry exemplifies an industry with a narrow latitude for failure due to its capital intensity, perishable nature, and the construction industry's high safety concerns. Ethiopia's and Nigeria's cement industries (2000s–2020s) exhibit distinct developmental trajectories. In Ethiopia, strong backward linkages to limestone mining and forward linkages to construction and infrastructure created a development sequence, with public–private partnerships encouraging investment in limestone quarrying, transport logistics, and housing. Nigeria's Dangote Group exemplified this approach on a pan-African scale by building cement plants across ten African countries (Nigeria, Senegal, Cameroon, Ghana, Ethiopia, Zambia, Tanzania, South Africa, Kenya, Congo) and integrated limestone quarries, captive power generation, and distribution networks. Dangote's vertical integration strategy spurred broader industrial activity: backward linkages to mining equipment, energy infrastructure, and coal/gas supply; forward linkages to real estate, roads, and housing construction; and horizontal spillovers through training local suppliers and contractors. Both cases demonstrate how cement's linkage-rich structure—high capital intensity yet continuous production process with "narrow latitude for performance" (Hirschman)—makes it strategically valuable for latecomers, catalysing investment sequences and industrial ecosystems beyond the sector itself, especially when firms achieve economies of scale across multiple markets.

The cement industry has strong links to the construction sector, aiding in job creation. It is driven by urbanisation and population growth, which significantly boosts the production of building materials. This industry is capital-intensive, depends on economies of scale, and is characterised by high energy usage. Africa remains a minor player in global cement consumption and production. Nevertheless, the African cement industry expanded more than threefold from 2000 to 2025. While the sector experienced modest growth from about 80 million to 150 million tonnes between 2000 and 2010, it saw substantial growth from 2010 to 2025, reaching 386 million tonnes annually. The main factors behind the rapid growth of the cement industry include modest economic development in many African countries, accelerated urbanisation, and increased infrastructure development (Oqubay 2015).[2]

Additionally, local industrial groups have successfully mobilised the necessary investments and selected the latest technology and production capabilities, allowing them to operate profitably. Nearly two-thirds of production capacity is supplied by local players, while the rest comes from foreign direct investment (FDI), including new entrants such as China. Almost all cement plants source their technology, machinery, and turnkey contractors from China, benefitting from lower investment costs, productivity improvements, and better capacity utilisation. Furthermore, significant value has been added, as limestone and other raw materials are abundant in most African countries. Nigeria leads the cement industry with an annual capacity of about 60 million tonnes, followed by Egypt, Morocco, Ethiopia, and South Africa. The main investor in the African cement industry has been the Nigerian Dangote Cement Group, which has invested in over 10 countries across Africa.

A key constraint has been the availability of power infrastructure, which has compelled firms to build their own captive power facilities, thereby increasing production costs. Underdeveloped road infrastructure also contributes to higher distribution costs, leading to the expansion of the transport industry and encouraging the establishment of new cement plants closer to consumption areas. African governments should promote the development of the cement industry, led by both domestic industrialists and foreign firms, and ensure that cement prices decrease to support growth in housing and infrastructure. The sector significantly contributes to tax revenues through corporate taxes from cement plants and VAT on cement sales. Although cement is a non-tradable product, some North African countries could become competitive in exporting certain outputs to European and other markets because of their geographic proximity. Governments should support decarbonisation efforts within the industry and improve access to raw material resources. The strategic goal for African governments should be to further develop the cement industry as a catalyst for growth, generating substantial spillover effects.

5 Fertiliser Industry

The development of the fertiliser industry is essential for transforming the agricultural sector, which is vital for food security, exports, and fostering inter-sectoral linkages, as African economies depend on agriculture as a

[2] See The Greening of African Economic Development (2025a, b, c, d, e, f).

major employer and contributor to national GDP. Significant challenges facing the African fertiliser industry include, firstly, the heavy dependence of African countries on imports, which makes them vulnerable to global market volatility, supply chain disruptions, price shocks, and geopolitical factors, as seen during the war in Ukraine. Second, African farmers use very little fertiliser and face high prices, along with frequent delays in shipment, port handling, and distribution, which limit fertiliser use and contribute to higher costs and volatility. Third, farmers struggle to access finance and scientific knowledge about fertiliser use, with an overreliance on generic application rather than precision methods supported by research and effective extension services. Fourth, African governments need to prioritise agricultural transformation; strategies and policies should be aimed at increasing fertiliser production capacity across the continent. Currently, many landlocked African countries spend significant foreign currency on importing fertiliser, which places enormous pressure on subsidising farmers, a practice that may not be sustainable in the long term. For instance, fertiliser imports represent the second-largest foreign-currency expense in Malawi. Due to their seasonal nature, importing becomes a logistical nightmare, as seen in Ethiopia's import experience.

Morocco possesses the world's largest phosphate deposit, and urea has been produced in limited quantities, with recent expansions in Nigeria. The African Union's leadership is ineffective in developing the African fertiliser industry, and all African governments should prioritise this sector. The aim should be not only to achieve self-reliance in food security but also to position Africa as the leading exporter of food and agricultural products. Attracting domestic and foreign firms to invest in fertiliser factories is central, and learning from international experiences from the Global South (such as Brazil, China, and India) and partnering with global fertiliser players is essential. A proactive and comprehensive strategy should prioritise attracting investors to the fertiliser industry, ensuring that policies support the development of the agricultural sector and assist farmers.[3]

6 Petrochemical Industry

African countries possess substantial oil and gas resources, and their economic strategies should leverage these endowments to accelerate industrialisation, build productive capacity, and promote economic diversification, thereby driving employment creation, exports, and industrial output. More than ten African economies depend heavily on oil and gas, including

[3] See The Greening of African Economic Development (2025a, b, c, d, e, f).

Nigeria, Angola, Algeria, Libya, Gabon, the Republic of Congo, Equatorial Guinea, and Chad. In principle, African nations have the sovereign right to develop their hydrocarbon resources, and this objective need not conflict with achieving net-zero targets if extraction revenues fund green industrial transitions and renewable energy infrastructure. Despite decades of oil and gas production, the results in promoting value addition and industrialisation have been profoundly limited. Beyond South Africa and Algeria, which established petrochemical industries in earlier decades, most oil-producing African countries failed to develop downstream processing. Nigeria's Dangote Industrial Complex—comprising a 650,000 barrels-per-day refinery and integrated petrochemical hub employing world-class technology—represents a landmark exception that became operational in 2024, yet its emergence after six decades of oil production underscores rather than contradicts the broader pattern of failure.

The rise of the global petrochemical industry offers a critical lens for analysis on two distinct, yet connected, levels:

First, the *macro-political economy level*: It highlights the "resource curse" dilemma, where oil-rich states often struggle to diversify their economies. The immense, low-effort rents from oil and gas exports can create political and economic structures that actively impede broader industrialisation, leading to entrenched overreliance on primary resource extraction.

Second, *the strategic industrial policy level*: It presents a counterpoint through the experience of resource-scarce nations. Here, the analysis focuses on the deliberate construction of competitive advantage. A prime example is Singapore, an oil-importer that built the world-class Jurong Island petrochemical supercluster. This case study revolves around specific policy challenges: strategic infrastructure investment, creating integrated value chains, attracting foreign capital and expertise, and leveraging geographic position to establish a globally competitive export-oriented hub.

By examining these two levels together, the development of petrochemicals becomes a powerful comparative tool. It contrasts the *passive constraints* of resource abundance with the *active creation* of industrial capacity, offering key insights into the political and policy determinants of economic development.[4]

[4] See The Greening of African Economic Development (2025a, b, c, d, e, f).

The Petro-State Paradox: Natural Wealth Versus Industrial Capacity?

A key question is why the oil and gas economies have failed to diversify and promote industrialisation. Five interconnected factors explain this ongoing failure. First, the "Dutch disease" phenomenon systematically weakened non-oil tradable sectors: oil revenues appreciated real exchange rates, making manufacturing internationally uncompetitive while directing investment, skilled labour, and entrepreneurial talent towards the rent-rich oil sector rather than productive industrial activities (Auty 1993; Gelb 1988). Second, the political economy of resource rents fostered powerful coalitions favouring continued extraction and rent distribution over the long-term, uncertain, and politically difficult investments needed for industrial diversification.

Di John's (2009) seminal work on Venezuela's oil economy demonstrates how oil wealth paradoxically diminished state capacity for industrial policy: resource rents allowed governments to avoid the fiscal bargains with domestic capitalists and organised labour that historically drove institutional development in successful industrialisers, while rent-seeking coalitions captured state institutions, preventing coherent, sustained efforts to implement diversification strategies. Third, weak state capacity and governance failures meant that even when governments articulated diversification strategies, they lacked the institutional capabilities for implementation: the reciprocity mechanisms, monitoring systems, and technical expertise in development banks that Amsden (1989, 2001) identifies as essential for successful industrial policy were systematically absent, allowing subsidies to become giveaways and protection to shield inefficiency rather than nurturing competitiveness (Mkandawire 2001).

Fourth, integration into global commodity markets as price-takers exposed these economies to extreme volatility in revenues and foreign exchange availability, creating macroeconomic instability that discouraged long-term investments, continuous learning, and incremental capability-building essential for industrialisation. Boom-bust cycles repeatedly disrupted emerging diversification efforts (Ross 2012; Venables 2016). Fifth, the structural adjustment programmes and Washington Consensus reforms of the 1980s–1990s dismantled already-weak state institutions, development banks, and industrial policy frameworks precisely when oil producers needed to strengthen them. Meanwhile, conditionalities actively discouraged the "getting prices wrong," targeted subsidies, and infant industry protection that successful late industrialisers employed. As Mkandawire (2001) argues, the ideological assault on developmental states and industrial policy in Africa coincided exactly with the period when resource-rich countries most required robust institutional capacity to transform windfall revenues into productive growth. As discussed above, addressing the political economy issue and developing the petrochemical hub are interconnected strategic matters.

African Petrochemical Hubs: The Pitfalls and Industrialisation Potential?

The challenges and constraints confronting the African petrochemical industry reveal systemic failures in implementing industrial policy, despite decades of recognition of the need for diversification. First, inadequate infrastructure—with poor transportation networks and limited storage capacity—leads to higher operational costs that hinder competitiveness, even when production facilities meet international standards. Second, over-reliance on coal or natural gas as primary feedstocks makes the industry susceptible to supply disruptions, price volatility, and high carbon emissions, as exemplified by South Africa's Sasol Secunda plant, the world's largest coal-to-liquids facility, which faces increasing pressure to decarbonise yet lacks viable transition pathways. Third, developing and modernising oil refineries requires substantial capital investment, but funding remains severely restricted by decarbonisation pressures from international financial institutions that impose overly strict conditions on African nations, while being more accommodating towards fossil fuel investments in developed economies—evident in the controversies surrounding.

Uganda's oil projects and the East African Crude Oil Pipeline. Fourth, political and economic pressures from entrenched interest groups and established international oil companies actively impede new investments and create supply chain vulnerabilities to protect existing rents. The Dangote Industrial Complex, for instance, confronted considerable political obstacles from oil majors and trading firms which initially refused to supply crude oil and downstream product off-take agreements, illustrating how incumbent interests mobilise to block new entrants that threaten long-standing oligopolies (Thurber et al. 2011). Fifth, outdated technologies and a lack of economies of scale in existing refineries and plants—compounded by skills and technological gaps—result in chronically low-capacity utilisation, rendering facilities economically unviable even when operational.

This sharp contrast underscores the pivotal role of strategic state intervention in overcoming initial resource and capital constraints. The exemplary cases of two *oil-poor* and historically *import-dependent* Asian economies are instructive:

Singapore transformed from a fuel importer into the architect of Jurong Island, a globally integrated petrochemical superhub. Its success was founded on meticulous state planning, world-class infrastructure, and policies designed to attract leading multinational capital and technology. India, a net crude oil importer, pursued a parallel path of technological capacity-building. It has now emerged as a global supplier of industrial technology and project expertise. This evolution is powerfully symbolised by its role as a key machinery supplier and builder for the Dangote Refinery and Petrochemical Complex in Nigeria—an ironic case of a once-dependent nation now enabling industrial development in a resource-rich African state.

Together, these cases demonstrate that successful petrochemical industrialisation is not a function of resource endowment but of sustained, sophisticated industrial policy.

The Jurong Island Petrochemical Hub in Singapore exemplifies deliberate, coordinated industrial policy: starting in the 1990s, the Singaporean government reclaimed seven offshore islands to create a 32-square-kilometre integrated petrochemical complex, invested heavily in world-class infrastructure, including underground pipeline networks connecting 95 plants, attracted key investments from global majors (ExxonMobil, Shell, Chevron), and simultaneously developed specialised technical education programmes to ensure a skilled workforce (Coe & Yeung 2016). The hub achieved critical mass swiftly because the government provided not just land and infrastructure but also coordinated logistics, streamlined regulatory approvals, and guaranteed long-term policy stability—the "three-pronged investments" in production facilities, distribution networks, and organisational capabilities that Chandler (1990) highlights as essential. Crucially, Singapore leveraged its petrochemical base to advance up the value chain into speciality chemicals and pharmaceutical ingredients, demonstrating how initial resource processing can catalyse broader industrial upgrading when supported by coherent capability-building policies.

India's petrochemical journey offers lessons more directly relevant to African contexts, given shared initial conditions of limited resources and weak industrial bases. Starting in the 1960s, India established public sector petrochemical complexes through strategic partnerships: Indian Petrochemicals Corporation Limited (IPCL, now part of Reliance Industries) began with government ownership and technical collaboration with Japan's Mitsubishi, facilitating technology transfer and capacity building. The government provided long-term development financing via specialised institutions, protected the domestic market during the learning phase, and mandated backward integration to develop local supply chains—precisely the reciprocity-based industrial policy that Amsden (1989) documents in East Asia.

Importantly, India's strategy evolved: initial public sector dominance shifted towards private sector dynamism as capabilities matured, exemplified by Reliance Industries' rise as a globally competitive, integrated petrochemical producer. The crucial factor was sequencing—developing capabilities through protected learning before liberalising, rather than exposing firms prematurely to international competition. India's experience also highlights the importance of scale: Reliance's Jamnagar complex, with a refining capacity of 1.24 million barrels per day, achieves economies of scale that enable competitiveness even as a late entrant (Sutton and Kellow 2010). African petrochemical development has failed to replicate either Singapore's coordinated infrastructure-led model or India's sequenced capability-building approach, instead oscillating between ineffective state-owned enterprises lacking commercial discipline and failed attempts to attract private investment without providing the necessary complementary infrastructure and policy support.

Although the governments of oil-producing economies face resource constraints in developing the petrochemical industry, strategic prioritisation and learning from successful models can overcome these limitations. Concentrating on attracting investors from the Global South—particularly from China, India, and Gulf states with relevant technological capabilities and experience operating in developing country contexts—offers advantages over traditional partnerships with Western multinationals that often limit technology transfer and local capability development (UNCTAD 2020). Partnering with established industry leaders through joint ventures that mandate technology transfer and skills development, following the Indian model, provides pathways to capability acquisition. Governments take proactive leadership in three critical areas: first, providing integrated infrastructure that reduces operational costs and enables scale economies, as Singapore demonstrated; second, establishing credible development finance institutions operating on reciprocity principles to channel oil revenues into productive investment rather than consumption or capital flight; third, building technical and managerial capabilities through specialised training programmes and public–private collaboration in R&D, recognising that organisational capabilities rather than just physical capital determine competitive success (Di John 2020; Mkandawire 2001). This window of opportunity is time-sensitive: global energy transition pressures are closing access to international finance for fossil fuel infrastructure, yet African countries still need to capture value from existing hydrocarbon endowments to finance their broader industrial transformation. Ensuring speed in policy formulation and scale in initial investments—learning from the Dangote Complex's breakthrough despite political obstacles and from Asian successes in achieving rapid critical mass—will be vital for success before the window closes entirely.

7 Textiles and Apparel: An Unexploited Launchpad for Early Industrialisation?

Africa has opportunities and advantages in light manufacturing, especially in the textile and apparel sector, which is labour-intensive, export-focused, yet connects to domestic markets and has strong backward linkages to agriculture. This sector is the largest employment sector worldwide and is integrated into buyer-led global value chains. Almost all industrialising nations, from the first Industrial Revolution in England to late industrialisers in Asia, have utilised this sector to learn about industrialisation and progress. The industry is primarily dominated by China and other Asian producers, largely due to their low labour costs, which serve as a competitive edge, and well-developed supply chains.

The Bangladesh apparel and textile sector (1980s–2020s) expanded, benefitting from the Multi-Fibre Agreement's quota access to Western markets, which compelled local firms to meet strict lead times and quality standards, and accelerated learning in production management, logistics, and compliance. Even as wages remained low, the export discipline drove productivity gains. The industry has faced several challenges and currently employs about 4.5 million people (and over 10 million indirectly), with exports valued at over US$47 billion in 2023. Similarly, Sri Lanka exports more than US$5.5 billion and employs nearly half a million, developing a vertically integrated industry. In both cases, foreign firms, such as South Korea's Daewoo in the 1980s and 1990s, and YoungOne Group (which currently employs 70,000 workers in Bangladesh) and global brands and buyers, contributed to developing the sector.

Africa's share is only 1% in the global textiles industry and 2% in the global apparel or clothing sector. Regional and subnational value chains have yet to develop in this highly competitive market. Consumer preferences—favouring quick market delivery and sustainability—drive competition in the industry. African countries previously enjoyed duty-free access to the European market and, under AGOA, to the US markets. However, these preferences have now been withdrawn by the Trump administration, which introduced new tariffs on all African nations. Africa's apparel and textile industry is concentrated in around a dozen countries, including Mauritius, Morocco, Egypt, Madagascar, Lesotho, Ethiopia, and Kenya.

The main challenges of building a vibrant textile and apparel sector are: first, the inability to compete by establishing high economies of scale and the industry's vertical integration to maximise speed to market and cost competitiveness, which can rival Asian manufacturing champions. Second, developing an industrial workforce to ensure sustained skill development and productivity growth. Evidence shows that what matters most is neither lower labour costs nor an abundance of labour, but the ability to translate these into high productivity. Many African countries struggle to build a productive industrial workforce as they transition from a rural society and establish workforce discipline and an industrial culture. Third, industrial policies and government support for the textile and apparel sector have been guided by ineffective measures that fail to provide consistent and coherent support for the sector. In some cases, the textile and apparel sector has not been regarded as a strategically important industry despite its potential for job creation. Many local firms are unable to secure industrial financing and lack the necessary support (Oqubay 2019a).

Fourth, accelerating the growth of the textile and apparel industry requires establishing industrial hubs and platforms to develop an ecosystem that encourages inter-firm learning, cooperation, specialisation, and production linkages. Often, apparel or textile firms operate outside industrial parks and within industrial hubs that are not specialised or sector-specific. Experiences in Asia and recent initiatives in Ethiopia demonstrate that creating specialised industrial hubs enables economies of scale and specialisation, attracts new investment, generates market opportunities, and enhances the resilience of supply chains. Fifth, ensuring social and sustainability compliance has become a critical trend in the industry over the past two decades. Sustainability involves developing sustainable cotton, ensuring traceability, and utilising recycled inputs. It also requires the use of clean energy, a zero-liquid discharge waste management system, and sustainable industrial hubs (Oqubay 2025a, b).

Furthermore, high transportation and logistics costs have created a significant obstacle, especially for landlocked countries. In summary, the textile and apparel sector is a strategic industry for many African nations, owing to demand from domestic and regional markets, its role in boosting exports, and the need to generate employment amidst a growing population. This mission is challenging and demands effective strategies that consider global changes.

8 Agro-industries, Horticulture, Food and Beverage Industries

Agro-industries and high-value agriculture are broad terms that cover various industries. A shared feature of these activities is their dependence on agriculture and their ability to promote industrialisation. Agro-industries include a variety of products, such as foods and beverages like processed cashew nuts, roasted coffee, and cocoa. They may also include breweries that can create backward linkages, such as the malt sub-industry and the production of high-quality malt barley. The floriculture and horticulture industries significantly contribute to exports and boost production capacity. These industries require effective extension systems, the transformation of agricultural practices, and substantial R&D focused on specific sectors, along with expertise in biotechnologies. They also stimulate investment in other sectors, such as fertilisers and packaging.

Furthermore, these industries continually enhance quality standards and phytosanitary requirements. The agro-industrial and food sectors have considerable market opportunities in both domestic and intra-African markets, driven by economic growth and demographic change. Additionally, African countries need to address protectionist policies, especially in European markets, as well as trade and non-trade barriers within intra-African trade.

Ethiopia's floriculture sector (2000s–2010s) experienced rapid export growth, creating winners such as large-scale commercial farms and export logistics firms. At the same time, losers included smallholders displaced or facing competition for water and land. The sector contributed to nearly 250,000 jobs and generated significant exports, positioning Ethiopia as the world's fourth-largest exporter of roses. Social tensions and labour disputes were managed through gradual policy adjustments rather than elimination, exemplifying Hirschman's "muddling through' approach to addressing inherent distributional conflicts during transformation.[5]

Vietnam's agro-processing sector, including coffee, rice, and cashew processing, from the 2000s to the 2020s generated demand for sorting machines, packaging equipment, and cold storage (manufacturing inputs). It also absorbed agricultural surplus and increased export revenue. This interdependence—rather than rivalry—between agriculture and manufacturing drove Vietnam's broader industrialisation. Agriculture is increasingly adopting high-technology, including outputs of biotechnological advances, as seen in Holland's agriculture and high-scale farming in Brazil.

The main challenges and constraints in these broadly defined industries are as follows: First, there is a lack of prioritisation of agriculture as a vital sector with significant potential for stimulating industrialisation, exports, and job creation. This neglect is evidenced by an insufficient national budget allocation, the failure to identify competitive industries and sub-industries, and weaknesses in the design and implementation of effective industrial policies. It is also connected to the structural constraints faced by small-scale subsistence farmers. Second, there is a low level of consistency in the quality of agricultural products, traceability, and the ability to produce on an industrial scale while ensuring a reliable supply to international markets. Third, there is low value addition (as seen in the cases of cashew nuts and cocoa in Côte d'Ivoire and Ghana, and coffee in Ethiopia and Uganda), resulting in the export of raw materials and an inability to attract investors to process these commodities. Fourth, there are weak production linkages and a failure to develop policies and capacity to stimulate them. Additionally, there is limited capability in quality assurance systems and phytosanitary testing, which meet the ever-changing international standards, ensuring health requirements are complied with and branding is developed. This does not pose health risks to consumers and also addresses phytosanitary and hygienic requirements, including regulatory and quality-control challenges.

Fifth, a major constraint in political economy is making land available for commercial and industrial-scale production to harness technological

[5] On linkages to aviation and expansion of Ethiopian Airlines, as a component of Ethiopian industrial policy, see African Airlines Association (AFRAA) (2023), IATA (2023).

advancements such as mechanisation, modern irrigation systems, and other innovations. Furthermore, poor logistics, inadequate transportation, and limited cold chain facilities greatly increase transportation costs and waste during the post-harvesting phase. Despite these significant challenges, numerous success stories exist across Africa, showcasing examples of international best practices. Between 2005 and 2015, Ethiopia emerged as a leading flower grower and exporter, employing around 200,000 people and attaining exports worth $500 million. Uganda has successfully built a thriving dairy industry, becoming one of Africa's top milk producers on an industrial scale, with production reaching 5.5 billion litres in 2024. This success is supported by over a hundred dairy processing plants connected to milk sheds. However, logistical hurdles and limited access to foreign markets remain substantial barriers. Ethiopia also developed one of the fastest-growing brewery industries, expanding quickly due to high economic growth after 2005. Many European brands entered the market, creating backwards linkages with malt plants linked to a large number of barley growers.[6]

A key issue is that transforming agriculture and agro-industries requires a comprehensive industrial policy approach tailored to each country's specific traits, such as comparative advantage, performance, political economy, and political commitment, to ensure food security, supply inputs for industries, and increase exports. International examples from Brazil, India, Vietnam, China, and many others provide valuable policy insights (Oqubay 2015).

9 Automotive Industry

The African automotive industry mainly focuses on South Africa and Morocco, where established industrial chains exist. However, many automotive assembly plants across various African countries operate on a small scale, providing limited value addition and localisation. The South African automotive sector comprises numerous manufacturers from Europe, the United States, Japan, and South Korea, supplying not only the domestic market but also other regions, including Africa, the Middle East, and Europe. Renault and Peugeot lead Morocco's automotive industry, which prospers due to proactive industrial policies, with over 90% of its output exported to European markets (see

[6] Cheru, Cramer, and Oqubay (2019), Shiferaw and Söderbom (2019), Manyazewal and Admasu (2019), Oqubay (2019a, b).

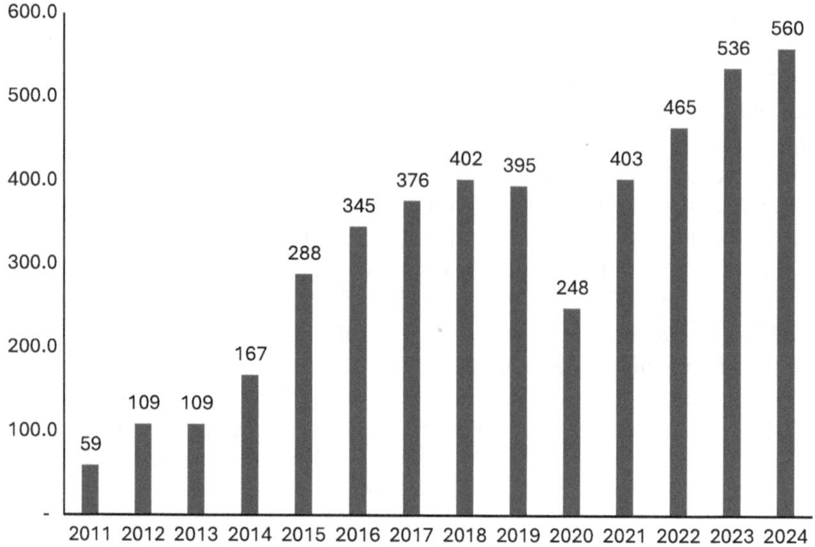

Fig. 5.1 Vehicle production in Morocco (2011 to 2023), thousands. (Source of data: International Organization of Motor Vehicle Manufacturers (cars and commercial vehicles))

Figs. 5.1 and 5.2). Africa mainly depends on imported vehicles, including those from South Africa, highlighting the market potential within the African Continental Free Trade Area. The industry sees significant growth opportunities driven by expanding domestic markets and high demand for two-wheeled and three-wheeled vehicles. Nonetheless, the global automotive industry remains concentrated, dominated by a few multinational corporations and characterised by integrated global value chains.[7]

Morocco's automotive sector (2000s–2020s) experienced significant FDI from Renault and PSA, which fostered a booming export industry. However, limited domestic supplier integration and R&D meant technological spillovers remained modest. The imbalance favouring FDI over domestic capability-building highlights the challenge of transforming FDI presence into genuine innovation-driven growth—addressing this imbalance requires deliberate policies for local content and training. The development of the automotive industry was made possible by a combination of proximity to Europe and government's extensive industrial policy

[7] See Nolan (2014), Porter (1998), The Greening of African Economic Development (2025a, b, c, d, e, f).

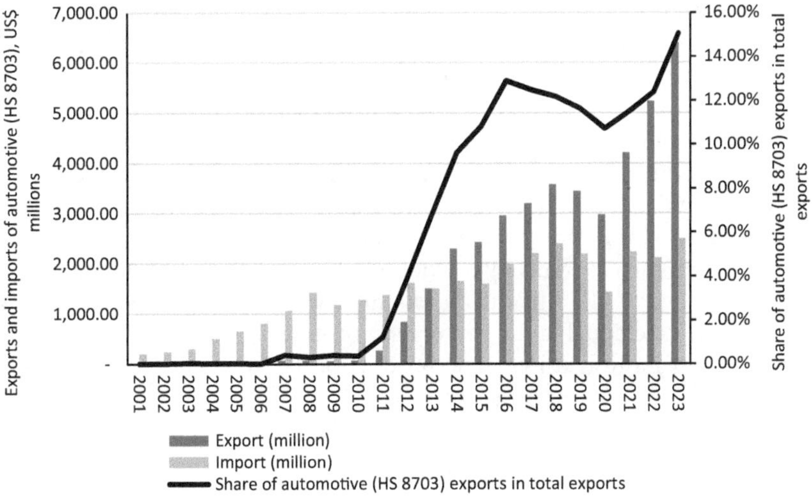

Fig. 5.2 Morocco's export-import of motor vehicles and share (2001 to 2023) in million US$. (Source of data: UN Comtrade database)

interventions, including the development of the world-class Tanger-Med Port and Industrial Complex, incentives, skill development, and domestic linkages in second and third tiers.

The main challenges facing the African automotive industry are: first, the market size is limited and highly fragmented, which restricts large-scale industrial growth. Second, the development of a globally competitive automotive industry is driven by multinational corporations (MNCs) whose headquarters are located in regions dominated by existing automotive players. Additionally, localisation and the development of the industrial chain are limited despite advances made in South Africa and Morocco. Third, skills development and the availability of talent present a significant challenge, particularly at professional and managerial levels. Furthermore, no R&D activities are conducted in these hubs. However, the biggest challenge is that the automotive industry is at a crossroads, moving in two directions: legacy automotive players continue to manufacture internal combustion engine vehicles (ICE) by traditional automakers (primarily from the United States, Europe, Japan, and South Korea), which account for over 80% of total production. The other path involves the automotive industry adopting new energy sources, such as electric vehicles, that emerged after 2000, primarily driven by Chinese EV and battery cell manufacturers, which account for approximately 60% of global production. The price of electric vehicles (EVs) has decreased rapidly, with many Chinese manufacturers exporting to African markets.

This shift and disruptions present both threats and opportunities. For example, some existing manufacturers might close certain plants to optimise their production costs and strategies. Many petroleum-importing countries, such as Ethiopia, could benefit from promoting electric vehicles (EVs) within their markets by providing incentives and investing in charging infrastructure. EV manufacturers may adopt aggressive strategies to develop new regional hubs for emerging energy markets, especially in Western and Eastern Africa. The production of two- and three-wheelers offers significant market prospects.

10 Conclusions on the Diagnosis of Industrial Chains

The diagnosis of these various sectors highlights the diversity of industries, and challenges differ markedly across countries. Several industries are crucial for Africa's industrialisation, such as e-commerce, tourism, and aviation, where some nations have achieved success and can concentrate on these areas. Emerging industries may also present opportunities, depending on each country's comparative advantages, like green energy. This chapter seeks to demonstrate that a sectoral approach to understanding challenges and opportunities is vital for Africa's industrial development. Therefore, African nations should develop strategies customised to their unique circumstances and strengths, recognising that the automotive industry is at a crossroads and requires a long-term focus on carbon-neutral pathways, technological trends, and growth prospects.

A sectoral analysis of six key industries shows that the challenges and policies needed for industrialisation in Africa are varied, requiring customised, strategic actions rather than one-size-fits-all solutions. The main cross-sector challenges and strategic priorities are outlined as follows.

Overcoming import dependency and building resilience: A significant vulnerability affects several sectors. The pharmaceutical industry (highly reliant on imports), the fertiliser sector, and the automotive sector are constrained by this dependence, making them susceptible to global supply shocks. The strategic approach should involve establishing regional hubs that benefit from economies of scale, as proposed for the pharmaceutical industry and demonstrated by the cement industry's growth. Additionally, it should actively promote local value addition, especially in agro-industries (e.g., coffee, cocoa) and the petrochemical sector.

The central role of industrial policy and state coordination: Success depends heavily on proactive, consistent government strategies. The lack of prioritisation and regulatory fragmentation hinders the pharmaceutical and agro-industrial sectors, whereas an effective industrial policy is essential to Morocco's achievements in the automotive industry. The analysis emphasises that strategic success demands high-level political commitment to coordinate policies, attract investment, and support emerging industries, including leveraging international agreements such as the TRIPS waiver for pharmaceuticals.

Addressing Infrastructure and Cost Competitiveness Bottlenecks: Physical infrastructure is a universal challenge. The cement and petrochemical industries face high expenses due to underdeveloped power and transport networks. For textiles and agro-industries, increased logistics and transportation costs, especially for landlocked countries, significantly reduce competitiveness. This calls for targeted investments in energy, roads, and ports, alongside the development of industrial hubs to create efficient ecosystems.

Developing Productive Capacity and Workforce Capabilities: The availability of a skilled, productive workforce is a recurring challenge. The textile and apparel sector's struggle to establish an industrial culture and the automotive industry's skills shortage demonstrate that low labour costs alone are insufficient without high productivity. Meanwhile, technological and managerial capabilities are limited across sectors, from R&D in pharmaceuticals to outdated technologies in petrochemicals, necessitating a strategic focus on technical education, skills development, and technology transfer.

Navigating Market Fragmentation and Global Dynamics: The small, fragmented nature of national markets creates a significant obstacle for sectors such as pharmaceuticals and automotive. The African Continental Free Trade Area (AfCFTA) is therefore essential for achieving scale. Additionally, sectors adapt to global shifts. The textile industry has to meet sustainability standards, while the automotive sector faces a disruptive crossroads between internal combustion engines and electric vehicles, requiring strategic positioning.

Sector-specific strategic positioning is crucial across various industries. Pharmaceuticals and fertilisers need a regional, policy-driven approach to promote self-reliance and cut down on imports. Cement is a good example, driven by domestic investment and urbanisation, with government support necessary to lower costs and reduce carbon emissions. Textiles and agro-industries are vital for creating jobs and increasing exports. However, they require extensive backing in workforce training, industrial hubs, and value addition to overcome logistical and productivity issues. The petrochemical and automotive sectors are complex and capital-heavy, with success largely depending on proactive government leadership to attract substantial investments, handle technological disruptions, and strengthen local supply chains.

In summary, Africa's industrialisation trajectory varies across the continent. The way forward is grounded in a detailed, sector-specific understanding of constraints and opportunities, leveraging comparative advantages through strategic government intervention, regional cooperation, and a sustained focus on developing productive capabilities.

References

African Airlines Association (AFRAA). 2023. *African Aviation Performance Report*. Nairobi: AFRAA Publications.

Amsden, Alice H. 1989. *Asia's Next Giant: South Korea and Late Industrialization*. New York: Oxford University Press.

Amsden, Alice H. 2001. *The Rise of "The Rest": Challenges to the West from Late-Industrializing Economies*. Oxford/New York: Oxford University Press.

Andreoni, Antonio, and Ha-Joon Chang. 2019. The Political Economy of Industrial Policy: Structural Interdependencies, Policy Alignment and Conflict Management. *Structural Change and Economic Dynamics* 48:136–150.

Auty, Richard M. 1993. *Sustaining Development in Mineral Economies: The Resource Curse Thesis*. London: Routledge.

Chandler, Alfred D., Jr. 1990. *Scale and Scope: The Dynamics of Industrial Capitalism*. Cambridge, MA: Harvard University Press.

Chandler, Alfred D., Jr., and Takashi Hikino. 1997. The Large Industrial Enterprise and the Dynamics of Modern Economic Growth. In *Big Business and the Wealth of Nations*, ed. Alfred D. Chandler Jr., Franco Amatori, and Takashi Hikino, 24–57. Cambridge: Cambridge University Press.

Chang, Ha-Joon. 1994. *The Political Economy of Industrial Policy*. Basingstoke: Macmillan.

Chang, Ha-Joon. 2002. *Kicking Away the Ladder: Development Strategy in Historical Perspective*. London: Anthem Press.

Chang, Ha-Joon. 2003. *Kicking the Ladder: Developing Strategy in Historical Perspective*. Anthem.

Cheru, Fantu, Christopher Cramer, and Arkebe Oqubay, eds. 2019. *The Oxford Handbook of the Ethiopian Economy*. Oxford: Oxford University Press.

Coe, Neil M., and Henry Wai-chung Yeung. 2015. *Global Production Networks: Theorizing Economic Development in an Inter-connected World*. Oxford: Oxford University Press.

Coe, Neil M., and Henry Wai-chung Yeung. 2016. *Global Production Networks: Theorizing Economic Development in an Interconnected World*. Oxford University Press.

Di John, Jonathan. 2009. *From Windfall to Curse? Oil and Industrialization in Venezuela, 1920 to the Present*. University Park: Pennsylvania State University Press.

Di John, Jonathan. 2020. The Political Economy of Developing Banking. In *The Oxford Handbook of Industrial Policy*, eds. Oqubay, A., Cramer, C., Chan H.-J., Richard K.-W. Oxford University Press.

Dicken, Peter. 2015. *Global Shift: Mapping the Changing Contours of the World Economy*. 7th ed. SAGE Publications.

Ethiopian Airlines. 2024. *Annual Performance Report*. Addis Ababa.

Gay, Dan. 2018. Pharmaceutical Dreams: TRIPS and Drugs Policy in Bangladesh (PDF). https://www.researchgate.net/publication/325206579_Pharmaceutical_Dreams_TRIPS_and_drugs_policy_in_Bangladesh.

Gay, Daniel, and Kevin Gallagher. 2020. *The Need to Extend the WTO TRIPS Pharmaceuticals Transition Period for LDCs in the COVID-19 Era: Evidence from Bangladesh*, UN CDP Policy Review Series. https://www.un.org/development/desa/dpad/wp-content/uploads/sites/45/publication/CDP-review-2020-1.pdf.

Gelb, Alan and Associates. 1988. *Oil Windfalls: Blessing or Curse?* New York: Oxford University Press.

Gelb, Alan. 1988. *Oil Windfalls: Blessing or Curse*. Oxford University Press.

Gereffi, Gary. 2018. *Global Value Chains and Development: Redefining the Contours of 21st Century Capitalism*. Cambridge: Cambridge University Press.

IATA. 2023. *Air Transport Market Profile: Ethiopia*. Montreal: IATA Economics. International Air Transport Association.

Kaldor, N. 1967. *Strategic Factors in Economic Development*. Cornell University Press.

Lall, Sanjaya. 2000. The Technological Structure and Performance of Developing Country Manufactured Exports, 1985–98. *Oxford Development Studies* 28 (3): 337–369.

Manyazewal and Admasu. (2019). Economic Policy and Structural Transformation. In *The Oxford Handbook of the Ethiopian Economy*, eds. Cheru, F., Cramer, C., and Oqubay, A, (pp. 137–158). Oxford University Press.
Mkandawire, Thandika. 2001. Thinking About Developmental States in Africa. *Cambridge Journal of Economics* 25 (3): 289–314.
Mkandawire, Thandika, and Charles Soludo. 1999. *Our Continent, Our Future: African Perspectives on Structural Adjustment*. Trenton: Africa World Press.
Nolan, Peter. 2001. *China and the Global Business Revolution*. Palgrave Macmillan.
Nolan, Peter. 2014. *Chinese Firms, Global Firms: Industrial Policy in the Age of Globalization*. London: Routledge.
Oqubay, Arkebe. 2015. *Made in Africa: Industrial Policy in Ethiopia*. Oxford: Oxford University Press.
Oqubay, Arkebe. 2019a. Industrial Policy and Late Industrialization in Ethiopia. In *The Oxford Handbook of the Ethiopian Economy*, ed. Fantu Cheru, Christopher Cramer, and Arkebe Oqubay, 724–746. Oxford: Oxford University Press.
Oqubay, Arkebe. 2019b. The Structure and Performance of the Ethiopian Manufacturing Sector. In *The Oxford Handbook of the Ethiopian Economy*, ed. F. Cheru, C. Cramer, and A. Oqubay, 747–768. Oxford: Oxford University Press.
Oqubay, Arkebe. 2025a. *Industrial Policy and Economic Development: Theory, Strategy, and Practice*. London: Palgrave Macmillan.
Oqubay, Arkebe. 2025b. *Industrial Hubs and Economic Catch-up: Productive Transformation and Governance*. London: Palgrave Macmillan.
Oqubay, Arkebe, Christopher Cramer, Ha-Joon Chang, and Richard Kozul-Wright, eds. 2020. *The Oxford Handbook of Industrial Policy*. Oxford: Oxford University Press.
Porter, Michael E. 1990. *The Competitive Advantage of Nations*. Free Press.
Porter, Michael E. 1998. *The Competitive Advantage of Nations*. New York: Palgrave Macmillan.
Ross, Michael L. 2012. *The Oil Curse: How Petroleum Wealth Shapes the Development of Nations*. Princeton: Princeton University Press.
Schmitz, Hubert. 2007. Reducing Complexity in the Industrial Policy Debate. *Development Policy Review* 25 (4): 417–428.
Schwartz, Herman. 2010. *States Versus Markets: The Emergence of a Global Economy*. New York: Palgrave.
Shiferaw, Admasu, and M. Söderbom. 2019. The Ethiopian Manufacturing Sector: Productivity, Export, and Competitiveness. In *The Oxford Handbook of the Ethiopian Economy*, ed. Fantu Cheru, Christopher Cramer, and Arkebe Oqubay, 747–770. Oxford: Oxford University Press.
Sutton, J., and Kellow, N. 2010. *An Enterprise Map of Ethiopia*. International Growth Centre.

The Greening of African Economic Development. 2025a. *Automotive Industry Background Paper*. British Academy research project. SOAS University of London.

The Greening of African Economic Development. 2025b. *Cement Industry Background Paper*. British Academy research project. SOAS University of London.

The Greening of African Economic Development. 2025c. *Energy Sector Background Paper*. British Academy research project. SOAS University of London.

The Greening of African Economic Development. 2025d. *Fertiliser Industry Background Paper*. British Academy research project. SOAS University of London.

The Greening of African Economic Development. 2025e. *Petrochemical Industry Background Paper*. British Academy research project. SOAS University of London.

The Greening of African Economic Development. 2025f. *Textile and Apparel Industry Background Paper*. British Academy research project. SOAS University of London.

Thurber, M. C., Hults, D. R., Heller, P. R. P. et al. 2011. Exporting the Norwegian Model: The Effect of Administrative Design on Oil Sector Performance. *Energy Policy*39 (9), 5366–5378.

UNCTAD. 2020. *Investment World Report. International Production Beyond the Pandemic*. Geneva: United Nations.

United Nations. 2008. *International Standard Industrial Classification of All Economic Activities (ISIC), Rev. 4*, Statistical Papers Series M No. 4/Rev.4. New York: United Nations Statistics Division.

Venables, Anthony J. 2016. Using Natural Resources for Development: Why Has It Proven So Difficult? *Journal of Economic Perspectives* 30 (1): 161–184.

CHAPTER 6

Productive Transformation in Africa: Comparative Case Studies

1 Why Mauritius and Morocco?

The importance and feasibility of productive transformation and industrialisation can be understood from the economic development paths of several African countries. This chapter draws lessons from two case studies of African nations that have achieved significant productive transformations: Mauritius and Morocco. Mauritius has demonstrated decades of productive transformation since the early 1970s and is now an upper-middle-income economy. Morocco has undergone its most notable productive transformation since the early 2000s. Both cases highlight the challenges, differences in economic structures, and diverse pathways for economic transformation across different periods. In both instances—one being a small island economy and the other an oil-importing country—successive governments pursued development strategies and effective industrial policies to promote productive transformation.

The comparative examination of Mauritius and Morocco reveals fundamental insights into the dynamics of productive transformation in Africa. These cases demonstrate that economic transformation occurs through deliberate transition to more productive industries, driven by industrial policy that strategically targets specific sectors—establishing the "sectoral approach" as a core principle of successful development strategy. The diversity of their political economies and initial conditions underscores that productive transformation follows context-specific pathways rather

A. Oqubay, *Productive Transformation in Africa*,
https://doi.org/10.1007/978-3-032-23941-9_6

than a uniform template. Nevertheless, both cases converge on common critical elements: manufacturing as a foundation for structural change, export-led industrialisation as a growth engine, strategic management of productive foreign direct investment, and the systematic development of industrial ecosystems. Significantly, these experiences challenge deterministic pessimism about African development prospects. Neither country possessed substantial natural resource endowments at the outset. Yet both successfully transitioned from low-income status to middle-income status, demonstrating that productive transformation remains achievable across different historical periods and initial conditions. Their trajectories affirm that strategic policy choices, rather than resource abundance or fortuitous circumstances, constitute the decisive factor in economic transformation.

The chapter examines Mauritius's remarkable economic transformation, from a sugar-dependent monoculture at independence in 1968 to a diversified, upper-middle-income economy. Challenging narratives that attribute this success to an unexplained 'economic miracle' or to simple market liberalisation, this analysis, from a perspective of productive transformation policymaking, argues that deliberate, pragmatic, and adaptive industrial policies drove Mauritius's development. The analysis describes the phased process of this transformation, exploring the policy tools, institutional innovations, and political agreements that supported export-led industrialisation and economic diversification. It also addresses current challenges, including low productivity, skills shortages, and the middle-income trap, which threaten the sustainability of the Mauritian model. The key lesson from Mauritius is the vital role of strategic state intervention, policy learning, and productive state-business collaborations in achieving successful economic progress, offering valuable insights for other developing countries.

Furthermore, this chapter offers a comprehensive analysis of Morocco's economic transformation over the past 50 years, with a focus on productive transformation, industrial policy, and economic diversification. Using structuralist development economics, it examines Morocco's shift from import-substitution industrialisation to export-led growth, analysing the strategic role of state intervention in driving structural change. The chapter highlights Morocco's successes in developing its automotive, aerospace, and renewable energy sectors, while also recognising ongoing challenges, including the middle-income trap, limited technological progress, and demographic pressures. The analysis reveals that Morocco's experience offers valuable insights for African industrialisation, challenging pessimistic views about the continent's manufacturing potential and emphasising the ongoing importance of strategic industrial policies for economic catch-up.

However, countries that pursue and achieve productive transformation face significant challenges as they enter a new stage of development. For example, Mauritius now stands at a crossroads, facing the challenges of maturity. The model that brought success—focused on attracting investment into specific sectors—is revealing its limitations amid global competition and the need for innovation-driven growth. Mauritius's future depends on its ability to address critical gaps in skills, technology, and inclusive development. The lesson for other nations is twofold: adopt the pragmatic approach that underpinned Mauritius's success, but also remain aware of the challenges that follow once the easy gains from catch-up growth are realised. Ultimately, Mauritius demonstrates that economic transformation is an ongoing journey of learning, adaptation, and renewal.[1]

The following section discusses the productive transformation and development strategies in Mauritius, while the third examines the Moroccan case. The final section offers conclusions and insights on productive transformation and policymaking.

2 Economic Transformation and Development Strategy in Mauritius

Introduction and Overview

Mauritius stands out as a notable exception in the history of African economic development. When James Meade assessed the island's prospects in 1961, he predicted a bleak future constrained by vulnerability to terms-of-trade shocks, population pressures, and limited economic opportunities (Meade 1961). Contrary to these forecasts, Mauritius has, over the past 50 years, achieved a significant shift from a low-income, agriculture-based economy to an upper-middle-income country with a diversified economic base that includes manufacturing, tourism, financial services, and information and communication technology (ICT).

Conventional explanations, often promoted by international financial institutions, have attributed this success to the adoption of open economy policies and structural adjustment programmes (World Bank 1989). However, this view has been challenged by scholars who argue that it

[1] See Subramanian (2009), Brautigam and Diolle (2009).

reflects ideological bias and overlooks the nuanced realities of policymaking in practice.

This analysis challenges the 'miracle' thesis by emphasising that Mauritius's success was not due to luck but the result of a deliberate development strategy characterised by pragmatic industrial policies, active state intervention, and conscious policy learning, mainly derived from East Asian economies as demonstrated in research on the Mauritian development model. It will first outline the three distinct stages of economic transformation, highlighting the evolving policy focus in each phase. Second, it will analyse the structure of Mauritian industrial policy, focusing on its unique features and key instruments. Third, it will examine the crucial role of institutional frameworks and political economy in enabling this transformation. Finally, it will consider the current crossroads Mauritius faces, exploring the significant challenges that threaten its future progress. The main argument is that Mauritius's experience demonstrates that economic catch-up depends on deliberate policy decisions and state capacity, rather than being solely dictated by initial conditions or passive integration into the global economy.

The Phased Trajectory of Economic Transformation

Mauritius's structural transformation has followed a complex path, evolving through distinct phases with their own challenges and policy responses. Three main stages characterise this trajectory: early industrialisation, significant diversification, and maturity, followed by further diversification.

Nascent Industrialisation and Initial Transformation (1970s–mid-1990s)

At independence, Mauritius was a typical mono-crop economy, with sugar accounting for 35% of GDP, 96% of exports, and providing most employment (Oqubay 2025). Facing high unemployment and balance-of-payments problems, the government's initial response was import-substitution industrialisation (ISI). However, the small size of the domestic market soon proved restrictive. Inspired by the early successes of the East Asian "Tigers," policymakers decisively shifted towards export-led industrialisation (Campling and Oya 2025). The key element of this transition was the Export Processing Zone (EPZ) Act of 1970, which offered incentives such as tax holidays and duty-free imports to attract foreign direct investment (FDI), particularly from Hong Kong investors in the apparel and textile sectors.

Critical social and political developments also characterised this period. The government established a welfare state with universal benefits, including free education and healthcare, thereby contributing to political stability and enhancing human capital (Oqubay 2025). Furthermore, the pragmatic development of the tourism industry, including the founding of Air Mauritius as a joint venture, laid the groundwork for another primary export sector. This phase successfully diversified the economy away from sugar, created extensive employment, and established the principle of outward-oriented, pragmatic policymaking.

Profound Diversification (1990s–mid-2000s)

Building on the confidence gained from initial successes, Mauritius undertook a more profound structural transformation in the 1990s. This involved both upgrading within existing sectors and venturing into new, skill-intensive service industries, thereby intensifying structural transformation. The apparel sector faced intense pressure from lower-cost competitors and the phasing out of the Multi-Fibre Agreement (MFA) in 2005, prompting a shift towards higher-value, more flexible manufacturing (Oya et al. 2025). Simultaneously, the government strategically promoted new sectors, including financial services, ICT, and business process outsourcing (BPO), with the aim of establishing Mauritius as a business hub for the Indian Ocean and Africa.

This ambition was physically realised through projects like Ebene Cybercity, a world-class technology centre developed in partnership with India. The expansion of freeport zones improved the country's logistics capacities. This stage demonstrated the adaptive capacity to respond to global economic shifts. However, it also marked the beginning of the EPZ model's decline, which was officially phased out in 2005 as the apparel sector's dominance waned.

Maturity and Late Diversification (2000s–2020s)

The modern phase presents the typical challenges of a middle-income economy. Manufacturing's contribution to GDP declined significantly from 15.9% in 2010 to 12.5% in 2019, with apparel exports decreasing from a peak of US$1 billion to US$677 million (Oqubay 2025). Simultaneously, diversification has occurred into sectors such as real estate, aquaculture, and education, which raises questions about whether this indicates genuine technological deepening or a shift towards an innovation-driven economy. The growth of the real estate sector, while attracting FDI, is recognised as potentially unsustainable and posing a risk to the productive industry due to land inflation.

The COVID-19 pandemic exacerbated these vulnerabilities, resulting in a 15% economic contraction in 2020 and highlighting the economy's reliance on global flows, particularly in tourism. This phase is therefore characterised by a search for new, high-productivity growth drivers amid concerns about premature deindustrialisation and the sustainability of the current development model.

The Architecture of Pragmatic Industrial Policy

The success across these phases was not accidental but rooted in a distinctive approach to industrial policy characterised by several key features.

Distinctive Features of the Mauritian Approach

Several key features characterise Mauritian policymaking. First, employment creation was the principal and consistent goal, shaping sector choices and garnering social and political support. Second, the ongoing pursuit of diversification was essential, with the state actively exploring and developing new sectors, from textiles to financial services. Third, a strong focus on international markets provided the scale and demand necessary for growth, supported by targeted diplomacy and trade agreement management. Finally, and most importantly, policy was driven by pragmatism rather than ideology. The state demonstrated a willingness to learn from international best practices (e.g., EPZs from Taiwan, financial services from Singapore) and adapt them to local circumstances, as well as to change course when necessary, as illustrated by the swift shift from ISI to an export-oriented approach.

Industrial Policy Instruments

The government utilised a variety of targeted tools to influence investor behaviour. These were often embedded in legislation, such as the EPZ Act (1970) and subsequent Finance Acts, ensuring transparency and consistency. The incentives were notably selective and diverse, customised to meet the needs of specific sectors. They included:

- *Fiscal incentives:* Ten-year income tax exemptions, exemption from import duties on inputs and capital goods.
- *Development financing:* Low-interest loans from the Development Bank of Mauritius (DBM) for machinery procurement and investment allowances.
- *Support for competitiveness:* Subsidies for training and shipping costs.

A key element was the inclusion of sunset clauses and reciprocity principles, ensuring that support was temporary and performance-linked, thus avoiding perpetual dependency.

Institutional Innovation and Political Economy

The practical implementation of industrial policy was underpinned by robust institutions and a unique political settlement that fostered consensus and stability.

Evolving Industrial Policy Organisations

Mauritian institutions showed remarkable adaptability. The leading agencies for investment and export promotion transitioned from the Mauritius Export Development and Investment Authority (MEDIA) to the Board of Investment (BOI), and subsequently into the integrated Economic Development Board (EDB Mauritius). This institutional change reflected the evolving needs of the economy, shifting from a focus on manufacturing exports to a more comprehensive approach that included services and investment. However, the analysis highlights a comparative weakness in institutions dedicated to technological learning and skills development, a gap that has become a significant constraint.

Productive Government–Business Partnership

A key factor in Mauritius's success was effective dialogue between the state and the private sector. This was formalised through organisations like the Joint Economic Council (JEC), established in 1970, which served as a vital channel for policy negotiation. The private sector itself was unified, with ethnically based chambers merging into the Mauritius Chamber of Commerce and Industry (MCCI) in 1970. This cohesion, along with the sector's extensive transnational networks in Europe and Asia, played a crucial role in attracting FDI and accessing export markets. The partnership was based on a shared understanding of the island's vulnerability and a mutual interest in export-led growth.

The Political Settlement: Managing Diversity and Inequality
The political context was vital. Despite its diverse society, Mauritius has maintained political stability through inclusive electoral governance and coalition politics (Brautigam 1997). The constitution included mechanisms, such as the "best loser system," to ensure community representation, and policies, such as free education in several languages, that promoted national unity. The welfare state, offering universal pensions, healthcare, and education, created a broad social contract that legitimised the development model and ensured the benefits of growth were shared widely, thereby preserving social cohesion (Phaahla 2019).

Mauritius at a Crossroads: Contemporary Dilemmas and Challenges

Despite its historic achievements, Mauritius confronts significant challenges that threaten its future development path.

The Productivity and Skills Challenge
A significant weakness is the slow productivity growth, which has not kept pace with rising labour costs. There is a heavy and unsustainable reliance on expatriate labour across all skill levels, especially in STEM fields, indicating a failure of the domestic education and training system to meet the demands of a modern economy. A joint UNCTAD-Mauritian government study concluded that "Mauritian labour skills have failed to improve relative to global competitors" (UNCTAD and Mauritian Ministry of Industrial Development 2020, p. 36). This skills gap remains a primary obstacle to industrial upgrading and escaping the middle-income trap.

Inadequate Technological Capability and the Decline of Manufacturing
The Mauritian economy faces a significant challenge of slowing industrialisation. The rise of high-value, technology-intensive industries is not compensating for the decline in the manufacturing sector. Investment in research and development (R&D) remains stagnant at a modest 0.36% of GDP, well below that of regional competitors such as South Africa and the African average (UNCTAD and Mauritian Ministry of Industrial Development 2020). The growth of sectors like real estate and finance,

while contributing to GDP, does not generate the same level of productive employment or technological spillovers as advanced manufacturing, raising concerns about the quality and sustainability of future growth.

Persistent Socio-Political Constraints

Social challenges also loom large. Inequality is widening (Bunwaree 2014), and structural disparities persist. Women's participation in politics and economic leadership remains dismally low, and female labour force participation is under 40% (Ramtohul 2019a, b). Youth unemployment is high, exceeding 25% in 2020 (Statistics Mauritius 2020), despite the service sector's reliance on imported labour. Furthermore, an ageing population presents long-term fiscal challenges to the sustainability of the universal welfare state, prompting difficult discussions about targeting social benefits.

3 Productive Transformation and Industrial Policy in Morocco

Historical Evolution of Morocco's Economic Transformation

Morocco has established itself as one of Africa's most successful economic performers, making notable progress in economic transformation and green transition over the past quarter-century. With an average annual GDP growth of 4.13% from 1971 to 2023, surpassing the African average of 3.45%, Morocco's development trajectory provides valuable insights into the dynamics of late industrialisation (World Bank 2025). This analysis argues that Morocco's economic transformation has been driven by pragmatic industrial policy, proactive state intervention, and the gradual development of productive capacity, rather than solely by market liberalisation or passive integration into the global economy.

The Moroccan experience is significant for understanding how African economies can navigate the challenges of structural transformation. As El Aynaoui and Oqubay (2026) note, Morocco's goal of achieving high-income status by 2050 necessitates addressing key constraints, including the middle-income trap, demographic pressures, and the need for technological advancement. This analysis examines how industrial policy has guided Morocco's productive transformation and what lessons it offers to other African economies seeking to accelerate their industrialisation.

Morocco's economic development can be categorised into three distinct phases, each marked by different policy approaches and structural outcomes.

Early Industrialisation and Moroccanisation (1960s–1970s)
The immediate post-independence period was characterised by import-substitution industrialisation (ISI) and the *Moroccanisation* policy of 1973, which aimed to transfer economic control from foreign to domestic hands. This period saw the establishment of state-owned enterprises and efforts to build a national capitalist class. However, as Oualalou (2026) notes, the policy often concentrated economic power within elite circles connected to political patronage networks, limiting its transformative potential. The period from 1971 to 1980 witnessed solid growth, averaging 5.23%, laying the foundations for future industrial development.

Economic Liberalisation and Structural Adjustment (1980s–1990s)
The 1980s and 1990s marked a period of structural adjustment and liberalisation, driven by Washington Consensus policies. Morocco implemented significant tariff cuts, privatisation initiatives, and a currency devaluation under IMF and World Bank programmes. While these reforms enhanced macroeconomic stability, their impact on structural transformation was mixed. The 1990s saw slowed growth, averaging 3.19%, leading some commentators to describe this as a "lost decade" for industrial development (World Bank 1995, 2006).

Export-led Diversification and Industrial Catch-up (2000s–Present)
The most dynamic phase of Morocco's transformation began in the early 2000s, characterised by a shift towards targeted industrial policy and export-led diversification. This period witnessed the development of sector-specific strategies in the automotive, aerospace, and renewable energy sectors, supported by significant infrastructure investments, including the Tanger Med port complex. The government adopted a more proactive approach to industrial policy, blending macroeconomic stability with targeted sectoral measures.

Industrialisation and Productive Transformation

Manufacturing Performance and Structural Change

Morocco's manufacturing sector has demonstrated mixed performance over the past five decades. The share of manufacturing value added (MVA) in GDP averaged 16.96% between 1971 and 2023, fluctuating from a high of 19.41% in the 1980s to 14.81% in the 2010s (World Bank 2025). This exceeds the African average of 11–12% but remains below that of comparator countries such as Vietnam and China.

A concerning trend has been the relatively slow growth of manufacturing value added, which averaged 3.34% annually between 1971 and 2023—below overall GDP growth of 4.13% during the same period. This suggests that manufacturing has not served as the primary engine of growth in the manner described by Kaldor's laws of economic development. Employment patterns reinforce this picture: while agricultural employment declined from 46% to 30% between 2000 and 2023, much of this labour was absorbed by non-tradable sectors such as construction and services, rather than manufacturing (El Aynaoui and Dinh 2024, 2026; Agénor and El Aynaoui 2015).

Export Diversification and Technological Upgrading

Morocco has achieved significant success in export diversification, particularly since the early 2000s. The export basket has transformed from dependence on primary products and low-technology goods toward more sophisticated manufacturing exports. Notably, the automotive sector has experienced a significant increase, with its share of total exports rising from 12% in 2010 to 34% in 2023, and vehicle exports exceeding US$6.5 billion in 2024 (El Abassi et al. 2026; Mandri 2026).

The technological composition of exports reveals both progress and limitations. The share of medium-technology goods in exports increased dramatically from 9.1% in 2000 to 46.2% in 2023, reflecting successful upgrading in sectors like automotive and electronics. However, high-technology exports have remained stagnant at around 7–9%, indicating persistent challenges in developing advanced technological capabilities (UNCTAD 2023b).

The phosphate sector exemplifies successful vertical diversification: OCP Group has transformed from exporting raw phosphate rock to sophisticated derivatives, with value-added products increasing from 27% to 74% of total phosphate earnings. This demonstrates how natural resource wealth can be leveraged for industrial upgrading when combined with effective industrial policy.[2]

Productive Capacity Development
Morocco's productive capacity has shown steady improvement, with UNCTAD's Productive Capacity Index (PCI) increasing from 37 in 2000 to 46.5 in 2022—above the global average of 44.5 and significantly exceeding Africa's average of approximately 32 (UNCTAD 2023a). However, Morocco lags behind comparator countries in specific capabilities: its structural change index score of 61.7% trails Vietnam's 70.1%. At the same time, business sophistication ranks 107th globally according to the Global Innovation Index (WIPO 2024).

The Architecture of Moroccan Industrial Policy

Strategic Sectoral Targeting
Morocco's industrial policy has been characterised by pragmatic sectoral targeting, focusing on areas in which the country can leverage specific advantages. The automotive sector strategy has been particularly successful, attracting major multinational manufacturers through a combination of incentives, infrastructure development, and workforce training. Similarly, targeted policies in the aerospace sector have enabled Morocco to develop a niche in aircraft component manufacturing, with exports projected to reach 4–5% of total exports by 2023.

The renewable energy sector is another focal area, with Morocco leveraging its solar and wind resources to reduce dependence on energy import while building new industrial capabilities. Installed renewable capacity increased dramatically from minimal levels in 2000 to more than 4000 MW by 2024, with ambitious targets for further expansion (IRENA 2025).

Integration with Global Value Chains
Morocco has strategically positioned itself within global value chains, capitalising on its proximity to European markets. The country has signed numerous free trade agreements, including those with the EU (1996), the USA (2006), and Turkey, facilitating its integration into international production networks. However, this strategy has limitations: a heavy reliance on imported intermediates in sectors such as automotive production constrains domestic value addition. At the same time, dependence on

[2] See Ajbilou (2026), Haddad and Arbouch (2026).

European markets (71.8% of exports in 2023) creates vulnerability to regional economic fluctuations.

Institutional Coordination and Governance

Effective economic governance has been crucial to Morocco's industrial success. The country has maintained political stability and policy predictability, enabling long-term investment planning. Industrial policies have been implemented through coordinated efforts across ministries and agencies, with significant infrastructure investments supporting the development of the private sector. The monarchy has provided continuity while allowing for gradual political reforms, creating an environment conducive to economic transformation.

Implications for African Industrial Policymaking

Morocco's experience offers several important lessons for African industrialisation strategies. First, it demonstrates that deliberate industrial policy can drive structural transformation even in contexts of limited initial technological capabilities. The successful development of the automotive and aerospace sectors shows that African countries can move beyond simple resource extraction or low-technology manufacturing.

Second, Morocco's experience highlights the importance of integrating global initiatives with domestic capacity-building efforts. While trade agreements and foreign direct investment can provide necessary market access and technology transfer, they need to be complemented by efforts to deepen domestic linkages and enhance absorptive capacities.

Third, the Moroccan case challenges pessimistic narratives about African industrialisation. As Cramer, Sender, and Oqubay (2020) argue, the "African homogenisation" in development literature often reflects methodological biases rather than inherent limitations. Morocco's achievements in productive transformation demonstrate that Afro-pessimism is not justified by empirical evidence.

Finally, Morocco's gradual and pragmatic approach to industrial policy offers a model that may be more suitable for African contexts than the rapid liberalisation often prescribed by international financial institutions. The sequencing of reforms—from initial stabilisation to targeted industrial policies—provides valuable insights for other African economies.

Contemporary Challenges and Crossroads

As Morocco makes significant progress, the nature of its challenges has evolved. Morocco faces critical challenges, including the risk of falling into the middle-income trap, the need for technological upgrading, structural constraints in labour markets, and the transition to a greener economy.

The Middle-Income Trap and Technological Upgrading

Morocco faces the classic challenges of a middle-income economy seeking to advance to high-income status. With a per capita GDP of approximately US$4300 in 2025, the country faces the middle-income trap by accelerating productivity growth and technological upgrading. Current weaknesses in research and development (R&D) investment—at just 0.71% of GDP according to recent estimates—represent a significant constraint on innovation-led growth (El Aynaoui and Oqubay 2026).

The limited progress in high-technology exports and continued dependence on medium-technology manufacturing suggest challenges in moving up the value and technology chains. As Lee (2019) argues, escaping the middle-income trap requires developing distinctive technological capabilities rather than merely improving existing ones.

Structural Constraints in Labour Markets

Morocco confronts significant demographic and labour market challenges. Unemployment remains high, particularly among youth and women, while informality is widespread. Paradoxically, declining fertility rates—now below replacement level at 1.97 children per woman—threaten future labour supply despite current unemployment. The outward migration of skilled workers further compounds challenges to human capital (Tritah 2026).

The structure of employment growth reveals deeper structural issues: tradable manufacturing sectors have grown more slowly (at 3% annually) than non-tradable services (at 3.8%), limiting the productivity benefits typically associated with manufacturing-led growth (El Aynaoui and Dinh 2026).

Green Transition and Sustainable Development

Morocco has positioned itself as a leader in Africa's green transition, particularly through its development of renewable energy. However, the economy's carbon intensity remains significant, with electricity generation still 66% coal-dependent in 2021 (IRENA 2025). The green transition presents both challenges and opportunities. While it requires substantial investment, it also offers opportunities to develop new industrial capabilities in areas such as green hydrogen and sustainable agriculture.

4 Challenging Afro-Pessimism and Lessons for Development Strategies

Progress in Productive Transformation

A key feature of the Mauritian story is that economic transformation arises from a deliberate strategy rather than from fate. The island's success is best explained by pragmatic and adaptable industrial policy, effectively implemented by a capable state in partnership with a cohesive private sector, all within a stable political settlement that emphasised social cohesion. The Mauritian experience strongly supports the arguments of development economists like Albert Hirschman (1958) that a country's economic prospects are shaped more by what it does than by its initial endowments. The lessons for other developing economies are significant. First, purposeful integration into the global economy, guided by industrial policy, is more effective than passive liberalisation. Second, building state capacity and fostering constructive dialogue with the private sector are vital for policy design and implementation. Third, investing in social cohesion and political stability through inclusive institutions and social protection is not a distraction from growth but a foundation for it.

Morocco's economic transformation is a notable achievement in African industrialisation, underscoring the potential of purposeful state intervention to promote structural change. The country has successfully diversified its economy, enhanced its export capacity, and laid a foundation for sustained growth. However, significant challenges remain, particularly in advancing technological development, addressing labour market imbalances, and managing the green transition. The Moroccan experience emphasises the enduring importance of industrial policy for economic advancement, especially in middle-income countries. As the government aims to achieve high-income status by 2050, it will need to enhance its technological capabilities, boost productivity, and overcome structural barriers within its development strategy. The success of these initiatives will carry substantial implications not only for Morocco's future but also for the broader landscape of African industrialisation in the twenty-first century. Morocco's journey demonstrates that economic transformation is neither automatic nor inevitable; it results from deliberate policy choices, institutional capacity, and ongoing learning and adaptation. Therefore, it offers both inspiration and practical lessons for other African economies aiming to accelerate their development through productive transformation and industrial upgrading.

Afro-Pessimism or Hirschman's "Possibilism" as a Development Mindset

The persistent idea of an "African homogenisation" variable in development literature has long suggested inherent limitations on the continent's economic progress (Cramer et al. 2020; Jerven 2011, 2013). This Afro-pessimism often argues that the export-led industrialisation that was successful in Asia cannot be replicated in Africa. However, the real achievements of countries such as Mauritius and Morocco directly challenge this perspective, showing that purposeful policy, rather than preconditions or luck, drives successful economic change.

The example of Mauritius is particularly illustrative. In the 1960s, economist James Meade predicted an "ultimate catastrophe" for the island nation, citing population pressure, ethnic tensions, and a mono-crop sugar economy (Meade 1961). Contrary to this prediction, Mauritius has become a stable, middle-income democracy with a GDP per capita surpassing $12,500, now facing labour shortages rather than a population crisis. While some describe this as an unexplainable "miracle" (Stiglitz 2011; Rodrik 2012), such views overlook the deliberate manufacturing and export-led industrial strategy that drove its transformation. Considering it an exception aligns with the same orthodox, neoliberal perspectives that have historically undervalued the importance of activist industrial policies and the developmental state.

A more constructive framework is found in Albert Hirschman's concept of "possibilism," which emphasises strategies that mobilise "scattered and backward resources" (Hirschman 1958). This view, supported by historical evidence, suggests that latecomer economies can catch up by learning from their predecessors and adopting institutional innovations—a phenomenon Gerschenkron (1963) referred to as the "advantage of backwardness." From the rise of the US and Japan to the East Asian Tigers and China, industrial policy has consistently catalysed catch-up growth

(Amsden 1989; List 1841). These strategies are not about indiscriminate state intervention but about targeted actions to accelerate productive transformation, develop technological capability, and foster productive ecosystems.

Prospects for Sustainable Structural Transformation

Morocco exemplifies this approach within the African context. Its consistent, context-specific industrial policies, guided by continuous learning, have resulted in significant economic diversification. The country's experience supports the structuralist perspective that manufacturing acts as a catalyst for growth and structural change (Kaldor 1967). Exports are crucial not only in alleviating balance-of-payments constraints and achieving economies of scale but also as an essential source of international learning. Morocco's experience demonstrates that export-led and import-substitution strategies are not mutually exclusive but can coexist across sectors and stages of development.

The key lesson from both Mauritius and Morocco is that successful industrial policy depends heavily on effective governance and a moderately conducive political economy. It requires a developmental state that fosters constructive dialogue with the private sector and promotes social cohesion. The quality of policymaking—its design and implementation—is essential. While Mauritian economic transformation was driven by industrial policy, its current challenges arise from weaknesses in those same policies, emphasising the ongoing need for adaptation.

Looking ahead, African development strategies, including Morocco's, benefit in prioritising prioritise sustainability and green growth as central drivers of economic transformation. The green transition—covering renewable energy, green hydrogen, and green ammonia—presents an opportunity to develop new industrial capabilities. Furthermore, harnessing Africa's demographic potential through enhanced continental integration, such as the African Continental Free Trade Area (AfCFTA), and strengthening partnerships within the rising Global South are vital priorities.

In summary, the experiences of Mauritius and Morocco fundamentally challenge Afro-pessimism. They show that development outcomes depend not on geography or initial resources but on deliberate policy choices and vision. The main message for Africa is the ongoing importance of pragmatic, learning-focused industrial policy led by a capable developmental state. Sustainable and inclusive development can be achieved, but it relies on purposeful action rather than luck or destiny.

5 Conclusions from Comparative Insights

The Mauritian and Moroccan comparative cases yield several fundamental insights for understanding productive transformation in Africa. First, they demonstrate that economic transformation occurs through deliberate transition to more productive industries rather than through spontaneous market forces alone. Second, both experiences validate the centrality of industrial policy that strategically targets specific sectors, establishing the "sectoral approach" as an essential principle of development strategy. Third, the diversity of their political economies and divergent starting points underscores that productive transformation follows multiple pathways, each shaped by specific historical and institutional contexts.

Despite these differences, both cases converge on common critical elements of successful transformation: manufacturing serves as the foundation for structural change; export-led industrialisation functions as the primary growth engine; strategic management of productive foreign direct investment accelerates capability development; and the systematic cultivation of industrial ecosystems sustains competitive advantage. These commonalities suggest underlying principles that transcend specific contexts.

Most significantly, these experiences provide compelling grounds for optimism about African industrialisation. Neither country initially possessed substantial natural resource endowments, yet both successfully transitioned from low-income status to middle- or upper-middle-income economies. This achievement demonstrates that productive transformation remains possible across different historical periods and diverse initial conditions. The decisive factor is neither resource abundance nor fortuitous circumstances, but rather the capacity for strategic policymaking, institutional adaptation, and sustained commitment to industrialisation. The Mauritian and Moroccan cases thus affirm that Africa's development trajectory depends fundamentally on policy choices and state capacity—variables that remain within the agency of African nations themselves.

This chapter conducts a comparative analysis of Mauritius and Morocco to challenge Afro-pessimism, proposing a dynamic theory of productive transformation in which purposeful state action is the key variable. Moving beyond simple case studies, the analysis is grounded in a structuralist development model that explicitly rejects neoliberal and exceptionalist explanations of economic success. It shows that the development paths of both countries were not the result of passive market liberalisation but of deliberate, state-led industrial policy characterised by adaptive implementation and pragmatic execution. The main argument introduces a "developmental symbiosis"—a mutually reinforcing relationship between purposeful state intervention, ongoing policy learning, and productive collaboration between the state and business—as the crucial process for driving export-led growth and economic diversification. Importantly, comparing Mauritius, a small island economy, with Morocco, a larger continental country, demonstrates that this principle of purposeful state leadership goes beyond specific geographic and structural contexts, revealing a universal, though not identical, logic of successful development.

The analytical distinction between the two pathways is sharpened to reveal more profound insights into state capacity. Mauritius exemplifies a model of institutionalised adaptive learning, where the state's role evolved through phased experimentation, building robust institutions and political consensus to move away from a sugar monoculture. Morocco, in contrast, exemplifies a model of deliberate sectoral leadership, in which the state acts as an architect, shifting the economy from import substitution to targeted integration into global value chains, thereby fostering high-value sectors such as automotive and aerospace. The chapter also introduces a critical dialectical perspective, framing development as a nonlinear process in which each stage of success generates its own subsequent contradictions. The middle-income trap is thus analysed not merely as a hurdle but as the inherent tension between the exhausted model of catch-up growth and the emerging imperative for innovation-driven competitiveness.

The study offers a threefold theoretical and practical contribution. First, it empirically confirms productive transformation as a viable, policy-dependent process in Africa, fundamentally challenging deterministic narratives of underdevelopment. Second, it develops the concept of contingent convergence, demonstrating that although the principle of purposeful state intervention is universal, its implementation varies across contexts and pathways. Third, and most importantly, it proposes a model of development as an ongoing journey of purposeful renewal. The key lesson is that the state's capacity for dynamic policy learning—its ability to adapt strategies and facilitate a shift from factor-driven to innovation-driven growth—is crucial to sustainable development in the twenty-first century, providing a vital blueprint for the Global South.

References

Agénor, Pierre-Richard, and Karim El Aynaoui. 2015. *Morocco: Growth Strategy for 2025 in an Evolving International Environment.* Rabat: Policy Centre for the New South. https://www.policycenter.ma/publications/morocco-growth-strategy-2025-evolving-international-environment. Accessed 21 July 2025.

Ajbilou, A. 2026. The demographic transition and the Moroccan economy, in El Aynaoui, K., and Oqubay, A. (eds). *The Oxford Handbook of the Moroccan Economy.* Oxford University Press. pp 184–199.

Amsden, Alice. 1989. *Asia's Next Giant: South Korea and Late Industrialization.* New York: Oxford University Press.

Brautigam, Deborah. 1997. Institutions, Economic Reform, and Democratic Consolidation in Mauritius. *Comparative Politics* 30 (1): 45–62.

Brautigam, D., and Diolle, T. 2009. Coalitions, Capitalists and Credibility: Overcoming the Crisis of Confidence at Independence in Mauritius. *Developmental Leadership Program. 1* April. Research Paper 04.

Bunwaree, Sheila. 2014. The Fading Developmental State: Growing Inequality in Mauritius. *Development* 57 (3–4): 578–590. https://doi.org/10.1057/dev.2015.40.

Campling, Liam, and Carlos Oya. 2025. Why Mauritius? The Political Economy of Structural Transformation in a Small Island: Questions and Debates. In *The Oxford Handbook of the Mauritian Economy*, ed. Carlos Oya, Ramola Ramtohul, and Verena Tandrayen-Ragoobur, 20–45. Oxford: Oxford University Press.

Cramer, Christopher, John Sender, and Arkebe Oqubay. 2020. *African Economic Development: Evidence, Theory, Policy.* Oxford: Oxford University Press.

El Abassi, Idriss, Aziz Ragbi, and Said Tounsi. 2026. Fiscal Policy in Morocco. In *The Oxford Handbook of the Moroccan Economy*, ed. Karim El Aynaoui and Arkebe Oqubay. Oxford: Oxford University Press.

El Aynaoui, Karim, and Hinh T. Dinh. 2024. *Economic Development of the New South After the Washington Consensus*, Policy Paper. 20 December. Rabat: Policy Centre for the New South. https://www.policycenter.ma/publications/economic-development-new-south-after-washington-consensus. Accessed 21 July 2025.

El Aynaoui, Karim, and Hinh T. Dinh. 2026. Growth and Structural Transformation in Morocco. In *The Oxford Handbook of the Moroccan Economy*, ed. Karim El Aynaoui and Arkebe Oqubay. Oxford: Oxford University Press.

El Aynaoui, Karim, and Arkebe Oqubay, eds. 2026. *The Oxford Handbook of the Moroccan Economy.* Oxford: Oxford University Press.

Gerschenkron, A. 1963. *Economic backwardness in historical perspective.* Harvard University Press.

Haddad, E., and Arbouch, M. 2026. Regional economic development in Morocco in El Aynaoui, K. (eds). *The Oxford Handbook of the Moroccan Economy*(pp 238–257). Oxford University Press.

Hirschman, Albert. 1958. *The Strategy of Economic Development*. New Haven: Yale University Press.

International Renewable Energy Agency (IRENA). 2025. *Renewable Energy Trends*. IRENA Database.

Jerven, Morten. 2011. *Africa: Why Economists Get It Wrong*. London: Zed Publishers.

Jerven, Morten. 2013. *Poor Numbers: How We Are Misled by African Development Statistics and What to Do About It*. Cornell: Cornell University Press.

Kaldor, Nicholas. 1967. *Strategic Factors in Economic Development*. Ithaca: New York State School of Industrial and Labour Relations, Cornell University.

Lee, Keun. 2019. *The Art of Economic Catch-up*. Cambridge: Cambridge University Press.

List, Frederick. [1841] 1856. *The National System of Political Economy*. Vol. I–IV. Memphis: Lippincott

Mandri, Badr. 2026. The External Sector of the Moroccan Economy. In *The Oxford Handbook of the Moroccan Economy*, ed. Karim El Aynaoui and Arkebe Oqubay. Oxford: Oxford University Press.

Meade, James. 1961. *The Economic and Social Structure of Mauritius*. Methuen.

Oualalou, Fathallah. 2026. Economic History of Morocco. In *The Oxford Handbook of the Moroccan Economy*, ed. Karim El Aynaoui and Arkebe Oqubay. Oxford: Oxford University Press.

Oqubay. 2025. *Industrial Policy and Economic Development: Theory, Strategy, and Practice*. Palgrave Macmillan.

Oya, Carlos, Ramola Ramtohul, and Verena Tandrayen-Ragoobur, eds. 2025. *The Oxford Handbook of the Mauritian Economy*. Oxford: Oxford University Press.

Phaahla, Elias. 2019. Mauritius' Competitive Party Politics and Social Democratic Welfare Outcomes after Independence. *Strategic Review for Southern Africa* 41:1–18.

Ramtohul, Ramola. 2019a. Mauritius: Still a Long Journey Ahead. In *The Palgrave Handbook of Women's Political Rights. Gender and Politics*, ed. S. Franceschet, M. Krook, and N. Tan, 547–562. London: Palgrave Macmillan. https://doi.org/10.1057/978-1-137-59074-9_37.

Ramtohul, Ramola. 2019b. Why Very Few Women Go into Politics in Mauritius. *The Conversation*, 30 December. https://theconversation.com/why-very-few-women-go-into-politics-in-mauritius-128579.

Rodrik, Dani. 2012. *The Globalisation Paradox: Why Global Markets, States, and Democracy Can't Coexist*. Oxford: Oxford University Press.

Statistics Mauritius. 2020. Labour Force, Employment and Unemployment—First Quarter 2020. https://statsmauritius.govmu.org/Documents/Statistics/ESI/2020/EI1528/LF_Em_Unemp_1Qtr20.pdf.

Stiglitz, Joseph E. 2011. The Mauritius Miracle. *Project Syndicate.* Online. http://www.project-syndicate.org/commentary/the-mauritius-miracle.

Subramanian, A. 2009. The Mauritian success story and its lessons 'WIDER Research Paper, No. 2009/36.

Tritah, Ahmed. 2026. Moroccan Migration Dynamics. In *The Oxford Handbook of the Moroccan Economy*, ed. Karim El Aynaoui and Arkebe Oqubay. Oxford: Oxford University Press.

UNCTAD. 2023a. *Productive Capacity Index.* Geneva: United Nations.

UNCTAD. 2023b. *Technology and Innovation Report 2023. Opening Green Windows: Technological Opportunities for a Low-Carbon World.* Geneva: United Nations.

UNCTAD and Mauritian Ministry of Industrial Development. 2020. *Industrial Policy and Strategic Plan (2020–2025): Revitalising Mauritius Economic Growth.* Geneva: United Nations Conference on Trade and Development and the Mauritian Ministry of Industrial Development.

WIPO. 2024. *Global Innovation Index. World Intellectual Property Organization.* Geneva: United Nations.

World Bank. 1989. *Mauritius managing success.* A World Bank Country Study. World Bank.

World Bank. 1995. *Kingdom of Morocco. Country Economic Memorandum: Towards Higher Growth and Employment*, Report No. 14155-MOR.

World Bank. 2006. *Kingdom of Morocco: Country Economic Memorandum. Fostering Growth and Employment with Productive Diversification and Competitiveness*, Report No. 32948-MOR.

World Bank. 2025. *Enterprise Survey.* IFC. Washington, DC: The World Bank Group.

PART III

The Path Forward

CHAPTER 7

Productive Transformation: An Engine of Africa's Economic Integration and the AfC FTA

1 The Genesis of African Economic Integration

Economic integration in Africa continues to be crucial for the continent's productive transformation. Since the early 1960s, African nations have pursued economic integration, emphasising political unity, economic cooperation, self-reliance, and Africa's assertive role on the global stage. However, progress has not been straightforward in practice. To understand the current status of the AfCFTA—its progress, challenges, and future prospects—it is essential to examine its historical development, origins, and political ambitions. This chapter offers comprehensive evidence on AfCFTA as a continuous political and economic endeavour shaping African productive transformation. UNECA has conducted research and advocacy on this issue for nearly five decades, work that has recently inspired numerous studies and publications (Ismail 2021; Luke 2023; Mangeni and Mold 2024; Ofori-Amoah 2024; Tarlac 2020). Research institutions and scholars have intensified their focus on AfCFTA, particularly on its implementation and its connection to Africa's structural transformation (Oqubay 2025a; Cramer et al. 2020).

From the OAU to the African Union: The Formative Decades

Economic and political union was a shared vision for post-independence Africa in the 1960s, ranging from an idealistic proposal by the Casablanca

A. Oqubay, *Productive Transformation in Africa*,
https://doi.org/10.1007/978-3-032-23941-9_7

Group (January 1961), which advocated a united pan-African political federation—"Africa without borders." A more cautious, yet realistic, stance, favouring gradual incremental integration, was agreed upon in May 1961 at Monrovia by over 20 African countries, leading to the establishment of the Organisation for African Unity (OAU) in 1963 in Addis Ababa. The primary aim of the Organisation of African Unity (OAU), as stated in its founding OAU charter signed on 25 May 1963 in Addis Ababa, was "To promote the unity and solidarity of the African States," with the purposes emphasising political and economic goals: "(a) To promote the unity and solidarity of the African States; (b) To coordinate and intensify their co-operation and efforts to achieve a better life for the peoples of Africa; (c) To defend their sovereignty, their territorial integrity and independence; (d) To eradicate all forms of colonialism from Africa."

A key summary of the aim for economic integration was outlined in the Lagos Plan of Action in 1980 and adopted in June 1991 through the Abuja Treaty, established by the African Economic Community. The main goal of the Abuja Treaty, formally called the Treaty Establishing the African Economic Community (AEC), is ambitious: "The Community shall have as its prime objectives the promotion of: (a) economic, social and cultural development and the integration of African economies to increase economic self-reliance and foster endogenous and sustainable development." These objectives are set out in Article 4: The Community shall aim to: (a) promote economic, social, and cultural growth and integrate African economies to boost self-reliance and support endogenous development; (b) develop a continent-wide framework for the mobilisation and utilisation of Africa's human and material resources; (c) encourage cooperation across all sectors to improve living standards, ensure economic stability, foster peaceful relations among Member States, and promote progress and integration on the continent; and (d) coordinate and harmonise the policies of existing and future economic communities to facilitate the gradual formation of the Community.

Essentially, the Abuja Treaty of 1991 served as the formal blueprint for establishing the African Economic Community through a gradual process spanning over three decades, culminating in a continent-wide common market and economic union. This treaty provided the foundational legal framework that subsequently advanced into the African Union's Agenda 2063 and the African Continental Free Trade Area (AfCFTA).

The African Union Reform and NEPAD

Two key developments that advanced the alignment and progress of the AfCFTA were the New Partnership for Africa's Development (NEPAD), launched in 2001 by African leaders, and the African Continental Free Trade Area (AfCFTA). NEPAD was an initiative promoting economic transformation, strategic development plans, and a confident African voice in global debates. This was further strengthened by the African Peer Review Mechanism (APRM), which aims to critically assess African development experiences and encourage peer learning among nations. Another critical step was transforming the Organisation of African Unity (OAU) into a new institutional structure, the African Union Commission, which enabled more effective cooperation in a changing global environment. This culminated on 9 July 2002 with the establishment of the African Union Commission (AUC). The African Union was founded on the same day, succeeding the Organisation of African Unity (OAU). The Commission evolved from the OAU Secretariat, which was dissolved to create the more influential AUC. The first Commissioners of the new African Union Commission were appointed and sworn in in 2003.

NEPAD was officially established and adopted by the Organisation of African Unity (OAU) during an extraordinary summit in July 2001 and was later ratified by the African Union (AU) in 2002, becoming its principal development framework. NEPAD aims to eradicate poverty, promote sustainable growth and development, prevent Africa's marginalisation in globalisation, empower women and harness their potential, foster good political and economic governance, and enhance regional and continental integration while mobilising resources. It also seeks to implement a pioneering governance initiative called APRM, a voluntary system where African countries review each other's governance practices to improve stability, transparency, and accountability. In essence, NEPAD's goal was to provide a new, African-owned and led vision and framework for the continent's development, building on the shortcomings of previous initiatives by connecting economic growth with principles of good governance and regional cooperation. AU-NEPAD was innovative in shaping the outlook expressed in the vision for Agenda 2063, "The Africa We Want," endorsed in 2013, with structural transformation goals emphasising productive transformation, sustainability, and inclusiveness.

Vision: Agenda 2063 The Africa We Want

Agenda 2063 is the African Union's strategic framework and master plan for transforming Africa into a global power of the future. It is a 50-year vision, adopted in 2013, designed to guide the continent's development from 2013 to 2063. The goals are outlined through seven key "Aspirations" that reflect the main desires of the African people, which are then broken down into specific goals, targets, and flagship projects. The overarching goals and aspirations are:

First, a Prosperous Africa, founded on inclusive growth and sustainable development through modern agriculture to boost productivity, industrialisation, economic diversification, and technological innovation. It aims for Africa to become a significant global player. Second, an Integrated Continent, politically united and grounded in the ideals of Pan-Africanism and the vision of Africa's Renaissance, with seamless mobility of goods and people through the establishment of the African Continental Free Trade Area (AfCFTA) with its headquarters in Accra in 2022. Third, an Africa whose development is people-driven, relying on the potential of its people, especially women and youth, fosters good governance, democracy, respect for human rights, justice, and the rule of law through developmental states, good governance, and democratic participation.

Five flagship projects were launched to achieve these goals, including: the establishment of the African Continental Free Trade Area (AfCFTA), creating a single continental market for goods and services; the Single African Air Transport Market, liberalising air travel to improve connectivity and trade; the African Passport and Free Movement of People, enabling seamless travel across the continent; connecting Africa through the development of the Pan-African E-Network to boost digital connectivity; and developing a conflict-free Africa through the "Silencing the Guns" initiative. In essence, Agenda 2063 is the overarching, long-term vision that builds upon and integrates previous frameworks, such as NEPAD (now AUDA-NEPAD) and the Abuja Treaty, aiming to fully realise the potential of a united, prosperous, and peaceful Africa. However, these remain aspirations and shared goals, and their implementation demands strong political commitment and careful management of complex processes and challenges.

The AfCFTA was officially launched on 1 January 2021, having achieved the necessary number of ratifications following the agreement signed in March 2018 by the African Union Summit in Kigali, Rwanda. Its primary goal is to *create a single continental market for goods and services*, with free movement of businesspeople and investments, thereby promoting deeper economic integration across Africa. Its specific aims include establishing a single continental market and gradually removing tariffs and non-tariff barriers on the trade of goods and services—a vital measure to tackle the low intra-African trade rate of 15–18%. It also aims to encourage industrial development through diversification and regional value chain creation by enlarging the market for industrialisation. Furthermore, it seeks to enhance competitiveness, address the "spaghetti bowl" problem of overlapping regional trade agreements, and establish a unified set of trade rules.

Essentially, the AfCFTA acts as the practical means of realising the economic integration objectives outlined in both the Abuja Treaty (1991) and Agenda 2063.

The Regional Economic Communities

African regional economic communities (RECs) serve as the primary drivers of continental integration; however, their collective potential is hindered by institutional fragmentation and differing national interests. The African Union (2025) recognises these eight RECs, although progress among them has been uneven.

- Common Market for Eastern and Southern Africa (COMESA)
- East African Community (EAC)
- Economic Community of West African States (ECOWAS)
- Intergovernmental Authority on Development (IGAD)
- Southern African Development Community (SADC).
- Arab Maghreb Union (UMA)
- Community of Sahel–Saharan States (CEN–SAD)
- Economic Community of Central African States (ECCAS).

Formed across different decades, their influence varies considerably: the Economic Community of West African States (ECOWAS), established in 1975, is recognised for its strong political and security frameworks, while the East African Community (EAC), revitalised in 2000 after its

1967 predecessor collapsed, shows advanced trade integration. The Southern African Development Community (SADC), restructured in 1992 from its 1980 predecessor, wields considerable economic influence, whereas the Common Market for Eastern and Southern Africa (COMESA), founded in 1994, faces challenges due to overlapping memberships. Meanwhile, the Economic Community of Central African States (ECCAS, 1983) and the Arab Maghreb Union (AMU, 1989) are hindered by political stagnation and weak institutions, collectively exemplifying the difficulties in turning regional frameworks into cohesive continental progress. According to UNECA (2025a, 2025b, 2025c: 35), the share of intraregional exports in total exports in 2023 was 21% in SADC, 14% in EAC, 10% in COMESA and ECOWAS, and 1% in ECCAS.

Despite their fundamental role in African integration, the regional economic communities (RECs) display varying capacities and face significant challenges. ECOWAS exhibits strong supranational authority with its binding protocols on free movement and a standing military force for conflict resolution, although political turbulence tests its jurisdiction. SADC retains considerable economic influence but struggles with implementing its customs union agenda and remains hampered by poor infrastructure connectivity. The EAC stands out for its deeper integration, characterised by a standard external tariff and a supranational court; however, political tensions periodically threaten its cohesion. Conversely, ECCAS remains weakened by institutional deficiencies and regional instability, while the Arab Maghreb Union is less vibrant, mainly due to prolonged political disputes. COMESA, being one of the largest FTAs, faces the complications of overlapping memberships, as many of its members also belong to other RECs, resulting in conflicting regulatory commitments. This fragmentation, further exacerbated by weak protocol enforcement and infrastructure deficits, continues to hinder the realisation of a continent-wide market under the AfCFTA framework.

2 African Single Market: Perspectives and AfCFTA Progress

The AfCFTA and African Economic Integration

The African Continental Free Trade Area (AfCFTA) embodies a complex and contested approach to continental development that can be analysed through several key contrasts. First, it functions both as a tool of market liberalisation—eliminating tariffs and streamlining trade—and as a driver of broader economic transformation, which creates inherent tensions and trade-offs. The latter perspective sees AfCFTA not as an end point but as a strategic pathway to promote industrialisation, develop regional value chains, and reduce reliance on raw material exports. However, this transformative potential remains fundamentally influenced by the political economy of implementation, where the agency of African states risks being swayed by external interests advocating for a straightforward, unrestrained free trade.

Furthermore, AfCFTA's success relies on its complex relationship with existing regional economic communities (RECs) and bilateral agreements; it does not replace these layers but must coordinate a complex, multi-speed integration landscape where they coexist. Finally, the continental framework cannot propose a one-size-fits-all solution. A single continental industrial policy is neither practical nor desirable; instead, AfCFTA should facilitate a mosaic of complementary national and regional strategies that leverage comparative advantages, recognising that integration is a means to development, not an end in itself (Oqubay 2015, 2025a; Oqubay et al. 2020). Ultimately, for the AfCFTA to effectively accelerate Africa's structural transformation and support meaningful economic catch-up, it needs to strategically manage not merely as a technical trade agreement but as a decisive, continent-wide political endeavour.

Progress of AfCFTA

Between 2021 and 2025, the African Continental Free Trade Area (AfCFTA) pursued a concerted implementation plan to enhance market integration and industrialisation, establishing a single market by removing tariffs on 90% of goods and introducing measures to reduce widespread non-tariff barriers. This foundational phase made significant progress, including finalising Rules of Origin for 88% of tariff lines—although key sectors, such as automotive and textiles, experienced stalled negotiations—and working to harmonise varied regional trade policies to decrease regulatory fragmentation. At the same time, the agenda facilitated the development of regional value chains in strategic sectors, such as agro-processing and pharmaceuticals. They expedited digital trade facilitation through mechanisms like the Pan-African Payment and Settlement System (PAPSS). Capacity-building initiatives and the creation of the AfCFTA Secretariat backed these operational achievements. However, the initiative's transformative potential was limited by ongoing structural obstacles, including unresolved Rules of Origin, infrastructural deficiencies, and significant disparities in implementation among member states, which together constrained the agreement's overall effectiveness.

The implementation of the AfCFTA faces many deep-rooted challenges, including regulatory fragmentation and slow harmonisation of trade protocols, which make the business environment costly. This is exacerbated by significant gaps in infrastructure and connectivity, which significantly increase the costs of intra-African trade. Additionally, progress is limited by low value addition, as exports mainly consist of raw commodities, alongside ongoing shortages of financing and incomplete Rules of Origin that hinder the development of the value chain. These issues are worsened by legacy problems, such as distrust and colonial-era trade patterns, difficulties in formalising the large informal trade sector, a heavy dependence on external partners, and the slow adoption of vital digital solutions and empowerment policies. Overall, these issues and challenges have influenced the path of AfCFTA's implementation and Africa's economic transformation efforts, with steady—but limited—progress towards deeper integration by 2025.[1]

The Intra-African Trade

Intra-African trade accounts for approximately 16% of the total trade within Africa, indicating a lower level of integration compared to Asia (Oqubay 2020; UNECA 2025). Despite formal efforts to boost African market integration, significant barriers still exist. First, the ongoing presence of non-tariff barriers, such as complex bureaucracy and obstacles, significantly impedes intra-regional trade (African Union 2025). This problem is exacerbated by the weak and inconsistent enforcement of trade protocols, where agreements often fail to yield uniform administrative practices. Second, limited economic diversification and weak industrialisation, with many countries relying on similar raw material exports, hinder the development of complementary trade and regional value chains. Third, poor infrastructure and high logistics costs further diminish

[1] See Ismael (2019) African Union (2001).

competitiveness, while the low participation of SMEs, due to financing and regulatory challenges, restricts the inclusive growth benefits of integration. Therefore, it is essential to accelerate industrialisation, promote productive investment, develop infrastructure for cross-border activities, and continuously improve trade facilitation to expand and deepen the African market.

Fifth, operational obstacles such as limited payment system interoperability and restrictive visa policies hinder the movement of capital and people. Finally, the absence of harmonised standards and certifications for goods and agricultural products prevents economies of scale and raises compliance costs. Collectively, these challenges highlight that while policy frameworks like the AfCFTA represent significant progress, transforming Africa's trade performance requires a systematic approach to overcoming these foundational constraints, thereby enabling genuine regional market integration (UNECA 2025a, b, c).

Africa's Global Positioning: The Logic of Market Size and Scale

The AfCFTA is fundamentally built on the economic principle of market size, aiming to unite Africa's fragmented economies into a single, integrated market of over 1.4 billion people. This combined scale provides the strategic basis for tackling the continent's central issue: small, uncompetitive national economies within a highly competitive, globalising economy. The primary benefit and focus is to utilise this market *to attract productive investment* in value addition and domestic capacity, making investment facilitation a key policy objective. This, in turn, supports the development of *industrial ecosystems and regional value chains*, moving beyond the export of raw materials. The ultimate aim is to establish "intra-African competitiveness" as a crucial step towards strong *international competitiveness*, using internal trade as a foundation for global trade (Oqubay 2025b; Oqubay and Lin 2020).

However, this logic depends on overcoming significant physical and financial barriers. The lack of *cross-border infrastructure* in energy, transport, and digital communications remains a considerable challenge, making the integration of logistics and harmonised customs systems an immediate priority. At the same time, the financial framework needs a corresponding transformation. *Development finance* increased to bridge substantial infrastructure gaps and support trade facilitation. Additionally, the *digitisation* of commerce—with over 40% of Africans now connected—offers a transformative path for e-commerce and innovative financing, but depends on strong digital infrastructure. Lastly, resolving *payment system* inefficiencies, both within Africa and for global transactions, is crucial to reducing transaction costs and enabling seamless trade, thereby laying the groundwork for future discussions on deeper monetary integration.

Africa's role in global trade remains disproportionately small, contributing only 2.9% of worldwide merchandise trade in 2023, a figure that has seen little progress over recent decades. A structurally problematic composition characterises this small share, as exports are heavily dominated by unprocessed natural resources, including mineral fuels, ores, and precious metals, making economies vulnerable to fluctuations in commodity prices. Conversely, imports primarily consist of high-value manufactured goods, machinery, and food products, resulting in a persistent trade deficit in many countries and a continuous outflow of foreign exchange. This pattern of trading raw materials for finished products highlights a more profound lack of industrial capacity and global competitiveness.

Significant external pressures worsen this marginal position. Africa's trade is increasingly influenced by geopolitics and geoeconomics, where trade is used as a political tool. Frameworks such as the US African Growth and Opportunity Act (AGOA) offer preferential access but foster dependency, while unilateral policies like the EU's Carbon Border Adjustment Mechanism (CBAM) introduce new forms of "green protectionism" that threaten future export revenues. However, this landscape also provides strategic opportunities for negotiation. The scale of China-Africa engagement and the EU's Everything But Arms (EBA) initiative offer leverage points (Oqubay 2020; Oqubay and Lin 2019). Africa benefits in shifting shift from a passive rule-taker to a strategic architect of its trade future, constructing partnerships that explicitly promote value addition, enhance productive capacities, and ultimately enable the continent to transform its vast resource wealth and strategic importance into sustainable economic sovereignty.

The AfCFTA's role as a collective platform for global repositioning can be summarised into three key strategic issues:

Internal economic transformation: The AfCFTA offers the essential foundation for diversifying Africa's trade by establishing a unified continental market. This scale facilitates the development of intricate regional value chains, shifting economies away from exporting raw materials and towards value-added production, which forms the core of global competitiveness.

Collective external leverage: By speaking with a unified voice, member states can transform the continent's fragmented negotiating power into a formidable instrument. This collective strength is vital for effectively countering external pressures—such as green protectionism that impacts African exports (e.g., the EU's Carbon Border Adjustment Mechanism, or CBAM)—and for achieving more equitable bilateral investment and trade deals.

Strategic rule-shaping agency: The platform transforms Africa from a passive rule-taker into an active architect of global governance. A united bloc can proactively participate in multilateral forums to influence the emerging rules on digital trade, intellectual property, and climate-related trade measures, ensuring they reflect continent-wide development priorities rather than being dictated from outside.

3 Structural Patterns of Intra-African Trade and International Trade

Structural Patterns of Intra-African Trade

The UNCTAD chart indicates that average non-tariff trade costs are considerably lower within African regional economic communities (RECs) than between them, highlighting both progress and ongoing fragmentation in intra-African trade integration.

Trade costs within major RECs—COMESA, EAC, ECOWAS, SADC—range from 1.35% to 2.83% ad valorem, significantly below inter-bloc trade costs, which often exceed 3% and reach as high as 4.13% between ECOWAS and EAC (see Table 7.1). The East African Community emerges as the most integrated group, with the lowest intra-bloc non-tariff trade costs (1.35%), indicating more seamless cross-border trade among its members compared to other RECs (AUC 2025a, 2025b; UNECA 2012, 2015). In contrast, trade between blocs remains hindered by higher costs due to ongoing issues, including differing customs procedures, regulatory mismatches, logistical inefficiencies, and indirect expenses related to currency, language, and transportation networks.

Evidence indicates that while regional integration has led to tangible cost savings within blocs, the divide between these blocs remains a

Table 7.1 Patterns of intra-Africa trade (within and among regional blocs)

Regional economic community (REC)	*Within bloc (%)*	*Trade with COMESA (%)*	*Trade with EAC (%)*	*Trade with ECOWAS (%)*	*Trade with SADC (%)*
Common Market for Eastern and Southern Africa (COMESA)	2.83	–	2.54	3.86	3.03
East African Community (EAC)	1.35	2.54	–	4.13	2.77
Economic Community of West African States (ECOWAS)	2.01	3.86	4.13	–	3.69
Southern African Development Community (SADC)	2.52	3.03	2.77	3.69	–

Source: UNCTAD (2025), Figure 10, page 19

significant barrier to establishing a truly unified continental market (UNCTAD 2025). The African Continental Free Trade Area (AfCFTA) explicitly seeks to overcome these obstacles by harmonising policies, reducing trade frictions, and encouraging deeper cross-bloc value chain integration. For AfCFTA to realise its full transformative potential, several crucial implications and priorities come to the fore. Firstly, concerning trade costs and convergence, reducing the disparity between intra- and inter-bloc trade expenses is essential to maximise the benefits of integration beyond individual RECs. This requires streamlining customs procedures, adopting interoperable standards, and enhancing logistics at border crossings.

Second, regarding infrastructure complementarity, reducing non-tariff costs is closely connected to improvements in physical infrastructure, particularly transport and energy, as logistical challenges increase trade costs between distant or poorly connected regions. Third, in terms of scale of opportunity, lowering cross-bloc trade costs would open larger markets, enabling economies of scale, increased specialisation, and the development of competitive regional value chains across Africa. Policymakers should focus on harmonising customs and trade facilitation frameworks, investing in transport corridors linking major blocs, and addressing soft barriers such as inconsistent documentation and non-harmonised regulatory regimes. Concentrating efforts to reduce the "distance" between RECs—both physical and regulatory—will be essential in creating an integrated African market that maximises the continent's diversity and scale.

Africa and International Trade

Three key trends emerge in Africa's role in global trade: a small share in international commerce; heterogeneity in trade orientation across RECs; diversification of trade with the EU and Asia playing major roles; and weak intra-Africa trade.

Marginal Share in Global Trade

Africa's share of global trade has consistently remained low, typically fluctuating between 2% and 3% for both merchandise exports and imports. In trade in services, the share is even smaller, usually around 2%. Despite housing over 17% of the world's population, the continent is underrepresented in global trade flows. Commodity price volatility, the COVID-19 pandemic, and ongoing structural challenges have shaped the period from 2015 to 2025. Africa's merchandise trade heavily relies on natural resources (oil, gas, minerals) and agricultural products, making it highly vulnerable to global commodity price swings. The share of global merchandise exports during this period was approximately 2.5%. Commodity overdependence, especially on oil, gas, and mining products, consistently accounts for more than 50% of Africa's total exports. The export of agricultural products has been characterised predominantly by low value addition (UNCTAD 2025).

This persistent marginalisation in global trade flows, coupled with commodity overdependence and minimal value addition, reinforces Africa's peripheral position in the international economic system and constrains the continent's capacity for autonomous development. The structural misalignment between Africa's demographic weight (17% of the global population) and its trade share (2–3%) signals both profound economic underperformance and substantial untapped potential. This export concentration exposes African economies to external shocks beyond their control, limits fiscal stability, restricts employment generation in higher-productivity sectors, and perpetuates dependency relationships that inhibit industrial upgrading and technological capabilities—ultimately undermining the continent's prospects for sustainable productive transformation.

Heterogeneity in Trade Orientation

Regional economic communities display considerable diversity and have different trade priorities. For example, AMU and ECOWAS tend to favour Europe, while other groups such as EAC, COMESA, ECCAS, and SADC are becoming more focused on Asia. IGAD is notable for its relatively higher intra-African exports (see Fig. 7.1 and Table 7.2).

Regarding African export patterns, Asia is the leading destination for exports from nearly all RECs—especially ECCAS (68%), EAC (56%), and SADC (47%). Europe remains a significant trading partner for North and West Africa (for example, AMU: 67%, ECOWAS: 37%), reflecting historical and geographical ties. Intra-African exports are relatively low, averaging 16% across the continent, with IGAD (36%) and SADC (22%) surpassing this average. Smaller shares are exported to Latin America, North America, and Oceania (each under 10%), indicating limited diversification of export markets.

Regarding imports, Asia remains the primary source in Africa, with an average share of 45% across the continent. The EAC (64%), IGAD (62%), and COMESA (49%) are particularly dependent on it. Europe remains a significant player, accounting for 31% of total imports, with higher shares in the AMU (50%) and ECOWAS (31%). Intra-African imports remain low at 13%, indicating that ongoing structural barriers persist in regional production and trade links.

The evidence shows the regional makeup of imports and exports across Africa's eight recognised regional economic communities (RECs),

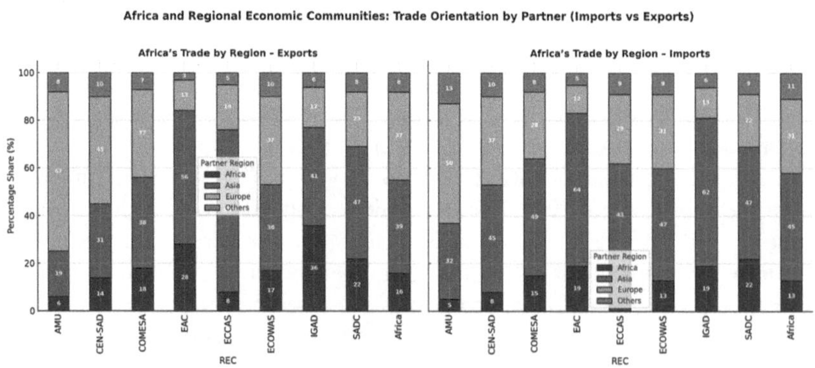

Fig. 7.1 Trade patterns of African exports and imports of merchandise goods in % (2019–23). (Source: UNECA (2025), Page 52–53 (Figure 1.3–1.4))

Table 7.2 Summary of export and import orientation trends

REC	*Export Trend*	*Import Trend*	*Observations*
AMU	Europe (67%) dominant	Europe (50%), Asia (32%)	Strong Euro-Maghreb ties; low African integration
CEN-SAD	Europe (45%), Asia (31%)	Asia (45%), Europe (37%)	Dual dependency; weak intra-African linkage
COMESA	Asia (38%)	Asia (49%)	Heavy Asian engagement; potential for regional consolidation
EAC	Asia (56%)	Asia (64%)	Strong Asia-Africa link; minimal diversification
ECOWAS	Asia (36%), Europe (37%)	Asia (47%), Europe (31%)	Balanced between Asia and Europe; intra-African trade modest
ECCAS	Asia (68%)	Asia (43%)	Over-dependence on Asian markets for exports (likely minerals, oil)
IGAD	Africa (36%), Asia (41%)	Asia (62%)	One of the highest intra-African export shares; promising integration
SADC	Asia (47%)	Asia (47%)	Balanced trade flows; relatively higher intra-African activity (22%)

Source: UNECA (2025)

including the AMU, CEN-SAD, COMESA, EAC, ECCAS, ECOWAS, IGAD, and SADC, as well as the African continental average and trading regions such as Asia, Europe, Latin America and the Caribbean, North America, and Oceania. The diagram depicts a dual trade pattern that reflects a legacy of historical European ties and a shift towards Asian markets and production centres. Despite the growth of regional economic organisations, Africa's trade pattern remains predominantly outward-focused. The AfCFTA's promising potential lies in changing this trend—transforming fragmented regional blocs into a unified, competitive continental market that can boost production, employment, and innovation.

Asia's Rising Role and Europe's Persistent Legacy

Both imports and exports are increasingly centred on Asia, emphasising Africa's shift towards China, India, and East Asia for manufactured goods and commodity exports. This trend further integrates Africa into Asia's production and consumption networks but reduces the value added locally. Despite Asia's rise, Europe remains a significant trade partner, especially for North and West Africa, owing to historic, linguistic, and institutional links (e.g., EU–ACP trade regimes, colonial ties). North America, Latin America, the Caribbean, and Oceania account for a smaller share.

Weak Intra-African Trade and Implications for AfCFTA

Intra-African trade makes up less than 18% of both imports and exports, highlighting ongoing regional fragmentation. This pattern results from low industrial complementarity among African nations, inadequate transport and logistics infrastructure, and non-tariff barriers across borders. The main challenges include continued reliance on external partners that hinders continental integration; infrastructure gaps, overlapping REC memberships, and trade facilitation issues that block cross-border movement; and structural imbalances between resource exporters and manufacturing importers that restrict reciprocal trade within Africa.

The African Continental Free Trade Area (AfCFTA) aims to unify fragmented regional markets and boost intra-African trade, thereby strengthening regional value chains (e.g., textiles, food processing, and automotive industries); reduce reliance on external sources by promoting continental supply linkages; and encourage industrial diversification and resilience against global shocks. Diversifying Africa's trade with other regions and promoting intra-African trade are crucial strategies. These include harmonising trade policies and customs procedures under the AfCFTA framework; investing in regional transport corridors (e.g., LAPSSET, North–South Corridor); encouraging industrial clustering within RECs to develop complementarity and economies of scale; and prioritising Africa-to-Africa value addition—particularly in energy, agriculture, and light manufacturing sectors.

It is notable that export-led industrialisation (ELI) supports productive transformation and the growth of the African single market. It plays an essential role in linking intra-African trade, international exports, and regional value chains by creating conditions for broad economic change through economies of scale, productivity improvements, and technological advancements. By focusing on exports, African countries can diversify beyond reliance on commodities, access larger external markets, and boost intra-African trade through regional value chains backed by the African Continental Free Trade Area (AfCFTA). This interconnectedness means that increased regional trade and value chain integration enhance international export competitiveness, generating positive cycles of industrialisation through specialisation, knowledge sharing, and investment across

African economies. Ultimately, ELI promotes resilience to external shocks, encourages employment growth, and raises income levels by connecting otherwise fragmented African markets into united platforms that benefit both the continent and the global economy.

4 Infrastructure Development as the Foundation for AfCFTA

Progress in African Infrastructure Development

Among the various constraints and challenges, infrastructure remains the most critical binding constraint and priority due to its strategic significance and the substantial financial investments, political commitment, and long-term planning requirements. Infrastructure integration is vital for unlocking the full potential of the AfCFTA, as it physically and economically links markets, reduces transaction costs, and strengthens regional value chains. The examples in energy, transport, and logistics illustrate how strategic, cross-border projects drive continental economic transformation when aligned with harmonised regulations and coordinated investment.

The AfCFTA aims to enhance intra-African trade, promote economic diversification, and strengthen regional value chains. However, the infrastructure gaps highlighted by UNCTAD (2025) emphasise the substantial barriers to achieving these aims.

- *Cross-border trade and logistics:* Insufficient transport integration raises the cost and challenges of moving goods within Africa, undermining the benefits expected from tariff liberalisation and harmonised trade regulations.
- *Industrial competitiveness is limited by* inadequate electricity supply and high energy costs, which hinder investment in export-led industries, thereby decreasing Africa's capacity to compete in both regional and global markets.
- *Regional value chains:* Without strong backbone infrastructure, the development of seamless regional value chains—the core of AfCFTA's transformative vision—remains limited.

Africa's infrastructure has seen notable improvements since 2005, as reflected in the composite Africa Infrastructure Development Index, with significant advances in ICT. However, major gaps still persist in the transport and electricity sectors. These disparities have profound implications for intra-African trade and the objectives of the African Continental Free Trade Area. Tackling these gaps requires continuous efforts to attract both public and private investment in physical (roads, rail, ports, and energy) and soft (customs, logistics, and regulation) infrastructure. Bridging these gaps will unlock trade potential, reduce barriers to the movement of goods and people, and markedly progress Africa's economic integration goals.

An analysis of the Africa Infrastructure Development Index (AIDI) from 2005 to 2022 reveals that the continent's uneven infrastructure growth poses a significant challenge to the African Continental Free Trade Area (AFCFTA). Although the overall index indicates progress, the sharply differing growth rates across sectors create a substantial mismatch between digital potential and physical trade capabilities. The data reveal that ICT develops the fastest, followed by electricity, while transport lags behind. While the advancement of ICT is crucial for trading digital services, the trade of merchandise goods is heavily limited by the substantial lag in transportation. Delays in electricity supply hinder both the exchange of goods and services, as production relies heavily on electricity and energy (see Fig. 7.2).

While the Africa Infrastructure Development Index grew steadily from 2005 to 2022, mainly due to the rapid expansion of the ICT sector after 2010, both the transport and electricity indices showed only modest improvements. Transport infrastructure, in particular, has remained essentially unchanged over this period, with only minor adjustments from its 2005 baseline. Electricity infrastructure also made limited progress, increasing slightly but lagging well behind ICT. This uneven development highlights a persistent structural bottleneck: basic physical connectivity and reliable power supply remain insufficient for much of the continent.

Infrastructure Regional Integration

Energy Sector Regional Integration

Cross-border electrification initiatives serve as a clear driver of regional integration, in terms of both market dynamics and industrial capacity

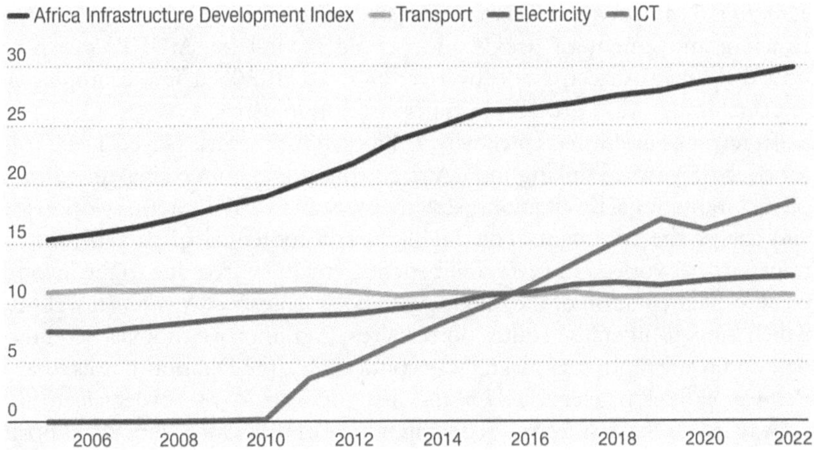

Fig. 7.2 Africa infrastructure development index 2005–2022. (Source: UNCTAD (2025), Figure 9, page 17)

building. This requires long-term planning, collaborative project development, and the implementation of adequate governance arrangements.

The Ethiopia–Kenya 500 kV Transmission Line, commissioned in 2022, connects renewable-rich power systems across East Africa, enabling the trade of surplus electricity generated by Ethiopia's hydropower resources. The Ethiopia–Djibouti 230 kV Interconnector provides a reliable power supply for Djibouti's port-centric economy, thereby reducing its dependence on costly thermal generation. The Ethiopia–Sudan Power Link enhances bilateral energy trade and helps stabilise Sudan's national electricity grid. Despite its economic and environmental importance as a significant renewable energy source, GERD has had to navigate complex geopolitical tensions related to the Nile River. As the largest hydropower project in Africa, generating over 5200 MW with a reservoir capacity of 75 billion cubic metres, and fully financed by domestic resources and the Ethiopian people, it has a transformative impact. It offers lessons for African countries (ENA 2025). With forecasts indicating Ethiopia's export capacity could exceed 4000 MW annually by 2030, these interconnectors lead to lower generation costs, improved reliability, and industrialisation benefits—crucial for competitive manufacturing under AfCFTA.

Regional Transport and Logistics Integration
Efficient movement of goods and people is vital for AfCFTA's aim of boosting intra-African trade by over 50% by 2030—a few examples of regional integration projects in transport and logistics.

In terms of aviation connectivity, Ethiopian Airlines has played a vital role for over 65 years in linking intra-African routes and connecting Africa with other international destinations, serving more than 130 locations worldwide and across the continent. This highlights the potential of pan-African air transport networks. However, full benefits remain limited due to the incomplete implementation of the Single African Air Transport Market (SAATM), which aims to liberalise routes, lower fares, and improve mobility for business and tourism. In regional railway connectivity, the Djibouti–Addis Ababa Railway (752 km, electrified) is the first modern, cross-border electrified railway in sub-Saharan Africa, reducing transport times for Ethiopian imports and exports via Djibouti and decreasing logistics costs for manufacturing exporters. Various road connectivity projects, including those linking Ethiopia with Sudan, South Sudan, and Kenya, serve as further examples.

The Abidjan–Lagos Corridor, a 1028 km highway connecting five ECOWAS countries, is expected to boost regional trade by up to 50%, support logistics hubs, and foster coastal industrial clusters. *Rail integration, through the Tazara Railway* (1860 km), serves as a crucial route for mineral and commodity trade, linking Zambia's Copperbelt with Tanzania's port of Dar es Salaam, with potential extension to landlocked countries such as Malawi.

Therefore, the infrastructure gap, especially in transportation and energy, directly hampers intra-African trade. Reliable roads, railways, ports, and energy networks are essential for facilitating cross-border trade by reducing transaction costs, minimising delays, and enhancing supply chain resilience. The slow progress in developing transport infrastructure leaves many regions poorly connected to significant economic and trading hubs, limiting both the scale and scope of African value chain integration. Likewise, ongoing electricity shortages constrain industrialisation, agricultural value addition, and manufacturing—key sectors for increasing trade in higher-value goods under AfCFTA.

In summary, for such projects to realise the full potential of AfCFTA's economic integration goals, three key factors are essential. First, harmonised infrastructure planning is vital for aligning national infrastructure plans with regional economic corridors and preventing duplication and bottlenecks. Second, regulatory alignment is crucial to ensure streamlined customs and technical standards, thereby facilitating seamless cross-border operations. Third, investment coordination is necessary to mobilise the full potential of blended finance from African DFIs, sovereign funds, and private investors, promoting risk-sharing and sustainability. Ultimately, the combined strength of energy trade, transport corridors, and logistics networks enhances Africa's competitiveness by integrating markets, unlocking economies of scale, and supporting industrial clusters—core objectives of the AfCFTA. While these are vital and desirable, adherence is often challenging, as other factors can create tensions in practice. It largely depends on political will and the championing of developmental ambitions.

5 Economic Integration as a Political Project

The African Continental Free Trade Area (AfCFTA) is more than just a typical trade agreement; it embodies Africa's most ambitious political effort directed at the continent's economic sovereignty and structural change. This initiative emphasises a key duality: while acting as a technical mechanism for market liberalisation, its broader promise is to actively promote structural transformation, industrialisation, and a fair green transition. This transformative aim makes AfCFTA not only a final objective but also a dynamic path to redefine Africa's global economic position through regional value chains and a decrease in reliance on commodities (AUC et al. 2025).

Drawing strategic lessons from other blocs is instructive, but they are considered within their specific context. The European Union's seven-decade journey from a peace initiative to a sophisticated, rules-based union demonstrates the potential of deep institutionalism. However, its perceived democratic shortcomings and rigid supranationalism serve as cautionary lessons for African models of sovereignty. Conversely, the Association of Southeast Asian Nations (ASEAN)'s consensus-driven approach, which facilitated export-led industrialisation through regional value chains, offers a more flexible framework for Africa's diverse political economies. ASEAN has ten member states: Brunei Darussalam, Cambodia, Indonesia, Laos, Malaysia, Myanmar, the Philippines, Singapore, Thailand, and Vietnam. It was founded in 1967 to encourage economic growth, social progress, cultural development, and peace and stability. It collectively represents a major global economy, with a combined GDP of over £4 trillion in 2025, making it roughly the fourth-largest economy in the world and China's largest trading partner, estimated at over US$1 trillion in 2024.

The stark difference between intra-EU and intra-ASEAN trade and supply chain integration mainly stems from institutional and structural factors. The EU's well-established legal and regulatory alignment, single market integration, and centralised policy frameworks have promoted intra-regional trade exceeding 60%, supported by extensive cross-border value chain activities and more diverse economies. In contrast, intra-ASEAN trade has plateaued at around 21–22% due to ongoing infrastructure deficiencies, less harmonised standards, differing tariffs, non-tariff barriers, and "bottom-up" market-driven dynamics combined with member states' strong focus on global markets. While ASEAN's flexibility allows countries such as Vietnam, Thailand, and Malaysia to attract investment and reposition within global supply chains as geopolitical shocks prompt corporate diversification, the lack of deeper supranational integration limits intra-regional value chain development. As a result, ASEAN faces greater external dependence and unequal spillovers among members compared to the EU's more integrated approach.

Nevertheless, the African integration pathway faces specific structural and political challenges. Rising protectionism and populism, evident in bilateral disputes within the EAC, combined with significant political divisions—such as ECOWAS's stance against military-led governments in the Sahel—highlight an apparent lack of effective dispute resolution mechanisms on the continent. Furthermore, institutional fragmentation—visible in coordination issues between the AU Commission and the AfCFTA Secretariat, as well as between continental and REC mandates—undermines cohesive implementation.

A single industrial policy remains unfeasible; instead, the AfCFTA can manage a mix of complementary national and regional strategies that utilise comparative advantages while embedding sustainability as a key element of its competitive approach (Oqubay 2016, 2020, 2025; UNECA 2016). Ultimately, the AfCFTA's success relies on moving beyond its technical aspects to be recognised as a continent-wide political initiative. Its potential to stimulate structural transformation and economic catch-up remains unrealised without addressing governance uncertainties and establishing a unified political purpose that asserts African agency against external influences and internal divisions.

In conclusion, this analysis presents two contrasting interpretations. If deep regional integration genuinely lays the foundation for productive transformation, the protracted timeline required for its realisation offers limited short-term prospects for such transformation. Alternatively, integration may be understood as inherently complex and gradual—a realistic expectation—but one that becomes increasingly feasible once productive transformation gains momentum. Such a transformation would foster more diversified economies, deepen markets beyond demographic scale to encompass purchasing power, and broaden the scope for complementarity. This perspective suggests that integration is not the foundation for transformation but rather its consequence and reinforcement. Therefore, the priority for African governments should be to accelerate the structural transformation of their economies, which will concurrently strengthen domestic productive capacity and enhance the continent's international standing, thereby creating more favourable conditions for meaningful regional integration.

References

African Union. 2001. *New Partnership for Africa's Development (NEPAD), Declaration on Democracy, Political and Economic Governance*. Lusaka. https://sarpn.org/NEPAD/july2002/declaration/declaration.pdf.

African Union. 2015. *Agenda 2063, "The Africa We Want"*. Final edition. http://www.un.org/en/africa/osaa/pdf/au/agenda2063.pdf.

African Union Commission. 2025a. *African Integration Report 2025. Strengthening the Implementation of Regional Frameworks to Leverage Continental Achievements Fully*. Addis Ababa: African Union Commission.

African Union Commission. 2025b. Regional Economic Communities. Regional Economic Communities. Established under the African Economic Community, as per the Abuja Treaty (1991). https://au.int/en/recs.

African Union Commission, United Nations Economic Commission for Africa (ECA), and African Development Bank (AfDB). 2025. *African Integration Report 2025: Delivering on the African Economic Community — Towards an African Continental Customs Union and African Continental Common Market*, Main Report. Addis Ababa.

Cramer, Christopher, John Sender, and Arkebe Oqubay. 2020. *African Economic Development: Evidence, Theory, Policy*. Oxford: Oxford University Press.

ENA. 2025. *Speech of Presidents of Kenya and Djibouti on Regional Economic Integration at the Inauguration of Grand Ethiopian Renaissance Dam*. 9 September. Ethiopian News Agency. https://youtu.be/QDODzfHbang?si=qXyGSTrefw2UTROU.

Ismail, Faizel. 2019. A Developmental Regionalism Approach to the African Continental Free Trade Area (AfCTA). *Journal of Reviews on Global Economics* 8:1771–1785. https://www.lifescienceglobal.com/JRGEV8A159-Ismail.pdf.

Ismail, Faizel. 2021. *The African Continental Free Trade Area (AfCFTA) and Developmental Regionalism. A Handbook*. Trade & Industrial Policy Strategies (TIPS).

Luke, David, ed. 2023. *How Africa Trades*. London: LSE Press.
Mangeni, Francis, and Andrew Mold. 2024. *Borderless Africa: A Sceptic's Guide to the Continental Free Trade Area*. London: Hurst Publishers.
Ofori-Amoah, Benjamin. 2024. *The African Continental Free Trade Area: Prospects, Problems and Challenges*. London: Springer.
Oqubay, Arkebe. 2015. *Made in Africa*. Oxford: Oxford University Press.
Oqubay, Arkebe. 2020. Africa's Economic Transformation and the Future of EU-Africa Cooperation. *CESifo Forum* 21:3–11. https://www.ifo.de/DocDL/CESifo-Forum-2020-2-oqubay-africas-economic-transformation.pdf.
Oqubay, Arkebe. 2025a. *Industrial Policy and Economic Development: Theory, Strategy, and Practice*. London: Palgrave Macmillan.
Oqubay, Arkebe. 2025b. *Industrial Hubs and Economic Catch-up: Productive Transformation and Governance*. London: Palgrave Macmillan.
Oqubay, Arkebe, and Justin Yifu Lin, eds. 2019. *China-Africa and an Economic Transformation*. Oxford: Oxford University Press.
Oqubay, Arkebe, and Justin Yifu Lin, eds. 2020. *The Oxford Handbook of Industrial Hubs and Economic Development*. Oxford: Oxford University Press.
Oqubay, Arkebe, Christopher Cramer, Ha-Joon Chang, and Richard Kozul-Wright. 2020. *The Oxford Handbook of Industrial Policy*. Oxford: Oxford University Press.
TARLAC. 2020. *The Africa Continental Free Trade Area. A Tarlac Guide*. 7th ed. https://www.africannewspage.net/wp-content/uploads/2021/03/AfCFTA-a-tralac-guide-7th-edition-August-2020.pdf.
UNCTAD. 2025. *Economic Development in Africa Report 2024. Unlocking Africa's Trade Potential, Boosting Regional Markets, and Reducing Risks. Overview*. Geneva: UNCTAD.
UNECA. 2012. *Boosting Intra-African Trade*. Addis Ababa: UNECA.
UNECA. 2015. *Economic Report on Africa: Industrialising through Trade*. Addis Ababa: United Nations Economic Commission for Africa.
UNECA. 2016. *Transformative Industrial Policy for Africa*. Addis Ababa: United Nations Economic Commission for Africa.
UNECA. 2025a. *Advancing the Implementation of the African Continental Free Trade Area: Proposing Transformative Strategic Actions. Economic Report on Africa*. Addis Ababa: UNECA.
UNECA. 2025b. *Assessing Regional Integration in Africa: ARIA XI. Delivering on the African Economic Community: Towards an African Continental Customs Union and African Continental Common Market*. Addis Ababa: UNECA.
UNECA. 2025c. *Economic Report Africa: Advancing the Implementation of the Agreement Establishing the African Continental Free Trade Area: Proposing Transformative Strategic Actions*. Addis Ababa: UNECA

CHAPTER 8

The Future of African Industrialisation

This chapter examines the future of African industrialisation by analysing key perspectives and strategies as pathways to development. It emphasises productive transformation as the central framework and underscores the importance of adapting to shifts in the global economy. This entails addressing challenges and capitalising on opportunities presented by global factors such as digital transformation, green initiatives, and uncertainties or crises stemming from geopolitical tensions affecting Africa.

1 The Prospects for Productive Transformation and Industrialisation Strategies

Perspectives of Productive Transformation

Accelerating Africa's industrialisation is vital for transforming the continent and enhancing the livelihoods of Africans. Additionally, it will create substantial positive spillover effects, supporting global growth and sustainable development. However, African industrialisation might not follow the same development paths as frontrunners and may display its own distinctive features.

First, in the African context, accelerated industrialisation will bridge gaps in structural transformation, achieve economic diversification, promote industrial transformation, and support economic catch-up in several

A. Oqubay, *Productive Transformation in Africa*,
https://doi.org/10.1007/978-3-032-23941-9_8

countries. This process will also improve the resilience of many African economies to withstand global crises and the increasing volatility of the global economy, as well as sluggish growth, which has significantly highlighted Africa's vulnerabilities. Recognising that industrialisation is the only pathway is essential so that political will and state capacity can be aligned towards this overarching goal.

Nonetheless, industrialisation should be viewed in a broader sense rather than from a traditional static perspective. It should primarily focus on manufacturing industries due to the *special* properties outlined by Kaldor (1967), which remain relevant. Modern agricultural activities utilise advanced technologies and economies of scale, which contribute to exports and foster strong production linkages with manufacturing industries (Cramer et al. 2020). In the services sector, high-value and tradable services should be integrated within the broader industrialisation process, maximising technological capacity, enhancing productivity, and fostering new linkages. Recent technological developments have increasingly blurred the lines between different sectors. Therefore, a new and practical approach, rather than a dogmatic definition, is crucial.

Furthermore, industrial policy should be understood broadly to include not only the conventional interpretation of "industrial policies" but also to cover productive transformation policies, which incorporate strategies, policies, institutions, and practices. Productive transformation policies encompass industrial, trade, and technological capabilities, as well as complementary macroeconomic policies and targeted infrastructure development. This approach encourages complementarity and promotes a more comprehensive policy framework, leading to better outcomes. It should be emphasised that African governments should develop their own development paths, strategies, and policies that reflect their unique local conditions; in some cases, subnational contexts may be essential and require different policies. Policies need to be tailored to specific sectors or industries, and approaches are likely to differ across various strategic phases. A dynamic design and implementation will demand an approach open to policy learning, which requires a different mindset and perspective.

Perspectives on Africa's Industrialisation

While the book avoids prescribing specific policies or strategic sectors, as African countries display different characteristics—such as levels of development, experiences with industrial policies, political economy, and natural endowments—it constructs its argument through a detailed analysis of industrial chains and policies. It posits that five key trends present opportunities for African industrialisation in the twenty-first century. First among these is the continent's unique demographic outlook, characterised by rapid urbanisation and a population projected to reach 2.5 billion by 2050. This trajectory will furnish Africa with the world's youngest workforce—a distinct competitive advantage amid the ageing populations and declining fertility rates of advanced and other emerging economies. Concurrently, urbanisation is set to fundamentally shape industrial development, with African cities expected to absorb nearly 1.6 billion people, almost two-thirds of the continent's total population. This demographic shift has significant policy implications, requiring the creation of 30 million decent jobs each year, attracting productive investment, and building substantial productive capacity to utilise a market expected to expand to over $15 trillion by 2050. Ultimately, as a demographic powerhouse, Africa needs to design its development strategies to capitalise on this potential, addressing the attendant challenges to maximise the benefits. In the long term, these demographic trends, coupled with technological advances, will be the primary drivers of structural economic change.

Second, technological progress presents a dual opportunity for African industrialisation: it offers a significant growth lever but also introduces major challenges. This dynamic encapsulates the "advantage of backwardness," where latecomers can leapfrog stages of development, yet pioneers still maintain a competitive edge. To harness this, developing robust technological capabilities is essential across all targeted sectors. The successful economic catch-up of South Korea and China demonstrates that systematic investment in R&D, including at the enterprise level, is a critical success factor. Consequently, a strategic approach is imperative, requiring early investment in R&D for selected areas, the development of systems to monitor technological trends, and a focus on building absorptive capacity. For instance, investing in biotechnology is crucial for transforming Africa's agricultural sector. Ultimately, this ensures that technological capability, industrial upgrading, and strategic financing are central pillars of a coherent industrialisation policy.

Furthermore, the creation of the African Continental Free Trade Area (AfCFTA), which began implementation in 2021, is a strategic necessity for the continent's economic transformation. Although this ambitious single-market initiative is still in its early stages and faces considerable challenges, external pressures—such as the unilateral US global tariff war and the possible non-renewal of AGOA—have highlighted the urgent need to increase intra-African trade and speed up regional integration. The AfCFTA's framework recognises that success depends not just on liberalising trade but on a focused strategy of adding domestic value, strengthening production connections, and building regional value chains to promote industrialisation. At the same time, the broader geopolitical shift, marked by the rise of Asia and the Global South, offers a complementary opportunity to diversify trade partnerships, attract productive investment, and deepen South–South economic cooperation.

Designing Industrial Policies

The analysis identifies five strategic considerations in the design and execution of industrial policy. First, creating a solid foundation for protecting investments and ensuring fair treatment of firms is essential. Establishing policy predictability and legislation is urgent and a significant initiative for African industrialisation. The practical implementation of vital national projects and essential comprehensive reforms that require a longer execution period than the periodic national election cycles is a critical task that demands building consensus among political parties, but remains difficult in practice. This should be supported by a strong political consensus within the highest legislative body and executed with resolute determination. Improving the business environment should align with international competitiveness while utilising the best available practices and adapting to local conditions. Deepening reforms should be regarded as a continuous mission and a top political priority.

Second, the industrial development strategy should align with the respective government's broad national development path, which is regularly reviewed and adapted for optimal outcomes. Industrial development strategies and policies are not the sole responsibility of any single ministry or government agency. The highest political body has to champion the strategy, whether that be the Prime Minister or the President, depending on the executive head, adhered to by all government agencies.

Third, selecting strategic priority sectors and creating targeted incentives and support schemes form the foundation for establishing the principles of reciprocity, with these incentives tied to performance outcomes. The selection criteria for priority sectors should prioritise those with stronger *production linkages*, *technological capabilities*, employment generation, and export growth, depending on the specific context, including the size of the domestic market, locational advantages, and available resources. While ensuring that sectors are grounded in existing comparative advantages, the ongoing aim should be to develop competitive advantages in existing or emerging sectors. Emphasising technological capabilities across sectors is essential to avoid premature deindustrialisation and escape from the middle-income trap (Lee 2019).

Fourth, proactive leadership from the state and effective coordination among government institutions should be continuously nurtured and upheld. While the state plays a strategic developmental role, the primary focus should be on ensuring that the private sector acts as an engine of industrialisation. The government and private sector should foster a productive partnership, supported by regular dialogue platforms within and across industries.

Fifth, according to research, despite the focus of industrial policy on specific sectors, the outcomes are likely to be uneven for three reasons: differences in the industrial structure (the economic and technological features) of each sector; the political economy of industries; and variations in linkage effectiveness (Oqubay 2015). It is essential that these considerations underpin industrial policies for the specific priority sectors. Due to policy or other external factors, sector outcomes continue to change. They never remain static, and the success of industrial policies coexists with seeds of failure or issues that require new policy decisions. Therefore, regular review and research of policies and outcomes are highly recommended to ensure that industrial policies are adapted or revised as necessary.

2 Global Drivers and Prospects for Africa's Industrialisation

The prospects for African industrialisation are heavily influenced by a changing global landscape, characterised by digitalisation, the green transformation, and geopolitical realignments. Understanding this context is vital for developing an effective strategy. First, rapid technological progress is fundamentally disrupting industrial sectors. The widespread global adoption of frontier technologies is evident in over one million patents for Industry 4.0 fields and more than 600,000 for green technologies between 2000 and 2023 (UNCTAD 2025b). Second, a slow yet unpredictable global economy, marked by uncertainty and climate collapse, worsens systemic vulnerabilities. This situation highlights the need for Africa to quicken its own industrial and technological transformation to build resilience. Lastly, the geopolitical factor is the economic rise of Asia and the Global South, which is reshaping global economic and green development trends.

Africa's contemporary industrialisation trajectory is being fundamentally reshaped by the global forces of digitalisation, which presents a dual-edged sword of opportunity and risk. Theoretically, digitalisation offers a pathway to technological leapfrogging, enabling the adoption of smart manufacturing, optimised logistics, and the proliferation of digital services and e-commerce, thereby bypassing traditional industrial stages. Conversely, the persistent digital divides—manifest in inadequate infrastructure, low digital literacy, and nascent data governance frameworks—threaten to exclude African economies from these very benefits. This exclusion risk would not merely maintain but deepen structural vulnerabilities, cementing a peripheral role in the global digital economy. Consequently, a proactive and strategic state response is imperative. African governments orchestrate this transition through strategic public investment in digital infrastructure, the creation of regulatory certainty, and targeted incentives to attract talent and capital. Critical to this effort is the deployment of industrial policy instruments, such as developing innovation clusters and high-technology parks, to systematically build technological capability. Furthermore, the transformation demands a parallel evolution in higher education, requiring universities to urgently adapt curricula and research to cultivate a workforce capable of driving and sustaining this digital shift.

The global shift towards green transformation—driven by climate commitments, carbon regulations, and changing consumer preferences—presents both challenges and opportunities for African industrialisation.[1] On the one hand, carbon border adjustment mechanisms (CABMs), stricter environmental standards, and the phase-out of fossil fuels can limit market access and funding for carbon-intensive sectors in Africa. On the other hand, Africa's abundant renewable energy resources and vital minerals (e.g., lithium, cobalt) present opportunities for green manufacturing, clean-tech investment, and leadership in low-carbon industrial value chains. Taking advantage of these opportunities will require conscious industrial policies and investments in green infrastructure, skills, and

[1] Mathews and Oqubay (2025), Oqubay (2025a, b).

innovation. The emergence of green and digital technologies creates prospects in new industries that could generate jobs and promote economic diversification (such as developing industrial chains in critical minerals) and technological advances. Infrastructure and energy systems are increasingly becoming affordable and easily accessible.

Geopolitical shifts, such as the increasing US-China rivalry, renewed interest in Africa from Gulf states, India, and Turkey, and the fragmentation of global supply chains, are reshaping the strategic landscape for African industrialisation. This realignment creates new opportunities for investment, trade partnerships, and leverage for African nations to negotiate better terms within global production networks. However, these geopolitical rivalries also risk assigning African countries into asymmetric dependencies, as foreign powers pursue resource extraction or infrastructure deals that lack long-term developmental benefits. Managing these relationships to protect strategic autonomy and industrial goals demands careful balancing.

In response, African countries are adopting a variety of policy measures to navigate these complex dynamics. Regional initiatives such as the African Continental Free Trade Area (AfCFTA) aim to develop continental value chains, reduce external reliance, and promote industrial diversification. National governments are investing in digital infrastructure, supporting green industrial parks, and designing local content regulations and fiscal incentives to attract high-quality investment in strategic sectors. Some countries are integrating green industrialisation into national development plans, while others are strengthening institutions for digital governance and industrial policy coordination. However, implementation capacity remains inconsistent, emphasising the need for enhanced regional cooperation, capacity-building, and adaptive policy learning to fully exploit the benefits of these transformative global shifts.

3 Green Transformation and Sustainable Industrialisation in Africa

The rationale for pursuing sustainable industrialisation in Africa should rest on an examination of fundamental factors, which will have strategic implications for Africa's structural transformation. African countries face a challenging decision between continuing the business-as-usual approach of "brown industrialisation," where environmental sustainability and climate neutrality are sidelined. However, African governments can opt for carbon-neutral industrialisation by leveraging new opportunities for various reasons.[2]

Since the first Industrial Revolution in the mid-eighteenth century, all advanced economies and newly industrialising catch-up economies have actively employed industrial policies, and their core nature has remained largely unchanged—the key lies in developmental state intervention to promote productive transformation and accelerate structural change and catch-up (Chang 1994). However, the implementation of an activist industrial policy tailored to the specific national context while also considering shifts in the external environment, such as economic and technological changes. List (1841) highlights productive capability as central to industrial policy: "First, to prefer constantly the importation of productive power to that of commodities; second, to maintain and carefully protect the development of productive power; third, to import only raw materials and agricultural products, and to export only manufactured articles." Amsden (1989) stresses, "diversity notwithstanding, all late industrializers have in common industrialization on the basis of learning, which conditioned how they behaved." These perspectives remain pertinent to African industrialisation and policymaking today.

One of the significant shifts in the early twenty-first century is the increasing importance of environmental sustainability and green development. As Table 8.1 shows, industrial policy should not be regarded as static, and a carbon-neutral path is essential for African industrialisation. Although industrial policy is not new, green industrial policy is a recent development that has gained momentum over the past two or three decades. Traditionally, industrial policies have focused on growth and economic catch-up and accelerating structural transformation without taking environmental sustainability into account, often guided by the "growth first and clean later" perspective.[3]

However, green industrial policy is based on the idea that industrial transformation and systems can be both sustainable and highly productive simultaneously. Its application has expanded to include energy systems as a key part of greening economic development. Energy has become a matter of national security influenced by geopolitical tensions, resource monopolies, and diminishing supplies. Green industrial policy involves developing innovation capabilities in green and digital technologies,

[2] See IRENA (2025) and UNCTAD (2025a).

[3] See Mathews and Oqubay (2020), Oqubay (2025a, b).

Table 8.1 Comparative matrix of industrial policies

Industrial policy remains unchanged	*Industrial policy is not static*
Purpose: Structural transformation and economic catch-up	Dual mission: Structural transformation and green development
Productive transformation: Industrial capacity, innovation, exports	Broader scope for industrial policy (energy and sectors, infrastructure, green finance)
Building on latecomer advantage and learning by doing and innovation	Sectoral boundaries blurred (manufacturing, services, agriculture)
Targeted, strategic sectors: production, investment, linkages	Distinction between brown and green industrial policy
Amsden's reciprocity and development banks	Driven by digital and green technologies
Role of state: Strategic, national champions, complementary	Governance for the green transition
Domestic value-addition, linkages, productive capabilities	New context: geopolitics, global crisis, advanced economies, alliance
Complementary macroeconomic policy, infrastructure development, education system	
Escaping middle-income trap: technological capability, deindustrialisation	
Institutional innovations and policy learning	

Source: Author's matrix

creating green industrial platforms, promoting the circular economy and green finance, which also give rise to new industries such as new energy vehicles and renewable energy. Implementing a green industrial policy necessitates a distinct approach to governance, encompassing broader partnerships and a more diverse range of stakeholders. Earlier industrial revolutions, from the seventeenth to the twentieth centuries, have been driven and powered by fossil fuel sources. In contrast, the twenty-first century is expected to witness a significant shift away from fossil fuels and towards various sources of clean and renewable energy. Green industrial policy encompasses a broader range of instruments, including infrastructure (such as charging infrastructure or sustainable mobility in public transportation) and sustainable urban development, all part of a wider ecosystem.

A recent global research publication, *The Oxford Handbook on the Greening of Economic Development* (Mathews and Oqubay 2025), seeks to provide the most comprehensive analysis, including practical examples from national economies and sectors, demonstrating the irreversible patterns of global economic development. The main argument is that the greening of economic development marks the next major transformation, similar to Polanyi's seminal work, *The Great Transformation* (1944), in which we emphasise the "coming into being of a greener economy, one that is more sustainable, closer to emulating life processes, where energy is renewable and resources flow in a circular pattern" (Mathews and Oqubay 2025: 799), exemplified by China's leadership in global green development. This transformation entails a comprehensive restructuring of the world order, a complete shift away from fossil fuels, a fundamental shift in resource flows from linear to circular, and a broad movement towards green finance.

The Rationale and Diverse Strategies

It is essential to recognise that greening economic development should follow divergent pathways that reflect the specific context of the sector, its natural endowments, and its development stage, based on several key premises. Firstly, Africa is the most vulnerable region to climate change, as clearly shown by the United Nations' findings on the Paris Agreement, Agenda 2030, and the IPCC Synthesis Report VI. Pursuing sustainable industrialisation could help reduce Africa's vulnerability to climate change (United Nations 2015; IPCC 2025). The continent shares a common interest and responsibility in achieving the Sustainable Development Goals.

Second, Africa's prospective industrial trajectory is inextricably linked to global environmental imperatives. Although currently a marginal participant in global industrial output, the continent's anticipated industrial expansion in the coming decades marks a critical strategic crossroads. It can either emulate the historically costly "grow now and clean later" model of its predecessors or forge a new, sustainable industrial base from the outset. The former approach is structurally unviable; it is not only environmentally detrimental but also economically obsolete in an era where access to global markets is increasingly contingent on low-carbon and sustainable production standards. This imperative is compounded by Africa's acute vulnerability to climate change—a disproportionate burden highlighted in frameworks like the Paris Agreement (2015), despite the continent's minimal historical contributions. Consequently, pursuing a green industrial pathway is not merely an ethical choice but a strategic necessity for Africa's resilient and competitive integration into the global economy.

Third, green development represents a strategic opportunity to harness emerging industries and sustainable practices, thereby accelerating Africa's ongoing industrial and economic transformation. This pathway is becoming increasingly economically viable, as evidenced by the declining costs and technological advancements in renewable energy, battery storage, and electric vehicles. Therefore, green development provides a pragmatic framework for establishing a carbon-neutral industrial base, while simultaneously addressing the immense economic pressures generated by Africa's unprecedented demographic growth.

Fourth, energy has moved beyond its traditional role to become a dual imperative for industrial competitiveness and national security. This strategic significance is further increased by rising demand factors, including the substantial energy needs of the digital and AI economies, rapid urbanisation, industrial growth, and expected increases in per capita energy consumption in the coming decades.

Pursuing carbon-neutral industrialisation constitutes a complex, multidimensional challenge for African nations, necessitating a strategic and integrated approach. This approach is guided by three core imperatives. First, the strategy is conceived as a dual transformation, simultaneously advancing structural economic transformation and securing a carbon-neutral future. Second, it has to be context-specific, acknowledging the continent's heterogeneity. African countries will need to design divergent pathways that reflect their unique national circumstances, natural endowments in sustainable resources, and sectoral compositions. This entails integrating decarbonisation processes into existing industrial frameworks while strategically fostering new green and emerging sectors. Third, the strategy has to be opportunity-driven, particularly in harnessing the growing global demand for critical and rare earth minerals. African nations should position themselves to capture greater value from these resources, utilising them as a catalyst for economic diversification, the development of complete industrial chains, and the enhancement of productive capacity. Underpinning all these efforts, targeted investment in research and development is indispensable, with a cross-sectoral focus on renewable energy applications and the systematic integration of sustainability studies.

Furthermore, a principled approach to carbon-neutral industrialisation recognises the sovereign right of African nations to develop their fossil fuel resources, thereby deepening economic diversification and enhancing productive capacity. The strategic response to climate change should therefore emphasise collaborative action within the Global South, promoting collective approaches to a common challenge. Several African nations are already implementing this dual-focused strategy. Ethiopia, for example, has made a deliberate shift towards renewable energy, directing significant investment into hydropower, wind power, and modernising the national grid to build a predominantly renewable energy foundation, financed mainly through domestic resources. The Grand Ethiopian Renaissance Dam (GERD), Africa's largest hydropower project, was entirely funded by the country. This base is being used to develop low-carbon industrial hubs, a crucial part of green industrialisation. Similarly, Kenya has implemented a strategy of targeted diversification, heavily investing in geothermal and solar power to considerably increase the share of clean energy in its national mix.

Similarly, Morocco has strategically shifted towards a green economy, actively expanding its solar and wind capacity, prioritising green hydrogen production, and establishing low-carbon industrial platforms. Likewise, South Africa is undertaking a significant energy transition by reallocating resources from coal-fired thermal power to renewable alternatives. This momentum extends to the transport sector, where many African nations are developing policies to promote sustainable mobility and new energy vehicles. A broader shift towards green industrialisation is clear across the African continent.

Meanwhile, the strategic importance of critical minerals—driven by global shortages and inspired by value-added models from leaders in the Global South, such as Indonesia and Chile—has spurred a new policy focus on developing domestic industrial supply chains. Collectively, these developments mark a substantial and strategic realignment of industrial policy towards a sustainable future.

4 The Global South as a Catalyst for Africa's Industrialisation

A significant reconfiguration of development cooperation is underway, characterised by the rise of multifaceted partnerships between African nations and other countries of the Global South, including India, Brazil, Turkey, and Gulf states. Among these, China-Africa cooperation stands as the most advanced and institutionalised, offering a formative model for South–South engagement. The Forum on China-Africa Cooperation (FOCAC), established in 2000, exemplifies this as a key institutional innovation, sustaining a vibrant and stable partnership founded on the principles of mutual respect, non-interference, and win-win cooperation. This platform has enabled both parties to cultivate new strengths and deepen their engagement.

Future collaboration among African nations and other countries of the Global South should extend beyond traditional areas, such as trade, investment, and development finance. Two key frontiers are essential: green development and digital transformation. The need to tackle climate change aligns with economic opportunities to develop new sectors, such as renewable energy and sustainable mobility. At the same time, the rapid progress of technologies—especially in artificial intelligence and digital infrastructure—requires a collaborative approach to ensure their widespread adoption across the Global South. Principles of open source in cutting-edge digital technologies, particularly in AI, present an opportunity for African countries to catch up. China's resurgence as a global leader in both green technologies and digital sectors (e-commerce, AI, and telecommunications) offers a crucial chance for latecomers to speed up their development.[4]

Financing development poses a strategic challenge for Africa's industrialisation because it is essential for industrial growth, economic transformation, the macroeconomy, and national sovereignty. This issue is examined by focusing on the underlying drivers and sustainable solutions to this problem. First, African countries should prioritise promoting economic growth to reduce pressure and increase domestic resources. In practice, the most effective strategy is to emphasise and prioritise domestically generated resources.

Many African nations are using their hard-earned foreign exchange and revenues to service external public debt, which decreases their budgets for education, health, and poverty alleviation, while also being burdened by high-interest external private loans. More than half of African countries allocate more funds to servicing external debt than to health and education. African governments should adopt policies that encourage savings, capital formation, and the development of financial institutions. According to many reputable surveys, the main obstacle for Africa's 50 million formal enterprises remains access to finance, with significant implications for employment creation, domestic capacity, and alleviating balance-of-payments constraints (IFC Enterprise Surveys 2024).

[4] Centre for International Knowledge on Development (CIKD) (2025), Development Research Centre of the State Council and World Bank (2022), Lin and Zhang (2019).

5 African Industrialisation and Productive Transformation Strategies

In summary, this book establishes that productive transformation in Africa is an attainable, yet demanding, imperative, contingent upon industrial policies designed to strategically build technological capabilities, human capital, and economies of scale. Compelling evidence from across the continent underscores this potential: SASOL in South Africa embodies technological mastery in complex resource processing; Morocco's automotive cluster and Tanger-Med port illustrate the efficacy of strategic industrial ecosystems; and the OCP Group exemplifies the transition from raw material extraction to industrial leadership. The expansion across Africa of the Dangote Industrial Group in the cement sector further demonstrates the capacity of indigenous firms to achieve global competitiveness in capital-intensive industries.

These cases are not merely isolated successes but models of strategic statecraft. Ethiopian Airlines operates as a disciplined instrument of industrial policy, catalysing high-value exports and securing economic sovereignty for a landlocked nation. This, alongside Ethiopia's domestically financed investment in monumental infrastructure, such as the Grand Ethiopian Renaissance Dam, affirms the foundational role of domestic resource mobilisation and visionary public investment in enabling industrial take-off.

Drawing these threads together, the book contends that Africa's industrial future hinges on a necessary dual transformation: the urgent pursuit of economic transformation yet intrinsically coupled with the greening of African economic development. Realising this vision demands context-specific strategies, pragmatic learning from both internal exemplars and external partnerships, and, above all, a profound political commitment to institutional reform, domestic finance mobilisation, and the development of a globally competitive industrial ecosystem. The African Continental Free Trade Area (AfCFTA) is, therefore, not merely a technical arrangement, but a central political project for the continent, one whose success is inextricably linked to a renewed, sustainable, and assertive industrial agenda. Africa's industrialisation in the twenty-first century is not a quest to emulate past models, but a defining opportunity to forge a distinct, resilient, and prosperous pathway of its own.

References

Amsden, Alice. 1989. *Asia's Next Giant: South Korea and Late Industrialization*. New York: Oxford University Press.

Centre for International Knowledge on Development (CIKD). 2025. *Global Development Report 2024. A World of Turbulence and Change: Cooperation to Address Global Common Languages*. Beijing: Foreign Language Press and China Development Press.

Chang, Ha-Joon. 1994. *The Political Economy of Industrial Policy*. Basingstoke: Macmillan.

Cramer, Christopher, John Sender, and Arkebe Oqubay. 2020. *African Economic Development: Evidence, Theory, Policy*. Oxford: Oxford University Press.

Development Research Centre of the State Council and World Bank. 2022. *Four Decades of Poverty Reduction in China: Drivers, Insights for the World, and the Way Ahead*. Beijing/Washington, DC: DRC of the State Council, People's Republic of China and the World Bank Group.

IFC. 2024. *IFC Enterprise Surveys 2024*. World Bank.

Intergovernmental Panel on Climate Change. 2025. Synthesis Report VI. https://www.ipcc.ch/report/ar6/syr/.

International Renewable Energy Agency (IRENA). 2025. *Renewable Energy Trends*. IRENA Database.

Kaldor, Nicholas. 1967. *Strategic Factors in Economic Development*. Ithaca: New York State School of Industrial and Labour Relations, Cornell University.

Lee, Keun. 2019. *The Art of Economic Catch-up*. Cambridge: Cambridge University Press.

Lin, Justin Yifu, and Jun Zhang. 2019. China: Learning to Catch Up in a Globalized World. In *How Nations Learn: Technological Learning, Industrial Policy, and Catch-Up*, ed. Arkebe Oqubay and Kenichi Ohno, 149–173. Oxford: Oxford University Press.

List, Frederick. [1841] 1856. *The National System of Political Economy*. Vol. I–IV. Memphis: Lippincott

Mathews, John, and Arkebe Oqubay, eds. 2025. *The Oxford Handbook on the Greening of Economic Development*. Oxford: Oxford University Press.

Oqubay, Arkebe. 2015. *Made in Africa: Industrial Policy in Ethiopia*. Oxford: Oxford University Press.

Oqubay, Arkebe. 2025a. *Industrial Policy and Economic Development: Theory, Strategy, and Practice*. London: Palgrave Macmillan.

Oqubay, Arkebe. 2025b. *Industrial Hubs and Economic Catch-up: Productive Transformation and Governance*. London: Palgrave Macmillan.

Polanyi, Karl. 1944. *The Great Transformation: The Political and Economic Origins of Our Time*. Boston: Beacon Press.

UNCTAD. 2025a. *Economic Development in Africa Report 2024. Unlocking Africa's Trade Potential, Boosting Regional Markets, and Reducing Risks. Overview*. Geneva: UNCTAD.

UNCTAD. 2025b. *Technology and Innovation Report 2025. Inclusive Artificial Intelligence for Development.* Geneva: UN Conference on Trade and Development.

United Nations. 2015. *Transforming our World: The 2030 Agenda for Sustainable Development.* New York: United Nations. https://sustainabledevelopment.un.org/post2015/transformingourworld/publication.

Védie, Henri Louis. 2010. *OCP Group: A Multifaceted Corporation*. English version by Abdelkrim Raddadi. Casablanca: La Croisée des Chemins, Morocco.

Bibliography

Abramovitz, Moses. 1986. Catching Up, Forging Ahead, and Falling Behind. *The Journal of Economic History* 46 (2): 385–406.

Ajbilou, A. 2026. The demographic transition and the Moroccan economy, in El Aynaoui, K., and Oqubay, A. (eds). *The Oxford Handbook of the Moroccan Economy*. Oxford University Press. pp 184–199.

African Airlines Association (AFRAA). 2023. *African Aviation Performance Report*. Nairobi: AFRAA Publications.

African Development Bank. 2025. *African Economic Outlook. Making Africa's Capital Work Better for Africa's Development*. Abidjan: AfDB.

African Union. 2001. *New Partnership for Africa's Development (NEPAD), Declaration on Democracy, Political and Economic Governance*. Lusaka. July. https://sarpn.org/NEPAD/july2002/declaration/declaration.pdf.

African Union. 2015. *Agenda 2063, "The Africa We Want"*. Final Edition. April. http://www.un.org/en/africa/osaa/pdf/au/agenda2063.pdf.

African Union. 2025a. *Agenda 2063: The Africa We Want*. https://au.int/en/ag enda2063/overview.

African Union. 2025b. The African Continental Free Trade Area. https://au.int/african-continental-free-trade-area.

African Union Commission. 2025a. *African Integration Report 2025. Strengthening the Implementation of Regional Frameworks to Leverage Continental Achievements Fully*. Addis Ababa: African Union Commission.

A. Oqubay, *Productive Transformation in Africa*, https://doi.org/10.1007/978-3-032-23941-9

African Union Commission. 2025b. Regional Economic Communities. Regional Economic Communities. Established under the African Economic Community, as per the Abuja Treaty (1991). https://au.int/en/recs.

Ajbilou, Aziz. 2026. The Demographic Transition and the Moroccan Economy. In *The Oxford Handbook of the Moroccan Economy*, ed. Karim El Aynaoui and Arkebe Oqubay. Oxford: Oxford University Press.

Akyűz, Yilmaz. 2017. *Playing with Fire: Deepened Financial Integration and Changing Vulnerabilities of the Global South*. Oxford: Oxford University Press.

Akyuz, Yilma, and Charles Gore. 1996. The Investment-Profit Nexus in East-Asian Industrialisation. *World Development* 24 (3): 461–470.

Amsden, Alice. 1989. *Asia's Next Giant: South Korea and Late Industrialization*. New York: Oxford University Press.

Amsden, Alice. 1997. Editorial: Bringing Production Back in—Understanding Government's Economic Role in Late Industrialization. *World Development* 25 (4): 469–480.

Amsden, Alice. 2001. *The Rise of the "Rest": Challenges to the West from Late-Industrializing Economies*. Oxford: Oxford University Press.

Amsden, Alice, and Wan-wen Chu. 2003. *Beyond Late Development: Taiwan's Upgrading Policies*. Cambridge, MA: MIT Press.

Andreoni, Antonio, and Ha-Joon Chang. 2017. Bringing Production and Employment Back into Development: Alice Amsden's Legacy for a New Developmentalist Agenda. *Cambridge Journal of Regions, Economy and Society* 10 (1): 173–187.

Andreoni, Antonio, and Ha-Joon Chang. 2019. The Political Economy of Industrial Policy: Structural Interdependencies, Policy Alignment and Conflict Management. *Structural Change and Economic Dynamics* 48:136–150.

Austin, Gareth, Ewout Frankema, and Morten Jerven. 2017. Patterns of Manufacturing Growth in Sub-Saharan Africa: From Colonization to the Present. In *The Spread of Modern Industry to the Periphery since 1871*, ed. Kevin H. O'Rourke and Jeffrey G. Williamson, 345–373. Oxford: Oxford University Press.

Auty, Richard M. 1993. *Sustaining Development in Mineral Economies: The Resource Curse Thesis*. London: Routledge.

El Aynaoui, Karim, and Hinh T. Dinh. 2024. *Economic Development of the New South after the Washington Consensus*. Policy Paper. 20 December. Rabat: Policy Centre for the New South. https://www.policycenter.ma/publications/economic-development-new-south-after-washington-consensus. Accessed 21 July 2025.

Bekele, Shiferaw. 2019. Ethiopia's Transition from a Traditional to a Developing Economy, 1890s–1960. In *The Oxford Handbook of the Ethiopian Economy*, ed. Fantu Cheru, Christopher Cramer, and Arkebe Oqubay. Oxford University Press.

Best, Michael. 2018. *How Growth Really Happens: The Making of Economic Miracles through Production, Governance, and Skills*. Princeton, NJ: Princeton University Press.

Boston University. 2025. *China's Global Power Database*. Chinese Loans Africa Database, Global Development Policy Centre. https://www.bu.edu/cgp/.

Brautigam, D., and Diolle, T. 2009. 'Coalitions, Capitalists and Credibility: Overcoming the Crisis of Confidence at Independence in Mauritius'. *Developmental Leadership Program. 1* April. Research Paper 04.

Brautigam, Deborah. 2019. Chinese Loans and African Structural Transformation. In *China–Africa and an Economic Transformation*, ed. Arkebe Oqubay and Justin Yifu Lin, 115–137. Oxford University Press.

Brautigam, Deborah, Toni Weis, and Xiaoyang Tang. 2018. Latent Advantage, Complex Challenges: Industrial Policy and Chinese Linkage in Ethiopia's Leather Sector. *China Economic Review* 48:158–169. https://doi.org/10.1016/j.chieco.2017.05.006.

Campling, Liam, and Carlos Oya. 2025. Why Mauritius? The Political Economy of Structural Transformation in a Small Island: Questions and Debates. In *The Oxford Handbook of the Mauritian Economy*, ed. Carlos Oya, Ramola Ramtohul, and Verena Tandrayen-Ragoobur, 20–45. Oxford: Oxford University Press.

Centre for International Knowledge on Development (CIKD). 2023. *China's Progress Report. China's Progress Report on Implementation of the 2030 Agenda for Sustainable Development*. Beijing: Centre for International Knowledge on Development.

Centre for International Knowledge on Development (CIKD). 2025. *Global Development Report 2024. A World of Turbulence and Change: Cooperation to Address Global Common Challenges*. Beijing: Foreign Language Press and China Development Press.

Chan, Stephen. 2025. *The Economic Transformation and Political Economy of Zambia: The Search for Modernity, Equity and Principle*. London: Palgrave Macmillan.

Chandler, Alfred. 2004. *Scale and Scope: The Dynamics of Industrial Capitalism*. Cambridge, MA: Harvard University Press.

Chandler, Alfred D., Jr. 1990. *Scale and Scope: The Dynamics of Industrial Capitalism*. Cambridge, MA: Harvard University Press.

Chandler, Alfred D., Jr., and Takashi Hikino. 1997. The Large Industrial Enterprise and the Dynamics of Modern Economic Growth. In *Big Business and the Wealth of Nations*, ed. Alfred D. Chandler Jr., Franco Amatori, and Takashi Hikino, 24–57. Cambridge: Cambridge University Press.

Chang, Ha-Joon. 1994. *The Political Economy of Industrial Policy*. Basingstoke: Macmillan.

Chang, Ha-Joon. 2002. *Kicking Away the Ladder: Development Strategy in Historical Perspective*. London: Anthem Press.

Chang, Ha-Joon. 2003. *Kicking the Ladder: Developing Strategy in Historical Perspective*. Anthem.

Cherif, Reda, and Fuad Hasanov. 2019. *The Return of the Policy That Shall Not Be Named: Principles of Industrial Policy*. IMF Working Paper WP/19/74. March.

Cheru, Fantu, and Arkebe Oqubay. 2019. Catalysing China–Africa Ties for Africa's Structural Transformation: Lessons from Ethiopia. In *China-Africa and an Economic Transformation*, ed. Arkebe Oqubay and Justin Yifu Lin, 282–309. Oxford: Oxford University Press.

Cheru, Fantu, Christopher Cramer, and Arkebe Oqubay. 2019. *The Oxford Handbook of the Ethiopian Economy*. Oxford: Oxford University Press.

China Development Bank. 2025. China-Africa Development Fund. https://www.cdb.com.cn/English/ywgl/zhjryw/zffzjjyxgs/.

China-Africa Research Initiative (CARI). 2025. China-Africa Data. http://www.sais-cari.org/data.

China-Africa Research Initiative (SAIS-CARI). 2023. *Chinese FDI in Ethiopia's Textile and Leather Sectors*. Washington, DC: Johns Hopkins University.

Clapham, Christopher. 1988. *Transformation and Continuity in Revolutionary Ethiopia*. Cambridge University Press.

Clapham, Christopher. 2019. The Political Economy of Ethiopia: From the Imperial Period to the Present. In *The Oxford Handbook of the Ethiopian Economy*, ed. Cheru Fantu, Cramer Christopher, and Oqubay Arkebe, 51–65. Oxford University Press.

Clarence-Smith, William Gervase. 2016. Colonial Industrialisation, 1840s–1960s. In *The Cambridge History of Capitalism, Volume 2: The Spread of Capitalism: From 1848 to the Present*, ed. Larry Neal and Jeffrey G. Williamson, 405–428. Cambridge: Cambridge University Press.

Coe, Neil M., and Henry Wai-chung Yeung. 2015. *Global Production Networks: Theorizing Economic Development in an Inter-connected World*. Oxford: Oxford University Press.

Coe, Neil M., and Henry Wai-chung Yeung. 2016. *Global Production Networks: Theorizing Economic Development in an Interconnected World*. Oxford University Press.

COMTRADE. 2025. *Trade database*. Geneva: COMTRADE.

Cramer, Christopher, and John Sender. 2019. Oranges Are Not Only Fruit: The Industrialization of Freshness and the Quality of Growth. In *The Quality of Growth in Africa*, ed. Ravi Kanbur, Akbar Noman, and Joseph Stiglitz, 209–233. New York: Columbia University Press.

Cramer, Christopher, John Sender, and Arkebe Oqubay. 2020. *African Economic Development: Evidence, Theory, Policy*. Oxford: Oxford University Press.

Deborah Brautigham. 2019. Chinese Loans and African Structural Transformation. In *China-Africa and an Economic Transformation*, ed. Arkebe Oqubay and Justin Yifu Lin, 29–146. Oxford: Oxford University Press.

Development Research Centre of the State Council and World Bank. 2022. *Four Decades of Poverty Reduction in China: Drivers, Insights for the World, and the Way Ahead*. Beijing/Washington, DC: DRC of the State Council, People's Republic of China and the World Bank Group.

Di John, Jonathan. 2009. *From Windfall to Curse? Oil and Industrialization in Venezuela, 1920 to the Present*. University Park: Pennsylvania State University Press.

Di John, Jonathan. 2020. The Political Economy of Development Banking. In *The Oxford Handbook of Industrial Policy*, ed. Arkebe Oqubay, Christopher Cramer, Ha-Joon Chang, and Richard Kozul-Wright, 292–318. Oxford: Oxford University Press.

Diamond, William. 1957. *Development Banks*. Baltimore: The Johns Hopkins Press (for the Economic Development Institute, International Bank for Reconstruction and Development).

Dicken, Peter. 2015. *Global Shift: Mapping the Changing Contours of the World Economy*. 7th ed. SAGE Publications.

El Abassi, Idriss, Aziz Ragbi, and Said Tounsi. 2026. Fiscal Policy in Morocco. In *The Oxford Handbook of the Moroccan Economy*, ed. Karim El Aynaoui and Arkebe Oqubay. Oxford: Oxford University Press.

El Aynaoui, Karim, and Hinh T. Dinh. 2026. Growth and Structural Transformation in Morocco. In *The Oxford Handbook of the Moroccan Economy*, ed. Karim El Aynaoui and Arkebe Oqubay. Oxford: Oxford University Press.

El Aynaoui, Karim, and Arkebe Oqubay. 2026. *The Oxford Handbook of the Moroccan Economy*. Oxford: Oxford University Press.

ENA. 2025. *Speech of Presidents of Kenya and Djibouti on Regional Economic Integration at the Inauguration of Grand Ethiopian Renaissance Dam*. Ethiopian News Agency. https://youtu.be/QDODzfHbang?si=qXyGSTrefw2UTROU

Ethiopian Airlines. 2024. *Annual Performance Report*. Addis Ababa.

FOCAC. 2024. *Beijing Declaration on Jointly Building an All-Weather China-Africa Community with a Shared Future for the New Era*. September 5. http://gb.china-embassy.gov.cn/eng/zgyw/202409/t20240905_11485993.htm.

Frankema, Ewout, Jeffrey G. Williamson, and Pieter Woltjer. 2018. An Economic Rationale for the African Scramble: The Commercial Transition and the Commodity Price Boom of 1845–1885. *The Journal of Economic History* 78 (2): 231–267.

Gay, Dan. 2018. Pharmaceutical Dreams: TRIPS and Drugs Policy in Bangladesh (PDF). https://www.researchgate.net/publication/325206579_Pharmaceutical_Dreams_TRIPS_and_drugs_policy_in_Bangladesh.

Gay, Daniel, and Kevin Gallagher. 2020. *The Need to Extend the WTO TRIPS Pharmaceuticals Transition Period for LDCs in the COVID-19 Era: Evidence from Bangladesh*. UN CDP Policy Review Series. https://www.un.org/development/desa/dpad/wp-content/uploads/sites/45/publication/CDP-review-2020-1.pdf.

Gebrechristos, Nigisty. 2025. *Industrialisation and Workforce Development: Policy Dynamics, Firms, and Industrial Ecosystems.* London: Palgrave Macmillan.

Gelb, Alan, and Associates. 1988. *Oil Windfalls: Blessing or Curse?* New York: Oxford University Press.

General Administration of Customs People's Republic of China. 2025. http://english.customs.gov.cn/Statistics/Statistics?ColumnId=1.

Gereffi, Gary. 2018a. *Global Value Chains and Development: Redefining the Contours of the World Economy.* Cambridge University Press.

Gereffi, Gary. 2018b. *Global Value Chains and Development: Redefining the Contours of 21st Century Capitalism.* Cambridge: Cambridge University Press.

Gerschenkron, Alexander. 1962. *Economic Backwardness in Historical Perspective: A Book of Essays.* Cambridge, MA: Harvard University Press.

Gerschenkron, A. 1963. *Economic backwardness in historical perspective.* Harvard University Press.

Green, Toby. 2019. *A Fistful of Shells: West Africa from the Rise of the Slave Trade to the Age of Revolution.* Chicago/London: University of Chicago Press/Allen Lane/Penguin.

Griffith-Jones, Stephany, and José Antonio Ocampo, eds. 2018. *The Future of National Development Banks.* Oxford: Oxford University Press.

Haddad, Eduardo A., and Mahmoud Arbouch. 2026. Regional Economic Development in Morocco. In *The Oxford Handbook of the Moroccan Economy*, ed. Karim El Aynaoui and Arkebe Oqubay. Oxford: Oxford University Press.

Hall, Peter. 1987. *Governing the Economy: The Politics of State Intervention in Britain and France.* Cambridge: Polity Press.

Hamilton, Alexander. 1934. *Papers on Public Credit, Commerce and Finance*, ed. Samuel McKee. New York: Columbia University Press.

Haddad, E., and Arbouch, M. 2026. Regional economic development in Morocco in El Aynaoui, K. (eds). *The Oxford Handbook of the Moroccan Economy.* Oxford University Press.pp 238–257.

Hirschman, Albert. 1958. *The Strategy of Economic Development.* New Haven: Yale University Press.

Hirschman, Albert O. 1967. *Development Projects Observed.* Washington, DC: The Brookings Institution.

Hirschman, Albert O. 1968. The Political Economy of Import-substitution Industrialization in Latin America. *Quarterly Journal of Economics* 82 (1): 2–32.

Hirschman, Albert. 1981. *Essays in Trespassing: Economics to Politics and Beyond.* Cambridge: Cambridge University Press.

IATA. 2023. *Air Transport Market Profile: Ethiopia.* Montreal: IATA Economics. International Air Transport Association.

IFC. 2024. *IFC Enterprise Surveys 2024.* World Bank.

ILO. 2023. *Employment Conditions in Ethiopia's Garment and Floriculture Sectors.* Geneva: International Labour Organization.

IMF. 2023a. *Regional Economic Outlook.* Sub-Saharan Africa: The Big Funding Squeeze. April.

IMF. 2023c. *Ethiopia: 2023 Article IV consultation report.* Washington, DC: International Monetary Fund (IMF).

IMF. 2025. *World Economic Outlook.* International Monetary Fund.

Intergovernmental Panel on Climate Change. 2025. Synthesis Report VI. https://www.ipcc.ch/report/ar6/syr/.

International Renewable Energy Agency (IRENA). 2025. *Renewable Energy Trends.* IRENA Database.

Ismail, Faizel. 2019. A Developmental Regionalism Approach to the African Continental Free Trade Area (AfCTA). *Journal of Reviews on Global Economics* 8:1771–1785. https://www.lifescienceglobal.com/JRGEV8A159-Ismail.pdf.

Ismail, Faizel. 2021. *The African Continental Free Trade Area (AfCFTA) and Developmental Regionalism. A Handbook.* Trade & Industrial Policy Strategies (TIPS).

Jerven, Morten. 2011. *Africa: Why Economists Get it Wrong.* London: Zed Publishers.

Jerven, Morten. 2013. *Poor Numbers: How we Are Misled by African Development Statistics and What to Do About It.* Cornell: Cornell University Press.

Johnson, Chalmers. 1982. *MITI and the Japanese Miracle: The Growth of Industrial Policy, 1925–1975.* Stanford: Stanford University Press.

Kaldor, Nicholas. 1967. *Strategic Factors in Economic Development.* Ithaca: New York State School of Industrial and Labour Relations, Cornell University.

Kaldor, Nicholas. 1980. *Essays on Economic Stability and Growth.* 2nd ed. New York: Holmes & Meier Publishers.

Krugman, Paul. 1994. *The Age of Diminished Expectations.* Cambridge, MA: MIT Press.

Lall, Sanjaya. 2000. The Technological Structure and Performance of Developing Country Manufactured Exports, 1985–98. *Oxford Development Studies* 28 (3): 337–369.

Lee, Keun. 2019. *The Art of Economic Catch-Up: Barriers, Detours and Leapfrogging in Innovation Systems.* Cambridge: Cambridge University Press.

Lin, Justin, and Volker Treichel. 2012. *Learning from China's Rise to Escape the Middle-Income Trap: A New Structural Economics Approach to Latin America*, Policy Research Working Paper, 6165. August.

Lin, Justin. 2016. The Latecomer Advantages and Disadvantages: A New Structural Economics Perspective. In *Diverse Development Paths and Structural Transformation in Escape from Poverty*, ed. Martin Andersson and Tobias Axelsson, 43–67. Oxford: University Press.

Lin, Justin Yifu, and Jiajun Xu. 2019. China's Light Manufacturing and Africa's Industrialization. In *China-Africa and an Economic Transformation*, ed. Arkebe Oqubay and Justin Yifu Lin, 265–281. Oxford: Oxford University Press.

Lin, Justin Yifu, and Jun Zhang. 2019. China: Learning to Catch up in a Globalized World. In *How Nations Learn: Technological Learning, Industrial Policy, and Catch-Up*, ed. Arkebe Oqubay and Kenichi Ohno, 149–173. Oxford: Oxford University Press.

List, Frederick. [1841] 1856. *The National System of Political Economy*. Vol. I–IV. Memphis: Lippincott

List, Friedrich. 1856. *National System of Political Economy*. Vol. I–IV. Memphis: Lippincott.

Luke, David, ed. 2023. *How Africa Trades*. London: LSE Press.

Mamo, Ayalew. 2024. *The Political Economy of Chinese FDI in Africa: Productive FDI and Industrialisation*. London: Palgrave Macmillan.

Mandri, Badr. 2026. The External Sector of the Moroccan Economy. In *The Oxford Handbook of the Moroccan Economy*, ed. Karim El Aynaoui and Arkebe Oqubay. Oxford: Oxford University Press.

Mangeni, Francis, and Andrew Mold. 2024. *Borderless Africa: A Sceptic's Guide to the Continental Free Trade Area*. London: Hurst Publishers.

Manyazewal, Mekonen, and Admasu Shiferaw. 2019. Economic Policy and Structural Transformation in Ethiopia. In *The Oxford Handbook of the Ethiopian Economy*, ed. Fantu Cheru, Christopher Cramer, and Arkebe Oqubay, 137–159. Oxford: Oxford University Press.

Marshall, Alfred. 1920. *Principles of Economics*. London: Palgrave Macmillan.

Mathews, John. 2017. *Global Green Shift: When CERES Meet GAIA*. London: Anthem Press.

Mathews, John, and Arkebe Oqubay, eds. 2025. *The Oxford Handbook on the Greening of Economic Development*. Oxford: Oxford University Press.

Mazzucato, Mariana. 2011. *The Entrepreneurial State: Debunking Public vs. Private Sector Myths*. London: Anthem Press.

Meade, James. 1961. *The Economic and Social Structure of Mauritius*. Methuen.

Ministry of Commerce of China. 2024. Keynote Address by Chinese President Xi Jinping, FOCAC Beijing Summit. http://english.customs.gov.cn/Statistics/Statistics?ColumnId=1.

Mkandawire, Thandika. 2001. Thinking About Developmental States in Africa. *Cambridge Journal of Economics* 25 (3): 289–314.

Mkandawire, Thandika, and Charles Soludo. 1999. *Our Continent, Our Future: African Perspectives on Structural Adjustment*. Trenton: Africa World Press.

Nolan, Peter. 2001. *China and the Global Business Revolution*. Palgrave Macmillan.

Nolan, Peter. 2014. *Chinese Firms, Global Firms: Industrial Policy in the Age of Globalization*. New York: Routledge.

Ocampo, J. Antonio. 2017. Dynamic Efficiency: Structural Dynamics and Structural Change in Developing Countries. In *Efficiency, Finance, and Varieties of Industrial Policy*, ed. A. Noman and J. E. Stiglitz. New York: Columbia University Press, chapter 3.

Ocampo, José Antonio, Cordina Rada, and Lance Taylor. 2009. *Growth and Policy in Developing Countries: A Structuralist Approach.* New York: Columbia University Press.

Ofori-Amoah, Benjamin. 2024. *The African Continental Free Trade Area: Prospects, Problems and Challenges.* London: Springer.

Oqubay, Arkebe. 2015. *Made in Africa: Industrial Policy in Ethiopia.* Oxford: Oxford University Press.

Oqubay, Arkebe. 2019a. Industrial Policy and Late Industrialization in Ethiopia. In *The Oxford Handbook of the Ethiopian Economy*, ed. Fantu Cheru, Christopher Cramer, and Arkebe Oqubay, 724–746. Oxford University Press.

Oqubay, Arkebe. 2019b. The Structure and Performance of the Ethiopian Manufacturing Sector. In *The Oxford Handbook of the Ethiopian Economy*, ed. F. Cheru, C. Cramer, and A. Oqubay, 747–768. Oxford University Press.

Oqubay, Arkebe. 2020. Africa's Economic Transformation and the Future of EU-Africa Cooperation. *CESifo Forum* 21:3–11. https://www.ifo.de/DocDL/CESifo-Forum-2020-2-oqubay-africas-economic-transformation.pdf.

Oqubay. 2025. *Industrial Policy and Economic Development: Theory, Strategy, and Practice.* Palgrave Macmillan.

Oqubay, Arkebe. 2025a. *Industrial Policy and Economic Development: Theory, Strategy, and Practice.* London: Palgrave Macmillan.

Oqubay, Arkebe. 2025b. *Industrial Hubs and Economic Catch-Up: Productive Transformation and Governance.* London: Palgrave Macmillan.

Oqubay, Arkebe. 2025c. Learning from Mauritius' Economic Transformation: A Policymaker's Perspective. In *The Oxford Handbook of the Mauritian Economy*, ed. Carlos Oya, Ramola Ramtohul, and Verena Tandrayen-Ragoobur, 435–462. Oxford: Oxford University Press.

Oqubay, Arkebe, and Justin Yifu Lin. 2019a. The Future of China–Africa Economic Ties: New Trajectory and Possibilities. In *China–Africa and an Economic Transformation*, ed. Arkebe Oqubay and Justin Yifu Lin, 367–383. Oxford: Oxford University Press.

Oqubay, Arkebe, and Justin Yifu Lin, eds. 2019b. *China-Africa and an Economic Transformation.* Oxford: Oxford University Press.

Oqubay, Arkebe, and Justin Yif Lin. 2020a. Industrial Hubs and Economic Development: Conclusion and Pathways to the Future. In *The Oxford Handbook of Industrial Hubs and Economic Development*, ed. Arkebe Oqubay and Justin Yifu Lin. Oxford University Press.

Oqubay, Arkebe, and Justin Yifu Lin, eds. 2020b. *The Oxford Handbook of Industrial Hubs and Economic Development.* Oxford: Oxford University Press.

Oqubay, Arkebe, and Kenichi Ohno, eds. 2019. *How Nations Learn: Technological Learning, Industrial Policy, and Catch-Up.* Oxford: Oxford University Press.

Oqubay, Arkebe, Christopher Cramer, Ha-Joon Chang, and Richard Kozul-Wright, eds. 2020. *The Oxford Handbook of Industrial Policy.* Oxford: Oxford University Press.

Oqubay, Arkebe, Fiona Tregenna, and Imraan Valodia (eds) (2021) *The Oxford Handbook of the South African Economy.*

Oualalou, Fathallah. 2026. Economic History of Morocco. In *The Oxford Handbook of the Moroccan Economy*, ed. Karim El Aynaoui and Arkebe Oqubay. Oxford: Oxford University Press.

Oya, Carlos. 2019a. Building an Industrial Workforce in Ethiopia. In *The Oxford Handbook of the Ethiopian Economy*, ed. Fantu Cheru, Christopher Cramer, and Arkebe Oqubay, 651–670. Oxford University Press.

Oya, Carlos. 2019b. Labour Regimes and Workplace Encounters between China and Africa. In *China-Africa and an Economic Transformation*, ed. Arkebe Oqubay and Justin Yifu Lin, 239–264. Oxford: Oxford University Press.

Oya, Carlos, Ramola Ramtohul, and Verena Tandrayen-Ragoobur. 2025. *The Oxford Handbook of the Mauritian Economy.* Oxford: Oxford University Press.

Pankhurst, Richard. 1996. *The History of Famine and Epidemics in Ethiopia: From Early Times to the Twentieth Century.* Addis Ababa: Haile Selassie I University Press.

Pasinetti, Luigi. 1981. *Structural Change and Economic Growth: A Theoretical Essay on the Dynamics of the Wealth of Nations.* Cambridge: Cambridge University Press.

Pasinetti, Luigi. 1993. *Structural Economic Dynamics: A Theory of the Economic Consequences of Human Learning.* Cambridge: Cambridge University Press.

Penrose, Edith. 1959. *The Theory of the Growth of the Firm.* Oxford: Oxford University Press.

Polanyi, Karl. 1944. *The Great Transformation: The Political and Economic Origins of Our Time.* Boston: Beacon Press.

Porter, M. 1990. *The Competitive Advantage of Nations.* Free Press.

Porter, Michael E. 1998. *The Competitive Advantage of Nations.* New York: Palgrave Macmillan.

Reinert, Erik. 2008. *How Rich Countries Get Rich and Why Poor Countries Stay Poor.* London: Constable.

Rodrik, Dani. 2012. *The Globalisation Paradox: Why Global Markets, States, and Democracy Can't Coexist.* Oxford: Oxford University Press.

Rodrik, Dani. 2015. *Premature Deindustrialization.* Paper Number 107, January.

Rodrik, Dani. 2018. *New Technologies, Global Value Chains, and the Developing Economies*, Pathways for Prosperity Commission Background Paper Series; no. 1. Oxford, UK.

Ross, Michael L. 2012. *The Oil Curse: How Petroleum Wealth Shapes the Development of Nations*. Princeton: Princeton University Press.

Schmitz, Hubert. 2007. Reducing Complexity in the Industrial Policy Debate. *Development Policy Review* 25 (4): 417–428.

Schumpeter, Joseph. [1934] 2017. *The Theory of Economic Development*. New York: Routledge.

Schumpeter, Joseph. 1950. *Capitalism, Socialism, and Democracy*. 3rd ed. New York: Harper and Brothers.

Schwartz, Herman. 2010. *States Versus Markets: The Emergence of a Global Economy*. 3rd ed. New York: Palgrave.

Shiferaw, Admasu, and M. Söderbom. 2019. The Ethiopian Manufacturing Sector: Productivity, Export, and Competitiveness. In *The Oxford Handbook of the Ethiopian Economy*, ed. Fantu Cheru, Chstopher Cramer, and Arkebe Oqubay, 747–770. Oxford: Oxford University Press.

Stein, Howard. 2020. Industrial Policy, Institutional Transformation, and the Development of Industrial Parks. In *The Oxford Handbook of Industrial Hubs and Economic Development*, ed. A. Oqubay and J. Y. Lin, 103–122. Oxford University Press.

Stiglitz, Joseph E. 2003. *Globalization and Its Discontents*. New York: Penguin.

Sutton, J., and Kellow, N. 2010. *An Enterprise Map of Ethiopia*. International Growth Centre.

TARLAC. 2020. *The Africa Continental Free Trade Area. A Tarlac Guide*. 7th ed. https://www.africannewspage.net/wp-content/uploads/2021/03/AfCFTA-a-tralac-guide-7th-edition-August-2020.pdf.

The Greening of African Economic Development. 2025a. *Automotive Industry Background Paper*. British Academy research project. SOAS University of London.

The Greening of African Economic Development. 2025b. *Cement Industry Background Paper*. British Academy research project. SOAS University of London.

The Greening of African Economic Development. 2025c. *Energy Sector Background Paper*. British Academy research project. SOAS University of London.

The Greening of African Economic Development. 2025d. *Fertiliser Industry Background Paper*. British Academy research project. SOAS University of London.

The Greening of African Economic Development. 2025e. *Petrochemical Industry Background Paper*. British Academy research project. SOAS University of London.

The Greening of African Economic Development. 2025f. *Textile and Apparel Industry Background Paper*. British Academy research project. SOAS University of London.

Thirlwall, Anthony. 2002. *The Nature of Economic Growth: An Alternative Framework for Understanding the Performance of Nations.* Cheltenham: Edward Elgar.

Thirlwall, Anthony. 2011. Balance of Payments Constrained Growth Models: History and Overview. *PSL Quarterly Review* 64 (259): 307–351.

Thirlwall, Anthony. 2013. *Economic Growth in an Open Developing Economy: The Role of Structure and Demand.* Cheltenham, UK: Edward Elgar.

Thurber, M.C., Hults, D.R., Heller, P.R.P., et al. 2011. Exporting the Norwegian Model: The Effect of Administrative Design on Oil Sector Performance. *Energy Policy 39* (9): 5366–5378.

Tregenna, F. 2009. Characterising Deindustrialisation: An Analysis of Changes in Manufacturing Employment and Output Internationally. *Cambridge Journal of Economics* 33 (3): 433–466.

Tregenna, Fiona. 2013. Deindustrialization and Reindustrialization. In *Pathways to Industrialization in the Twenty-First Century: New Challenges and Emerging Paradigms*, ed. Adam Szirmai, Wim Naudé, and Ludvico Alcorta. Oxford: Oxford University Press.

Tritah, Ahmed. 2026. Moroccan Migration Dynamics. In *The Oxford Handbook of the Moroccan Economy*, ed. Karim El Aynaoui and Arkebe Oqubay. Oxford: Oxford University Press.

UN DESA. 2025. World Population Prospects 2024. https://population.un.org/wpp/.

UNCTAD. 1996. Chapter 2, Export, Capital Formation and Growth. In *Trade and Development Report 1996,* 108. Geneva: UNCTAD.

UNCTAD. 2006a. *"Developing Productive Capacities", the Least Developed Countries Report.* Geneva: UN Conference on Trade and Development.

UNCTAD. 2006b. *Developing Productive Capacities. The Least Developed Countries Report 2006.* Geneva: United Nations.

UNCTAD. 2008. *Trade and Development Report, 2008. Domestic Sources of Finance and Investment in Productive Capacity, Chapter IV.* Geneva: UN Conference on Trade and Development.

UNCTAD. 2013. *World Investment Report 2013. Global Value Chains: Investment and Trade for Development.* Geneva: UN Conference on Trade and Development.

UNCTAD. 2016. *Structural Transformation for Inclusive and Sustained Growth. Trade and Development Report.* Geneva: United Nations.

UNCTAD. 2017. *Financing Development: Addressing the Challenges of Industrialization in Africa.* Geneva: UN Conference on Trade and Development.

UNCTAD. 2018. *World Investment Report: FDI and the Sustainable Development Goals.* Geneva: UN Conference on Trade and Development.

UNCTAD. 2019. *World Investment Report 2019. Special Economic Zones*. Geneva: UN Conference on Trade and Development.

UNCTAD. 2020. Investment World Report. *International Production Beyond the Pandemic*. Geneva: United Nations.

UNCTAD. 2023a. *Global Value Chains in Agribusiness: Ethiopia's Floriculture Case*. Geneva: UN Conference on Trade and Development.

UNCTAD. 2023b. *Technology and Innovation Report 2023. Opening Green Windows: Technological Opportunities for a Low-Carbon World*. Geneva: UN Conference on Trade and Development.

UNCTAD. 2023c. *Productive Capacity Index*. Geneva: United Nations.

UNCTAD. 2023d. *Trade and Development Report 2023. Growth, Debt and Climate: Realigning the Global Financial Architecture*. Geneva: UN Conference on Trade and Development.

UNCTAD. 2023e. *Technology and Innovation Report 2023. Opening Green Windows: Technological Opportunities for a Low-Carbon World*. Geneva: United Nations.

UNCTAD. 2024a. *Economic Development in Africa Report 2024. Unlocking Africa's Trade Potential: Boosting Regional Markets*. Geneva: United Nations.

UNCTAD. 2024b. *World Investment Report 2024. Investment Facilitation and Digital Government*. Geneva: UN Conference on Trade and Development.

UNCTAD. 2024c. *Technology and Innovation Report*. Geneva: UN Conference on Trade and Development.

UNCTAD. 2025a. *Economic Development in Africa Report 2024. Unlocking Africa's Trade Potential, Boosting Regional Markets, and Reducing Risks. Overview*. Geneva: UNCTAD.

UNCTAD. 2025b. *Technology and Innovation Report 2025. Inclusive Artificial Intelligence for Development*. Geneva: UN Conference on Trade and Development.

UNCTAD-UNIDO. 2011a. *Economic Development in Africa Report 2011: Fostering Industrial Development in Africa in the New Global Environment*. New York/Geneva: United Nations Industrial Development Organization and United Nations Conference on Trade and Development.

UNCTAD-UNIDO. 2011b. *Fostering Industrial Development in Africa in the New Global Environment*, Economic Development in Africa Report 2011. New York/Geneva: United Nations Industrial Development Organization and United Nations Conference on Trade and Development.

UNECA. 2012. *Boosting Intra-African Trade*. Addis Ababa: UNECA.

UNECA. 2015. *Economic Report on Africa: Industrialising Through Trade*. Addis Ababa: United Nations Economic Commission for Africa.

UNECA. 2016. *Transformative Industrial Policy for Africa*. Addis Ababa: United Nations Economic Commission for Africa.

UNECA. 2025a. *Advancing the Implementation of the African Continental Free Trade Area: Proposing Transformative Strategic Actions. Economic Report on Africa*. Addis Ababa: UNECA.

UNECA. 2025b. *Assessing Regional Integration in Africa: ARIA XI. Delivering on the African Economic Community: Towards an African Continental Customs Union and African Continental Common Market.* Addis Ababa: UNECA.

UNECA. 2025c. *Economic Report on Africa 2025: Advancing the Implementation of the Agreement Establishing the African Continental Free Trade Area*. Addis Ababa: UNECA.

United Nations. 2008. *International Standard Industrial Classification of All Economic Activities (ISIC), Rev. 4*, Statistical Papers Series M No. 4/Rev.4. New York: United Nations Statistics Division.

United Nations. 2025a. Agenda 2030. https://sdgs.un.org/2030agenda.

United Nations. 2025b. Climate Action. The Paris Agreement. https://www.un.org/en/climatechange/paris-agreement.

United Nations Department of Economic and Social Affairs. 2025. *World Population Prospects 2024. Data Portal.* New York: United Nations.

United Nations Industrial Development Organization (UNIDO). 2023. *Industrial Parks and Sustainability: The Case of Hawassa Industrial Park, Ethiopia*. UNIDO.

Védie, Henri Louis. 2010. *OCP Group: A Multifaceted Corporation.* English version by Abdelkrim Raddadi. Casablanca: La Croisée des Chemins, Morocco.

Venables, Anthony J. 2016. Using Natural Resources for Development: Why Has It Proven So Difficult? *Journal of Economic Perspectives* 30 (1): 161–184.

Wade, Robert. 2004. *Governing the Market: Economic Theory and the Role of the Government in East Asian Industrialization.* Princeton: Princeton University Press.

World Bank. 1989. *Mauritius managing success.* A World Bank Country Study. World Bank.

World Bank. 1995. *Kingdom of Morocco. Country Economic Memorandum: Towards Higher Growth and Employment.* Report No. 14155-MOR.

World Bank. 2006. *Kingdom of Morocco: Country Economic Memorandum. Fostering Growth and Employment with Productive Diversification and Competitiveness.* Report No. 32948-MOR.

World Bank. 2023a. *Enterprise Survey Database.* Washington, DC: The World Bank Group.

World Bank. 2023b. *Logistics and Trade Challenges in Ethiopia: A Case Study of the Port of Djibouti*. Washington, DC: World Bank.

World Bank. 2024. *World Development Indicators.* World Bank Group. Retrieved from https://data.worldbank.org.

World Bank. 2025a. *Development Indicators Database.* Washington, DC: World Bank.

World Bank. 2025b. *Enterprise Survey.* IFC. Washington, DC: The World Bank Group.

World Intellectual Property Organisation. 2024. *Global Innovation Index.* Geneva: United Nations.

Yasuda, Ayako. 1993. *The Performance and Roles of Japanese Development Banks*, Working Paper, May 1993.

Young, Allyn. 1928. Increasing Returns and Economic Progress. *Economic Journal* 38 (152): 527–542.

Zalk, Nimrod. 2021. Africa's Development Banks: The Urgent Need for Scale. *LSE Business Review*, November 17.

Zartman, I. William. 2026. Political Economy in Morocco. In *The Oxford Handbook of the Moroccan Economy*, ed. Karim El Aynaoui and Arkebe Oqubay. Oxford: Oxford University Press.

Zewde, Bahru. 2002. *A History of Modern Ethiopia: 1855–1991.* James Currey.

Index[1]

[1] Note: Page numbers followed by 'n' refer to notes.

A. Oqubay, *Productive Transformation in Africa*,
https://doi.org/10.1007/978-3-032-23941-9

FSC
www.fsc.org
MIX
Papier | Fördert gute Waldnutzung
FSC® C083411

Kolibri 360 GmbH
Ferdinand-Jühlke-Straße 7
99095 Erfurt, Deutschland
produktsicherheit@kolibri360.de